ESSAYS

CONTRIBUTED TO THE 'QUARTERLY REVIEW'

By SAMUEL WILBERFORCE, D.D.,
LATE LORD BISHOP OF WINCHESTER.

IN TWO VOLUMES.—Vol. II.

WIPF & STOCK · Eugene, Oregon

Wipf and Stock Publishers
199 W 8th Ave, Suite 3
Eugene, OR 97401

Essays Contributed to the Quarterly Review, Volume 2
By Wilberforce, Samuel
Softcover ISBN-13: 978-1-6667-0559-1
Hardcover ISBN-13: 978-1-6667-0560-7
eBook ISBN-13: 978-1-6667-0561-4
Publication date 3/10/2021
Previously published by John Murray, 1874

This edition is a scanned facsimile of the original edition published in 1874.

CONTENTS OF VOLUME II.

	PAGE
CLERICAL SUBSCRIPTION	1
THE GALLICAN CHURCH	42
THE CHURCH AND HER CURATES	84
ROYAL AUTHORSHIP	115
THE ARCHBISHOPS OF CANTERBURY OF THE REFORMATION	185
KEBLE'S BIOGRAPHY	228
EAST AFRICAN SLAVE TRADE	277

CLERICAL SUBSCRIPTION.*

(*April*, 1865.)

Most of our readers may have seen the effect of the stirring of some deep and stately stream by the sudden pouring into it on every side of the thousand freshets which have been awoke by an unwonted fall of rain. There is a rising up of dead and forgotten things from its tranquil depths which might stand for an acted parable of the great final awakening of all departed words, and thoughts, and actions. The present aspect of religious thought amongst ourselves seems to have been subjected to some such law of disturbance. There is scarcely a question of criticism or interpretation— scarcely a faint struggle over a principle, a regulation, or a creed, however deep it may seem to have been buried, however long the quiet waves have flowed over it, and babbled nothing of its presence—which is not being stirred up and brought to the surface of the present seething, eddying tide of theological thought.

There are some who see in all this nothing else than the signs of present vitality and the promise of future progress. Such is Dean Stanley's view, in his paper read at the monthly meeting of the London clergy, at the Rectory of St. James, in which he seeks to fix the character of what he terms the theology of the nineteenth century; but which we should

* Clerical Subscription Commission Report.

rather call the Dean's school of opinion. Judging its peculiarity and its promise to consist, as plain people would gather from his words, mainly in the subjection of all objective truth to speculation—ranging on its side not only its avowed supporters, but as 'being penetrated to a considerable degree with the modern spirit,' its most distinguished opponents, he finds seven distinct reasons for anticipating its final triumph, one of them being ' the calmness of its advocates '—a startling assertion to the readers of the debates in Convocation, unless the Dean's name has been inserted by a mistake for that of some fiery advocate of the other side, as the utterer of certain recent orations in the Jerusalem Chamber.

To others, the scene suggests very different impressions. They see little beside the muddy slime of the discoloured stream, the passionate whirlpools which disturb whilst they hasten its progress, and the froth and foam boiling around the strange collection of floating substances which for the most part deface the silvered surface that of old had given back the burnished rays of the sun, or mirrored in unbroken outline the encircling heavens. The truth probably lies between these two views of the times in which we live. Such disturbances of long-settled currents of thought are no proof either of depth or of power. They may be accounted for by the sudden rising of what are, after all, but transitory landsprings. There is no proof in such swellings of Jordan that the great depths have been broken up to add new volume to the ancient river. They promise no very magnificent or permanent results, yet they have in them nothing alarming (though the rising waters send abroad a few troublesome beasts of prey who had sheltered in their jungle), unless the river's banks are overhanging and unsound; and they may even have their utility in sweeping away old accumulations and preparing the cleansed stream for another and a purer calm.

One of these subjects which has now come again to the surface is that of Clerical Subscription. The question has recently been stirred somewhat roughly in the House of Commons. In July, 1863, Mr. Dodson called attention to a petition from certain members of the University of Oxford for the abolition of the requirement of subscription to formularies of Faith as a qualification for academical degrees; and in March, 1864, he moved the second reading of a Bill for the abolition of Subscription to the Thirty-nine Articles and to the three articles of the 36th Canon, now required as necessary conditions for the degree of Master of Arts or of Doctor in any faculty. These debates travelled, as might be expected, over far wider grounds than the mere academical question, and brought more or less under review the whole question of subscription to any test as the rule of a national Church.

'The strife,' Mr. Buxton told the House, 'was between the principle of religious subjection and the principle of religious liberty. It was impossible to understand the meaning of these tests, or even to imagine any feasible plea for them, unless they were regarded as parts of a great system which emanated in days gone by from the idea that uniformity of belief was the first essential. . . . That idea 300 years ago led the Government of almost every land in Christendom to attempt the extermination, by fire and sword, of all who broke through the required uniformity of belief. This test was in fact nothing else but a miserable rag and tatter of the system which issued from the idea that uniformity of belief was essential. . . . . Whilst he admitted the necessity of some such tests for the authorised teachers of a national Church, he strongly detested the tyrannical stringency of the existing subscriptions required of the clergy.'

The struggle which followed was severe, and the issue doubtful. In March the second reading of the Bill was carried by 211 ayes to 189 noes. On the next stage of the Bill in June, the going into Committee was carried in a much fuller House by a majority reduced from 22 to 10, the ayes being 236 to 226 noes; on the 1st of July an amendment to postpone the third reading till this day six months was lost by 10, the numbers being 140 to 150. On the same night, on the direct question of the third reading, the ayes and noes each reached 170, and the casting vote of the Speaker alone saved the Bill, which passed the same night through its last ordeal, on the question that the Bill do pass, by 173 to 171.

It was plain, after these debates and divisions, that the question could not be quietly shelved; and Lord Palmerston's Government, already touched with the enfeebling hand of age, flew to the familiar resource of a troubled ministry. It appointed a Royal Commission to inquire into the matter. The Commission, it was understood, was to consist of leading men of all schools and parties who were known to have taken interest in the subject, and who were not absolutely resolved either against all subscription or against all modification of that form of it which actually existed amongst ourselves. It required a long catalogue of names in any degree to exhaust such a list. The subject was one with which many men were officially, and some *officiously* connected; and their various representatives reached (in the Commission), by various graduations, from the Archbishop of Canterbury to Lord Ebury; from the Bishop of Oxford, Sir William Heathcote, and Sir John Coleridge, to Dr. Lushington, Mr. Napier, and Mr. Buxton; and from Dean Milman to Mr. Venn. It might have been thought at first that anything like an unanimous decision would be impossible from twenty-seven such counsellors* on such a subject.

---

* The entire list comprised the Archbishops of Canterbury, York, Armagh, and Dublin; the Earls Stanhope and Harrowby; the Bishops of London, Winchester,

For granting that some subscription was to be kept, yet how wide in their scope were the questions which remained behind, and invited diversity of judgment! Should subscription to the Thirty-nine Articles be still made obligatory on all clergymen? Might it not be urged that such subscription was altogether unnecessary as the safeguard for the essential doctrines of Christianity, which might be more safely and fully protected by other means; that it tended to create and keep alive, rather than to reconcile, religious differences; that the Articles were framed in an atmosphere of fierce controversy; that they treated of the most profound, abstruse, and agitated theological questions; that on these subjects, bristling with difficulties, they were throughout controversial—speaking, of necessity, the controversial language of their day—requiring very careful study and very wide knowledge of the disputes and opinions of the times in which they were composed, to be distinctly understood; that the calm and deep examination of all the questions involved in such knowledge is not to be expected from young men on entering the Holy Ministry, for that the range of such questions is immense, nay, almost infinite; that even when the definitions of our Articles concern the fundamental truths of our faith, and are—as they are—at once exquisitely subtle, and yet, for their subject-matter, remarkably distinct and clear, that still their dry logical form is the most unpropitious for teaching and avouching the doctrines they enunciate, but that, beside these fundamental truths, they branch out into profound subjects which modern wisdom has concluded to be beyond the verge of human thought, and the power of human

---

St. David's, and Oxford; Lords Lyttelton, Cranworth, and Ebury; Mr. Bouverie; Dr. Lushington; Mr. Walpole; Mr. Napier; Sir John Coleridge; Sir W. Heathcote; Mr. Buxton; the Deans of St. Paul's, Ely, and Lincoln; Archdeacon Sandford; Dr. Jacobson; Mr. Venn; and Mr. Humphry.

language; that their declarations concerning the sacraments are flavoured rather with the polemics of past days than with the enduring spirit of devotion; that thus they are poor teachers of the truth, and no bulwarks against new errors which have sprung up since their construction; that this infirmity has been revealed, whenever their strength for such service has been tested in our Courts; that they have notoriously failed to maintain uniformity of doctrine, since they have been subscribed, through successive generations, by men who are identified with all the different schools of religious opinion known amongst us; whilst the uncertainty in which the question of how far the subscriber is bound to believe, and not merely to acquiesce, in what he subscribes, is an immoral trial of the conscience—leading men, on the one hand, to tamper with sacred obligations, and, on the other, to fall into the paralysing torture of doubt? As wide as this, it might assuredly have been expected that the controversy must have opened on the members of this Commission. From its composition it could scarcely have been possible but that there were, amongst its members, those whose disapprobation of any subscription to the Thirty-nine Articles could not have fallen far short of such positions as we have noted above.

In the Report of the Commissioners there is no positive evidence of such difference of opinion having existed. A so-called religious newspaper, indeed, which throughout the sittings professed to have some interior sense of what was proceeding, was wont to whisper its suspicious notes of the internal discords of the Chamber; and when the Report appeared, with the signatures of all the Commissioners, it found, in the unreasoned but clearly-stated conclusions of which it consisted, a new evidence of the fierce dissensions which in their progress had burnt up all the surrounding verdure, and left the charred columns of the naked propositions alone as the surviving witnesses of past volcanic activity. But its information was questionable, and its instinct for suspecting notorious. Nothing has since appeared to justify its surmises. But we have had proof enough that, as might have been supposed, all these views found their advocates in the wide circle to whom the question had been submitted. The speech of the Dean of St. Paul's, published in the last number of 'Fraser's Magazine,' contains all the arguments which it appeared to us might probably have been urged against subscription to the Thirty-nine Articles. Mr. Napier, in his 'Answer,' whilst he admires the chivalry of 'a Dean errant,' deals unsparingly with what he conceives to have been the unproved and mischievous propositions of the speech, which was meant to show that the required subscription to the Articles and the Prayer-book, taken together, was a very dangerous, a very objectionable, and a very immoral trial of the conscience.* 'These,' says Mr. Napier, ' are hard words; but hard words are not a substitute for strong or sufficient reasons.'† Mr. Napier's reasons probably appeared to the Commission as they appear to us, 'strong and sufficient' enough to overpower the Dean's words; whilst enough is known by all of us of Dr. Milman, to make us feel sure that in those secret discussions he had something more to urge than the mere element of wordy war.

All of these opinions, then, had to be weighed and answered before any practical conclusions could be gained; and yet answered doubtless they were with a very unusual completeness of reply; since the signature of the author of the paper of objections, which look startling and extreme even in the pages of our contemporary, is subscribed without note of

* 'Clerical Subscription Commission, Answer to the Speech of the Dean of St. Paul's, by the Right Hon. Jos. Napier, D.C.L.,' p. 21.
† Mr. Napier's 'Answer,' p. 30.

reserve to the recommendation of the very subscription they impugn.

Nor would this be all. Very different estimates may undoubtedly be formed as to the history of subscription amongst ourselves; and those different estimates would inevitably lead to very different practical conclusions as to the nature and even purpose of any changes which should be introduced into it. It might be treated as a set of props and buttresses, which the events of former times had shown to be necessary for the support of the ancient fabric, and which it would be the height of rashness to touch incautiously, or to remove without supplying everywhere their place with similar defences. On the other hand, it might be argued, that in the settlement of these questions we had inherited the records of a fierce struggle, the victors in which had been severe, and harsh, and unapproachable; that our forms of subscription had been drawn up in that hour of bitter triumph, with a hard and ingenious exclusiveness, which it became us to sweep eagerly away to cover our fathers' shame and separate us from their sin.

The admirable paper of Mr. Walpole, which was printed in their Appendix by the Commissioners, and which we shall use freely in these pages, shows how thoroughly these questions were examined in the course of their inquiries.

That they arrived (as the signatures of all the Commissioners to their common recommendations prove them to have done) at a unanimous conclusion, is another proof of the completeness of their sifting of the subject. Nothing short of this could have drawn one harmonious voice out of all the discordant utterances with which such discussions must have opened. What that conclusion was, we will presently set before our readers; but for the present it will suffice to say, that should their recommendations be adopted, two considerable alterations of our present practice will have been effected· There will be first a great simplification and diminution in number of the oaths and declarations which are now binding on the clergy. This of itself will be a clear gain, since all needless oaths and all unnecessary declarations are of course an evil in themselves. But, further, there will be a considerable relaxation in the stringency of the declarations. This, too, seems to us a clear gain. All excessive stringency in such subscriptions destroys its own efficiency. For the assertion of an absolute unity of view, which is really incompatible with the inalienable freedom of the human mind, must introduce either conscious falsehood, which swallows the whole declaration at a gulp, or a latitude in the use of the common words, the limits of which, being left to the conscience of each individual, are practically wholly unrestricted. The words of our existing declarations, though patient, no doubt, of reasonable explanation and defence, can hardly be cleared from the charge of tending towards this dangerous extreme.

Of what uninspired book can it be safe to require of every beneficed clergyman (as we do in the case of the Book of Common Prayer) to declare that he gives his 'unfeigned assent and consent' to all and everything contained and prescribed in and by it? This form, the invention, be it remembered, of Parliament, and not of the clergy, bears on its front the marks of the unhappy time when it was enacted. The acts of that era (1662) are often spoken of as if they embodied only the violence of the restored party, and many hard words have in consequence been uttered against the leading Churchmen of that day. It is perfectly true that those were reactionary times, and that there was a hardness and violence in many towards the defeated faction which is worthy of all censure and regret. But this is far from being the whole statement of the case. Such an enactment as this witnesses quite as much to the sin of the provokers of such violence, as to the existence of that which they evoked. All the violence and fraud, all the dishonesties and cant by which the Puritans had ejected Churchmen from their benefices, and through which they now sought to keep out from their rights the returning claimants, are written broad in these rigid letters. No doubt there was something of the insolence of present triumph in such a declaration, but there was also the desire to frame something which it should be impossible for the loosest Puritan to utter, and so retain the post to which possession of doubtful legality was the only plea against the claims of returning and more rightful owners. This was, no doubt, the intention of Parliament in requiring so trenchant a declaration. But when the peculiar evils of the times which required, or seemed to require, such strait bonds to be laid upon all liberty of opinion, have passed away, it is surely desirable that this excessive strictness should be relaxed. Such has been the decision, and, we think, the wise decision, of the Commissioners. The case of this single declaration is a good example of the necessity of an accurate knowledge of the history of our existing forms of subscription as a preliminary to forming any sound judgment on the degree in which they can be safely altered or relaxed; and this history, at least in outline, it may be well, before going further into the question, to trace out. Two important facts appear distinctly in its course; first, that subscription marks a period of liberty; and secondly, that whenever it was strained to any extreme strictness, it was devised, not by the clergy, to coerce opinion amongst themselves, but by the laity, in their jealous care of the religious teaching of their established guides.

Before the Reformation no subscription was required from the body of the clergy, as none was necessary. The Bishops

at their consecration took an oath of obedience to the king, in which, besides promising subjection in matters temporal, they 'utterly renounced and clearly forsook all such clauses, words, sentences, and grants, which they had, or should have, of the Pope's Holiness that in any wise was hurtful or prejudicial to His Highness or His Estate Royal;' whilst to the Pope they bound themselves by oath to keep the rules of the Holy Fathers, the decrees, ordinances, sentences, dispositions, reservations, provisions, and commandments Apostolic, and to their powers to cause them to be kept by others.*
And as their command over their clergy was complete, and they could at once remove any who violated the established rule of opinion, no additional obligation or engagement from men under such strict discipline was requisite. The statement, therefore, that 'the Roman Catholic clergy, and the clergy of the Eastern Church, neither formerly, nor now, were bound by any definite forms of subscription; and that the unity of the Church is preserved there as the unity of the State is preserved everywhere, not by preliminary promises or oaths, but by the general laws of discipline and order;†' though true to the letter, is really wholly untrue in its application to the argument concerning subscriptions. For it is to the total absence of liberty, and to the severity of 'the general laws of discipline and order,' and not to a liberty greater than our own, that this absence of subscription is due.

In point of fact, the requirement of subscription from the clergy was coeval with the up-growth of liberty of opinion; whilst the circumstances of the English Reformation of religion made it essential to the success and the safety of that great movement. It was essential to its success; for as it

---

* Gibson's 'Codex,' vol. i. pp. 116, 117.
† 'Letter to Bishop of London,' by A. P. Stanley, p. 36.

was accomplished mainly by a numerical minority, both of the clergy and laity of the land, there could be no other guarantee for its maintenance than the assurance that its doctrines would be honestly taught, and its ritual observed by by the whole body of the conforming clergy.

Thus the Reformation subscriptions aimed at the prevention of covert Popery, a danger to which the Reforming laity felt that they were exposed by the strong wishes of a majority of their own class; by the undissembled bias of many of the parochial clergy; and by the secret bias of some even of the bishops; whilst the diminution of their absolute control over the clergy lessened the power of enforcing the new opinions when the bishop was sincerely attached to them.

The first and essential requirement of this era was a hearty renunciation of the usurped jurisdiction of the Bishop of Rome within the realm. The intensity of the conviction which then pervaded the Legislature of the greatness of this necessity may be measured by the extraordinary severity of the acts by which it was enjoined. The oath of the king's supremacy was passed, and it was made high treason for any ecclesiastical person to refuse to take it. This had been indeed for generations before the Reformation the continual battle-field between England and Rome. The statute book bears abundant witness to the vigorous struggles of the Plantagenets before the Reformation against the usurpations of the Roman Pontiff. It was but natural when the time of full emancipation came, that there should be a certain fierceness in assertion of the long-coveted independence. The feeling of the Puritan Bunyan to a great degree possessed the nation, and they triumphed over the 'old giant' in his decay, who had kept in his strength so ruthless a court and such terrible dungeons; though now, 'by reason of age, and also of the many shrewd brushes that he met with in his younger days, he was grown so crazy and stiff in his joints that he could do little more than sit in his cave's mouth grinning at pilgrims as they go by, and biting his nails because he cannot get at them.' * Nor did the stern resolution to have no more of these old usurpations in any degree die out. The Statutes of Henry VIII.† were indeed repealed in the reign of Philip and Mary; but amongst the first Acts of Elizabeth were those which restored to the Crown of England its ancient jurisdictions. The very title is indicative of the spirit in which the claim was made. It was the assertion of an ancient nationality with which the foreign Bishop had dared to interfere by constituting himself the fountain of jurisdiction in matters spiritual, and exempting so far as he could from their sovereign sway the persons and the causes of the clergy. The substitution of milder penalties in these Acts marked indeed that the time of spasm was passed, whilst they left no doubt as to the absolute determination of the framers of the Acts. The penalty for refusing to take the oath of supremacy was changed from high treason to the loss of promotion, benefice, and office.

The next great requirement of this æra was the use of the new ritual. There existed no doubt amongst many of the clergy a secret love for the old forms; and as on this point a large number of the common people sympathised with them, the authority of the Bishops would not suffice to introduce generally the reformed ritual. This accordingly was enforced by the Acts of Edward‡ and Elizabeth;§ and in the new ordinal the oath of the King's sovereignty was inserted with a view to bind by its obligation the consciences of all the

---

* 'Pilgrim's Progress,' p. 78, ed. 1760.
† 28 Henry VIII., c. 10, and 35 Henry VIII., c. 3.
‡ 2 & 3 Edward VI., c. 1, and 5 & 6 Edward VI., c. 1.
§ 1 Eliz., c. 2.

clergy. Strictly speaking, this was at first their only subscription, so far as actual law, whether of canon or of statute, reached. The liberty of the clergy was not yet complete, and the authority of the Bishops was deemed sufficient to require and to obtain the public reading of a declaration of his faith from every clergyman entering on his cure. For a time this authority sufficed; but growing freedom led to contentions between the clergy and their Bishops. The puritan element which was now beginning to work strongly in the House of Commons made it eager to enforce doctrinal subscriptions on the clergy, and in the 13th year of Elizabeth, when the violence of the Pope making her strong heart quail, she conceded something of her coveted religious independence of her Parliament, an Act was passed 'For the Ministers of the Church to be of Sound Religion,' requiring every minister under the degree of a bishop to declare his assent and subscribe to 'All the Articles of Religion which only concern the confession of the true Christian Faith and the doctrine of the Sacraments.' It has been ever since a moot point whether these words were intended to limit the subscription to certain of the Articles which concerned the fundamentals of the faith, or whether they were used as being at once a compendious description and a passing justification of the Articles. Selden said in his 'Table Talk,'* 'There is a secret concerning this. Of late ministers have subscribed to all of these, but by the Act of Parliament that confirmed them they ought only to subscribe to those Articles which contain matters of faith and the doctrine of the Sacraments.' The contrary practice, however, prevailed; mainly it seems through the vigorous sway of Archbishop Whitgift, whose 'Articles,' issued in 1583–4, required subscription from all preachers and licensed ministers to the three Articles which

* Title 'Articles,' pp. 3 and 4, quoted by Mr. Walpole in his paper.

are embodied in the 36th canon, and which distinctly name the whole Thirty-nine Articles as those to which subscription is made.* This use of Subscription well illustrates our position, that its strength increased with the growth of clerical liberty. That liberty was already expanding into a licence which the heavy hand of authority—and few hands were heavier than those of Queen Elizabeth—could scarcely curb. The feeble fingers and semi-Puritan inclinations of Archbishop Grindal had sown the wind, and Archbishops Parker, Whitgift, and Bancroft had to reap the whirlwind. That in the long and often irritating strife which followed, in an age to which the first principles of religious liberty were strange, they were never betrayed into words or acts of unnecessary severity, it is not necessary to assert. The very features of men who are breasting with determined contention the blast of a hurricane assume, unawares to themselves, something of unnatural severity; but this may safely be asserted, that whenever their opponents gained a temporary superiority they manifested a far greater violence. Whitgift did but enforce strictly a solemnly-adopted ritual; but the Presbyterians, even after the return of Charles II., sought to prohibit its use, even in the King's chapel, urging him, when they found him obstinate, at least 'to concede that he would not use it entirely, but only have some parts of it read, with mixture of of other good prayers;'† and Prynne, in his old age, reflecting probably on his own share in the treatment of Laud, admitted that if, when the Star Chamber, on Chief Justice Finch's motion, sentenced him to lose his ears, it had taken

---

* Those who wish to go further into the matter may refer to Gibson's 'Codex,' vol. i. 321. See also 'Hist. of the Puritans,' vol. i. pp. 175, 299, and 345; Fuller's 'Church Hist.,' book ix.; Hallam's 'Constitut. Hist.,' vol. ii. 191, 192; Hardwicke's 'History of Articles,' p. 277.

† Clarendon's 'Rebellion,' vii. 502.

off his head at once, it would not have exceeded his deserts. 'Having seen,' says Echard, 'a thousand unexpected calamities, and growing weary of himself, when he had in a manner no enemies to engage him, he began to look at and to repent of his former career, wishing that when they had cut off his ears they had cut off his head.'* On all sides the storm of these angry passions was now gathering blackly round. The removal of the old restraints of episcopal power bred a love of self-assertion in the clergy, which exactly accorded with the growing Puritanism of the time; and the latter part of Elizabeth's reign was disturbed by the contests to which this gave rise, and often by the victory of the insurgent clergy over all authority. 'The Brethren† (for so did they now style themselves), in their churches and charges would neither pray nor say service, nor baptise nor celebrate the Lord's Supper, nor do any other ecclesiastical duty, according to law, but after their own devices.' In this many of the Bishops, hopeless of success in resisting the rising tide, and shrinking from the annoyances to which Whitgift had been subjected, yielded a reluctant acquiescence.

In A.D. 1593 Bishop Bancroft wrote:—

'How carelessly subscription is executed in England I am ashamed to report. Such is the retchlessness of many of our Bishops on the one side, and their desire to be at ease and quietness over their own affairs; and on the other side such is the obstinacy and intolerable pride of that factious sort, as that betwixt both sides, subscription is not at all required, or if it be, the Bishops admit them so to qualify that it were better to be omitted altogether.'‡

Nor was this the complaint of an episcopal pen alone. Sir Walter Raleigh, in a passage§ Mr. Walpole has quoted in his

* Lawson's 'Life and Times of Archbishop Laud,' vol. ii. 184.
† 'Rogers on the XXXIX. Articles,' p. 10, reprinted by the Parker Society—quoted by Mr. Walpole.
‡ 'Rogers on Articles,' ut supra—quoted by Mr. Walpole.
§ 'First Part of the History of the World,' ch. v. sec. 1.

draft report, speaks quite as severely of the present, and with as much alarm for the future. Speaking of the Tabernacle and the Ark, he says:—

'The industry used in the framing thereof, and every and the least part thereof, the curious workmanship thereon bestowed, the exceeding charge and expense in the provisions, the dutiful observance in the laying up and preserving the Holy vessels, the solemn removing thereof, the vigilant attendance thereon, and the provident defence of the same, which all ages have in some degree imitated, is now so forgotten and cast away in this superfine age by those of the family, by the Anabaptist, Brownist, and other sectaries; as all cost and care bestowed and had of the Church, wherein God is to be served and worshipped, is accounted a kind of popery, and as proceeding from an idolatrous disposition; insomuch as time would soon bring to pass (if it were not resisted) that God would be turned out of Churches into barns, and from thence again into the fields and mountains, and under the hedges; and the officers of the ministry (robbed of all dignity and respect) be as contemptible as these places. All order, discipline, and church government left to newness of opinion and men's fancies; yea, and soon after, as many kinds of religion would spring up as there are parish churches within England; every contentious and ignorant person clothing his fancy with the Spirit of God, and his imagination with the gift of revelation; inasmuch as when the truth, which is but one, shall appear to the simple multitude no less variable than contrary to itself, the faith of men will soon after die away by degrees, and all religion be held in scorn and contempt.'

With the Queen's life expired even the shadowy authority of the Canons for Subscription, which, unconfirmed either by Convocation or Parliament, rested altogether on the sanction of the Bishops and the Crown. It was not too much to fear that universal anarchy was at hand.

In such heavy clouds, angry with the prophecy of future conflict, set the once proud light of the imperious Elizabeth. Nor did the immediate succession of the Crown promise any great improvement. It was not even clear that the new King might not bring with him from his northern Dominion a strong taint of its Presbyterian leaven, which might lift the Puritan section into the supremacy for which it thirsted, and enable it to vent all its animosity alike on Prelacy and Popery. These apprehensions, however, were speedily set at rest; and it was clear that, whatever might be the treatment of the Church of England by the Royal pedant who had mounted the throne, it would not be in favour of Puritanism that his influence would be exerted. The King's language and demeanour at the Hampton Court Conference must have violently dashed to the ground any hopes they had entertained from his Presbyterian nurture, the only effect of which from the unsparing rod of Buchanan in his boyhood down to the privileged invectives of the pulpit in his manhood, had evidently been to exasperate to the utmost pitch of undignified irritation his narrow and selfish nature. Even in the Conference he broke out into language unsuitable, in most men's judgment, for Royal lips. Mr. Walpole quotes from Neale's 'Puritans,' vol. i., 441, ed. 1857, the following choice morsel:—

'If you aim at a Scotch Presbytery, it agreeth as well with monarchy as God and the devil. Then Jack, and Tom, and Will, and Dick, shall meet and censure me and my Council. Therefore I reiterate my former speech Le Roy s'avisera: Stay, I pray, for one seven years, before you demand, and then if you find me grow pursy and fat, I may perchance hearken unto you, for that government will keep me in breath, and give me work enough.'[*]

The concluding words of his address to the Puritan ministers present at the Conference, as Neale records them, were no less vehement:—"If that be all your party hath to say I will make them conform themselves, or else I will harry them out of the land, or else do worse—only hang them—that's all.'[†]

In this temper the King was little disposed to see the

[*] Fuller's 'Church Hist.,' B. x. 18; Neale's 'Puritans,' vol. i. p. 441, edit. 1857.
[†] Neale's 'History of the Puritans,' vol. ii. p. 14, edit. 1822.

troubles which were evidently gathering in the days of the late Queen's decline, come unresisted to an head; and as it was impossible to restore to the Bishops their old autocratic authority over the clergy, he turned at once to the instrument of Subscription for the maintenance of uniformity of doctrine. Convocation was called together. At its meeting it revised the Canons of the Church and passed amongst them the three articles of Archbishop Whitgift. These were thereupon published with the sanction of the Royal Letters Patent; and, so far as the law spiritual is concerned, have from that time governed the subscription of the clergy as to the doctrines which they undertake to teach. The first of these three celebrated articles asserts the supremacy of the English Crown in moderate and well-weighed language; and whilst dropping the obnoxious title of head of the Church, it declares that the King's Majesty is, under God, the supreme governor of the realm, as well in all spiritual or ecclesiastical things or causes as temporal, and denies all jurisdiction within it to any foreign potentate or power. The second article declares that the Book of Common Prayer contains in it nothing contrary to the Word of God, and may lawfully be used; and the third allows the Thirty-nine Articles to be agreeable to the Word of God.

On this basis matters continued until the proscription of the Church of England under the Commonwealth. Then all the forebodings of the sagacious Raleigh, and all the fears of the pedant James, had been abundantly fulfilled. Crown and Altar, Prelate and Prince, had gone down in the common storm. Mr. Walpole quotes two striking passages, one from the Churchman Evelyn, one from the Presbyterian Edwards, describing the miserable results of the religious lawlessness which, to so great a degree, caused, and so surely accompanied the turbulent swellings of the great Rebellion.

'Things,' writes Edwards,* 'every day grow worse and worse; you can hardly imagine them so bad as they are; no kind of blasphemy, heresy, disorder, and confusion but it is found among us, or is coming in upon us. For we, instead of reformation, are grown from one extreme to another; fallen from Scylla to Charybdis; from Popish usurpations, superstitions, and prelatical tyranny to damnable heresies, horrid blasphemies, libertinism, and fearful anarchy. Our evils are not removed and cured, but only changed; one disease and devil hath left us, and another as bad is come in the room; many of the sects and sectaries in our days deny all principle of religion, are enemies to all holy duties, order, learning, overthrowing all; being vertiginosi spiritus, whirligig spirits. And the great opinion of an universal toleration tends to the laying all waste, and the dissolution of all religion and good manners.'

Instead of obtaining licence to act as the public teachers of the faith on the easy condition of subscribing their assent to certain carefully-constructed fundamental propositions, on which their general acceptance by the Church had already fixed a definite meaning, men had to satisfy the independent 'Triers,' judges marked by the grossest ignorance and the most unscrupulous dishonesty. The most learned divines were now ousted from their posts, to make room for some unlettered friend of the Triers or their party, on the plea of ignorance, by men who were innocent of all knowledge alike of the Greek of the New Testament, of the history of the Church, and of the writings of the Fathers. The use of the Book of Common Prayer was forbidden, under heavy penalties. Here then, again, in spite of the loud professions of republican liberty, it was indeed a time of tyranny which put an end to Subscription.

With the liberty which the restoration of the monarch restored subscription revived, but, as we have said already, with some new and marked features of severity. The Savoy Conference failed wholly to reconcile the conflicting parties, and the Church of England resumed her legal status, no

* Gangran, 'Epis. Ded.'

change having been introduced into her doctrine, her discipline, or her formularies, from the hope of comprehending objectors; and with no presence in her own body either of Presbyterians or Independents. The clergy would, it seems, have been content with the old and moderate canonical subscriptions. But the reactionary temper of the Parliament was violent and harsh. The members had suffered too much too recently from the sourness of Puritanical bigotry, to maintain a calm and judicial temper; and they resolved to leave no door open through which its preachers could, without renouncing their peculiarities, creep into the National Establishment. The Act of Uniformity bristles with such provisions. Its requirement of a declaration of unfeigned assent and consent to all and everything contained and prescribed in and by the Book of Common Prayer, itself stringent enough, was backed up by clauses specially aimed at the Puritan lecturers, who had established themselves in many churches, and who were now subjected to a far severer rule than that which governed the parochial clergy. They were to read over the whole Thirty-nine Articles aloud in the Bishop's presence before being licensed, and were never to preach unless they had just read, or at the least been present at the reading of the public office in the Prayer Book which belonged to that time of day.

All this extreme stringency was of lay devising; and so determined was it, that when the House of Lords, in which the Spiritualty was represented by the Bishops, desired to mitigate the severity of the declaration of 'assent and consent' to all and everything in the Book of Common Prayer, by interpreting it as applying only to the use, and not to the actual correctness of the book, the Commons, with a somewhat unwonted heat, declared at a conference that such a course had in it 'neither justice nor prudence,' and unceremoniously rejected the proposal.*

Thus, then, the present state of subscription amongst us has been reached, and it bears marks on every side of the accidental and transitory character of the influences by which it has been shaped. Though the Church of England and Ireland is by law united, different subscriptions and declarations are taken in the two Islands. Amongst other differences, a special renunciation of transubstantiation,† and an oath to keep a school for teaching English,‡ are still exacted of the Irish clergy; whilst both in England and Ireland, besides the oaths of allegiance and supremacy, and the oaths of canonical obedience and against simony on being licensed to a curacy or instituted to a living; separate and distinct declarations of conformity to the Liturgy and Articles are required by the Canons of the Church and the Statutes of the realm.

As to all of these, the Commissioners recommend that the subscriptions and declarations should be the same in England and Ireland; that the oaths of allegiance and supremacy, as being out of keeping with a devotional office, should be taken before and not during the Ordination and Consecration services; that a declaration should be substituted for the oath against simony; that the oath of canonical obedience should be retained; that the provisions of the acts of uniformity which specially affect 'Lecturers,' should be repealed; and that on every occasion on which a Subscription or Declaration shall be required to be made in England or Ireland, with reference to the Articles of Religion, or the Book of Common Prayer, the following form be used :—

---

* 'Lords' Journals,' vol. ii. pp. 553-557; 'Commons' Journals,' vol. viii. p. 555.
† 3 William and Mary, c. 2, § 5.
‡ 28 Henry VIII., c. 15 (Irish).

'I, A. B., do solemnly make the following declaration :—

'I assent to the Thirty-nine Articles of Religion, and to the Book of Common Prayer, and of Ordering of Bishops, Priests, and Deacons: I believe the doctrine of the United Church of England and Ireland, as therein set forth, to be agreeable to the Word of God : and in Public Prayer and Administration of the Sacraments I will use the form in the said Book prescribed, and none other, except so far as shall be ordered by lawful authority.'

As to most of these recommendations the Commissioners may expect perfect unanimity of opinion. No one would desire to maintain the peculiar Irish declarations, or to interrupt our most solemn services with semi-political oaths; and every one must agree that, as to such an offence as simony, which is so difficult legally to define, the greatest authorities not unfrequently differ whether a peculiar act is or is not simoniacal, it is most unwise to exact a general disavowal upon oath—a course little likely to restrain the corrupt, and almost certain to entangle tender consciences in distressing perplexities.

The recommendation which will be most eagerly canvassed is that which substitutes the new form for those already in use. On the point involved in this decision several courses, were open to them. They might have recommended the abolition of all Subscription, as tending to fetter the freedom of thought; or even if, with some of the Swiss and German sects, they retained the transitory shadow of its principle, they might have required a mere engagement that the clergy would faithfully teach their flocks out of the Word of God; or if they had been in love with feeble ambiguity they might have adopted Archbishop Tillotson's suggested form: 'I, A. B., do submit to the doctrine, discipline, and worship of the Church of England as it shall be established by law and promise to teach and practice accordingly ;'[*] or they might

[*] Birch's 'Life of Tillotson,' p. 169.

have fallen back upon the form contained in the 36th canon of 1603, and recommended the abolition or the alteration of the offensive 'assent and consent' of the Act of Uniformity.

A good deal is to be said for this last scheme. Amongst other recommendations of it is the fact that it was suggested in January, 1864, by a Committee of the Lower House of the Convocation of Canterbury, who recommended that no alteration should be made in the subscription required by the 36th Canon : 'a form,' say the Committee, ' which commends itself by the wisdom and moderation of its language ;' whilst as to the Declaration in the Act of Uniformity, the Lower House Committee recommended a substitution of ' a consent to the use of all and everything contained in and by the Book of Common Prayer for an unfeigned assent and consent to every part of it.' But, with all that there was to recommend this form, we are of opinion that the substitution of one wholly new is, on the whole, a wise suggestion. The old form newly adopted would, in effect, have been a fresh one so far as regards the force and effect of every word and expression contained in it. This would have made some change almost inevitable. After the quibbles of Mr. Wilson,* it would, for instance, have been impossible to leave the words 'he alloweth the Book of Articles ;' and the old declaration, taken simply as it stood, and merely re-enacted, might have seemed to favour the notion of there being some difference in the authority of the Articles and the Book of Common Prayer. Some change, therefore, there must have been, yet every change, because it was a change, would have assumed a disproportionate importance. A new form, therefore, was to be preferred; and if a new form was to be devised, it is not probable that one less open to exception could have been

* 'Letter to Bishop of London,' p. 12. Ibid., p. 13.

framed. It binds the subscriber to a simple assent to the Articles and Book of Common Prayer, to a belief in the agreement of the doctrine set forth in them with the Word of God, and to an obedient use of the prescribed Ritual. More than this—if this is honestly declared—subscription cannot effect: less than this would make it an unmeaning mockery.

This, of course, will not satisfy those whose real object is to abolish subscription altogether; who wish to leave the public teachers of a set of fixed doctrines free, not only to change their opinions on these points, but, having changed them, still to hold their preferment. Hitherto the almost unanimous voice of the laity has been clear against granting any such allowance to their teachers. Their English honesty and clear common sense has seen through the flimsy fallacy so often put forward, that subscription is a sore injury to men of high qualities and endowments; that it is constituting one set of subjects on which they are forbidden liberty, not of speech only or of action, but of thought. They know that there is no such tyranny—no such suffering; that, on the other hand, there is amongst us not permitted only, but encouraged, the largest allowance of free thought which is compatible with teaching honestly, not as an inquiring philosophy, but as revealed truth, any positive set of doctrines; and they have no wish that the clergy of their church should be at liberty to retain their office as its public teachers, if their absolute free thoughts have led them to conclusions at variance on material points with her doctrines. It has, indeed, been asserted both that many who have subscribed are groaning under their fetters, and that the known necessity of wearing them has prevented many young men, with deep yearnings for truth, from entering a ministry which would compel them to submit their necks to such a yoke. No proof of these confident assertions has ever been attempted; and we think with Dr. Hawkins, whose 'Sermon' and 'Notes,' * are marked throughout with his wonted, calm, and convincing accuracy, that 'the supposed restraints upon free and full inquiry into all religious questions within the Church of England are greatly exaggerated, and that generous spirits and intellects of the highest order have no just cause to refrain from entering into her service, from any dread of an undue restriction upon their private judgments.'

Nothing is more common than these 'exaggerations.' One favourite form of them is to represent the exceeding greatness of the difficulty which the very nature of the documents to be subscribed presents to their subscription. 'They consist,' Dean Stanley tells us, ' of a number of complicated propositions on many intricate and difficult questions—propositions discussed by men who lived three hundred years ago in the heat of vehement struggles which have long since passed away.' They contain, he tells us again—to aggravate the hardship of subscription—' at least six hundred propositions on the most intricate and complex subjects that can engage the human mind.'

No one can have dipped into the current literature upon this subject without being perfectly familiar with such charges as these, brought by men who, like the Dean of Westminster, draw one of their auguries for the success of their own party from the extreme calmness of its advocates. 'Men must,' we are told, 'either consciously say what they do not mean, or submit to have their individual intellects and spirits so deadened and utterly enslaved, as to bind themselves to assent and consent unfeignedly to everything contained and prescribed in and by a book which contains thousands of propositions on the most solemn subjects of thought and belief . . . . . which is inconsistent with itself . . . . . which is

* 'The Liberty of Private Judgment in the Church of England. A Sermon by the Rev. E. Hawkins, D.D.'—'Notes upon Subscription.' By the Same.

notoriously a compromise . . . . . the chief merit of which is thought by many to be in its inconsistency,' &c.* And yet what language can be more exaggerated than all this? The first great fallacy on which it rests has been admirably brought out by Dr. Hawkins in his 'Notes on Subscription,' in which he shows how distinctly, whilst requiring a real assent to both, the Church of England plainly distinguishes between propositions which express the essential truths of the creeds, the true Catholic faith, and those truths in a lower subject matter which are what Bishop Bramhall calls 'pious opinions, fitted for the preservation of unity.' Nor does he deal less ably with the second fallacy, which asserts that by subscription men bind themselves never more to enquire into truth or to modify their present views, showing that as 'to promises of *future* belief we have absolutely none,' and that all we have is that to which no honest man who is above casuistry can object, namely, a pledge that men will not, after '*material* changes in their opinions, retain any position in which they have been placed upon the faith of their subscriptions.'

Again, as to the multitude of the propositions to which it is asserted that our subscription extends, some of them, it is urged, notoriously contrary to fact, as, for instance, that the creed which bears his name was composed by St. Athanasius, or that the quotation in the 29th Article is rightly attributed to St. Augustine, Dr. Hawkins excellently well remarks, 'We do not subscribe to the correctness of the quotation, but to the truth of the article;' and these alleged mistakes, if they proved anything, would supply reasons not for altering subscription, but for correcting the articles. We do not subscribe to statements metaphysical, historical, political, or expository, although they may be incidentally and

* 'Letter to Bishop of London,' by Rev. H. Highton, late Principal of Cheltenham College, pp. 12, 13.

indirectly involved in the statements of the articles, but solely to those points which they directly propose for our assent, in order to 'the avoiding of diversities of opinion, and the establishing of consent *touching true religion.*'

But after all, the main objection to subscription, which underlies all these minor difficulties, is that which addresses itself to requiring from men a distinct declaration of their belief in the great doctrines of the Christian faith. It is, and always has been, a restless anxiety to be free from the obligation to believe on these great matters, which leads to the assault upon the practice of subscription. The Feathers Tavern petition, in 1772, in a few homely words, put forth the real claim; 'The undoubted right, as Protestants, of interpreting Scripture for themselves, without being bound by any human explications thereof, or required to acknowledge by subscription or declaration the truth of any formulary of religious faith and doctrine whatsoever, save Holy Scripture itself.' [*]

Here is the real objection. Nor would we deny that such difficulties, from the nature of the case, must exist as to the mysterious truths of the Trinity, the Incarnation, and the like; though, as Dr. Hawkins well reminds us, these difficulties are not in themselves greater or more difficult than some of those which belong to the truths of natural religion. We have the deepest sympathy with all who are tried by such difficulties; and we fear that there has been of late much to increase if not to cause such trials in 'vague floating notions of morality, to be taught apart from religion; of doctrines to be cherished as sentiments, not embodied in statements; of exalted ideas of our own faculties as being such as would constitute us fit judges of what revelation ought to be;' in the whole teaching, in fact, of the half-

---

[*] See a full account in Dr. Ogilvie's 'Subscription to the Thirty-nine Articles,' 1865, pp. 3, 4, &c.

CLERICAL SUBSCRIPTION. 29

unbelieving, half-sentimental, school which seeks to arrogate to itself the exclusive possession of breadth of view. But such difficulties are not caused by subscription and would not be lessened by its removal. This side of the question has been handled in a most remarkable pamphlet by the Rev. J. B. Mozley.

'It appears to me a point which has not been sufficiently attended to in our controversies on the subject of Subscription, that where the language of a doctrinal formulary and the language of the Bible are the same, whatever explanation we give, in case there is a difficulty, of the language of the Bible, is applicable to the language of the formulary as well; and that, therefore, in such a case, the statement in the formulary is no fresh difficulty, but only one which we have already surmounted in accepting the same statement in the Bible. In such a case the formulary is not, in truth, responsible for the apparently obnoxious nature of the assertion it makes; nor does a person who has already assented to the same declaration in Scripture incur any new responsibility when he assents to the formulary. This appears to be a very simple and natural rule, and yet it is one which a great many serious and most intelligent persons never think of applying when they encounter difficulties in our formularies. Their minds are in a different state and attitude when they read the Bible and when they read a doctrinal formulary. I do not mean simply that they know the Bible to be inspired, and the other document not, but that, as readers, they are freer, more natural, more liberal in interpreting the meaning of Scripture than they are in interpreting the meaning of a formulary, even when it is exactly the same language which is used in both. They come with the expectation of finding ugly and repulsive matter in the human document; and when, therefore, they do find what at first sight is such, they fasten upon it that *primâ facie* meaning as the true and real meaning of the formulary, and will not let it go. No; that is its meaning, and that shall be its meaning, and nobody shall persuade them that it is not. Whereas, when they came across the very same statement in the Bible, they accepted it with a natural and obvious qualification.

'To take the commonly-quoted instance of the damnatory clauses, as they are called, in the Athanasian Creed, which assert of the "Catholic faith" that "except a man believe it faithfully he cannot be saved." The difficulty which is felt about this assertion in the Athanasian Creed does not at all relate to the nature of the *credendum*, or subject-matter of belief—the doctrine of the Trinity—but to condemnation on account of simple belief. Yet this point of condemnation on account of belief is stated in Scripture as strongly as in this Creed. It is asserted in terms, absolutely and positively, "He that believeth and is baptized shall be saved; but he that believeth not shall be damned." How is it, then, that when those who object to the statement of condemnation on account of belief, when they meet it in the Athanasian Creed, did not object to the same statement when they encountered it in Scripture? The reason is obvious—that when they met this statement in Scripture they gave it the benefit of a liberal interpretation. They did not suppose for an instant that this text *could* mean that God, who is just and merciful, would condemn a man simply on account of his not believing certain truths, apart from all consideration of disadvantages of education, early prejudices, and want of opportunities and means of enlightment. They therefore regarded it immediately, I might say unconsciously, as containing the unexpressed condition of *moral* responsibility, and understood the condemnation only to apply to such as did not believe in consequence of faults of their own. But if they gave the assertion this liberal interpretation when they met it in the Bible, why cannot they give it the same interpretation when they meet it in the Athanasian Creed? And if they do, this assertion in the Creed can be no burden to them; it only asserts what Scripture asserts, and need only mean what Scripture means.

'The literal meaning is just the very opposite to that which it especially pretends to be—the *natural* meaning. It is an *un*natural meaning. It is artificial, when we know—know by familiar and practical experience—that language is a system of *understandings*, as well as of *expressions*, to insist, in all cases, upon the bare expression or the naked letter as its adequate exponent.'

And again, in answering the objection that the language of Holy Scripture on these mysterious subjects is, at all events, more simple, Mr. Mozley well asks:—

'But does the attribute of simplicity really belong to the scheme of human salvation, as described in the page of Scripture?—a scheme which, starting with a mysterious depravation of our nature, as mysteriously remedies it, and brings things to their issue by a circuitous process of rectification, instead of by a straight and direct course? I take the actual language of the Bible, as it meets my eye, and I say, it is not simple language. It is complicated language. It is language which expresses a complication of some kind or other in the Invisible world of man's relations to God and God's relations to man; something out of order in nature which requires to be met by supernatural means. And S. Paul discloses a human interior corresponding to this intricacy of Divine truth, and illuminates with his torch a cavern awful in its depth and recesses, when he reveals man to himself. And are there not oppositions which can only be harmonised by interpretation in that Volume, which expresses doctrinal truth by statement and counter-statement, but not always by simplicity and unity of statement?*

'It appears to me, then, that whatever became of the Articles, the self-same difficulties, and the self-same way of meeting them, would go on amongst us; that we should still accept a complicated mass of statement, and that we should accept that mass of statement in a variety of senses according to the particular school to which we belong. The Articles, are, many of them, but a reflection of Scripture, and their interpretation but the reflection of the interpretation of Scripture. Were the representative document to go, the original document itself would still remain to be the subject-matter of conflicting explanations, to be language accepted by all alike and understood by different sections differently, and to be the basis of doctrinal variety under the form of one and the same subscription.'

The following is Mr. Mozley's conclusion from the whole:

'The conclusion which I arrive at, then, is that, over the ground on which I have been travelling relief from subscription is not wanted. We may, I think, be quite sure, that a very large amount of forbearance will always be secured for the results of individual speculation by the natural operation of reasonable feelings in the members of the Church, without instituting any organic change. Our system is one which raises the greatest possible difficulties in the way of prosecution of individuals—not only formal difficulties, but difficulties of feeling. Ours is a system which encourages inquiry and sets minds to work. When, then, we have sanctioned an active principle of examination at the outset, and when we have lived side by side with the gradual growth of individual thought, in the same institution, under the same roof, the sanction of the process must, to a certain extent, affect us even in dealing with its results, when they are erroneous, and must operate as a great practical check upon the temper in which we condemn them. A limit, of course, there must be to freedom of opinion within a communion which professes a definite creed.'

Mr. Mozley's conclusion accords exactly with our view. There must be some limit to freedom of opinion within a communion which professes a definite creed. That limit may be fixed either by the severity of a penal system, which marks

* The Bishop of Oxford, speaking of our Formularies, says, 'Such a state of things is rather a combination than a compromise. And this is the special character of Catholic Truth. For all revealed religion rests upon certain great principles, which the human mind can hold together in what it knows to be a true concord, whilst yet it cannot always by its intellectual processes limit, define, and reconcile what its higher gift of intuition can harmonise.'—*Charge*, 1860.

instantly and chastises mercilessly every defection from the living tradition of belief; or by the mild and self-adjusting action of a reasonable system of subscription. It is precisely for this reason that the existence of such a system is at once a proof and a preservation of liberty. In the interests, therefore, both of liberty and of truth, it is of the utmost moment that our existing system should be preserved. Never, perhaps, was it for each of these high interests more essential than at the present moment. For there is, at this time, a strong current setting on towards unlimited speculation as to all revelation, which would, unchecked, soon bear us on to the boundless sea of unbelief. As this danger increases, there must always be the risk of devout minds seeking by some sacrifice of lawful liberty to save that possession of truth, which, almost alone, is better even than liberty itself. By such a reaction the liberty we have so long enjoyed might be dangerously menaced. But the more immediate and certain danger is undoubtedly on the other side. The volume lately published on the 'Ecclesiastical Judgments of the Privy Council,' under the sanction of the Bishop of London, little as it really answers the often-urged objections that the present supreme Court of Ecclesiastical Appeal has really drifted wide of the great appeal statutes of the Reformation era, tends certainly to discourage any tendency to appeal to our Courts, as they are now constituted, for the maintenance of the necessary limits of belief. We had better, perhaps, explain rather more fully our meaning. The great point on which the writers of this volume rely for the justification of the present Court, is the allegation that the actual composition of the old Court of Delegates gives no 'sanction to the theory that Ecclesiastical laws should be administered exclusively by Ecclesiastical persons.'[*] 'The authority usually quoted,' we are told, 'is that of Bishop

---

[*] 'Ecclesiastical Judgments,' &c., Introduction, p. xlvii.

Gibson,' who states that 'in fact there are no footsteps of any of the Nobility or Common Law Judges in Commissions till the year 1604 (*i. e.* for seventy years after the erection of the Court), nor from 1601 have they been joined in above one Commission in forty till the year 1634, from whence (*i. e* from the downfall of the Bishops and their Jurisdictions which ensued) we may date the present *rule* of mixtures in that Court.'*

The writer's object is to destroy the authority of this assertion. For this purpose he divides the whole time over which Bishop Gibson's statement ranges into three distinct periods; that from the foundation of the Court to 1604: from 1604 to 1640, and the time subsequent to the Reformation.

As to the third period, which is unimportant for the argument, he allows the correctness of the Bishop's statement; but as to the second period, his statement is asserted to be 'absolutely contrary to the fact; whilst, as to the first, the evidence which exists is against him.' These are grave charges; very grave to be adopted and made public by a Bishop of London against one of the greatest, the most learned, and, as till this day the world has believed, the most accurate of his predecessors in that chair of dignity. How, then, is the demolishing charge established? First, there is something rather too like a quibble in a half-ventured suggestion that the presence of civilians, *i. e.* ecclesiastical lawyers not in holy orders, on these Commissions, was not a fulfilment of Gibson's statement. 'Civilians, therefore, we are told, were not excluded, *even according to the statement of Bishop Gibson;* and civilians were often laymen, even in the time of Henry VIII.' Of course they were not excluded; but how does this touch the argument, or tend to invalidate the authority of Gibson, who laid down the rule that ecclesiastical laws were to be administered, not exclu-

* 'Ecclesiastical Judgments,' &c., Introduction, p. xviii.

sively by persons in holy orders, which no one has ever, so far as we are aware, advanced; but by ecclesiastical persons. For civilians, were, in every legal sense of the word, such ecclesiastical persons. They are the legal advisers of Convocation, as the judges are of the House of Lords. They were admitted to their office by rescript from the Archbishop of Canterbury, addressed to his official principal, who was also Dean of the Arches; after taking a solemn oath of allegiance to the Church of England, and being admitted to plead in virtue of their fealty to her.

But the main proof of the alleged falsehood of the Bishop's statement is said to be drawn from the last twenty years of the second period. Of it, the repertory book of the Court of Delegates gives full information. 'During those twenty years there were 1000 appeals in ecclesiastical causes. The Court was composed, in 872 cases, of civilians only; in 2 cases, of Bishops only; in 24 cases, of Bishops and civilians together, without nobility or Common Law Judges. On the other hand, in 110 of the Commissions, Judges alone are named with the civilians; in 59, Judges with Bishops and civilians; and in 13, temporal peers are found with the civilians, and with either Judges or Bishops. In the place, therefore, of Bishop Gibson's assertion, that the nobility or Common Law Judges were present in no more than 1 Commission out of 40, we have the fact that they were present in 182 Commissions out of 1080, being rather more than 1 in 6, and in more than 1 out of 10, they formed the only element in the Court besides the civilians.'

Having, as he conceives, proved this gross misstatement as to the second period, the writer thinks himself entitled to assume the probable presence of like errors as to the first; though the actual records of the Delegates are too scanty to allow of such proof as he tenders with regard to the former period.

But how, when it is closely scrutinised, does this showy list of causes justify so grave censure? To answer this question we must remember the constitution of the Spiritual Courts at that time. The Dean of the Arches received, and now receives, a merely nominal payment; and therefore to feed this high office it was held with the Judgeship of the Prerogative Court. In this latter Court, for reasons which we do not now stop to set out in detail, were tried all the most important testamentary causes originating in the province of Canterbury. In the Arches Court—so as has been stated—united with the Prerogative or Testamentary Court, were tried by appeal all the most important matrimonial causes in the same province. Thus there came before these Courts a multitude of causes which, though technically spiritual, yet really involved no point of the doctrine of the Church. Now, the whole question stripped of its ambiguities is, how many of these alleged 182 Commissions were really engaged with cases involving doctrinal decisions of any kind? For unless some real point of the Church's doctrines or discipline were involved, it would not be too much to anticipate that the Bishops would not sit, but would leave to the civilians, or others, the entire handling of the Commission. Before Bishops Gibson's assertion is so summarily disposed of, it should have been shown how many of these 182 Commissions which are quoted with such triumph, did indeed involve the settlement of any such spiritual question whatever. Such an investigation has been made, and it turns out that between the years 1603 and 1823, there have actually been *only four* spiritual causes, properly so called, tried before the Delegates :—

1. The Bishop of St. David's *v.* Lucy, 13th March, 1699.
2. Salter *v.* Davis, 10th November, 1691.
3. Pelling *v.* Dr. Bettesworth, 16th May, 1713.
4. Havard *v.* Evanson, 27th June, 1775.

In the first case *six* Bishops sat. In the second *three.* In the third *five.* In the fourth none, as a technical point of law alone was decided, and the merits were not heard. While on the other hand, as late as the year 1777, three Prelates were summoned as Delegates on an important cause of Nullity of Marriage. We have thought this matter so important that we have appended to this article a careful note of the names and professions of the Judges and Delegates in each of these cases. It is also to be observed that in these *four* cases, during an interval of more than two centuries, are included all the appeals from the province of York, and we believe from the Ecclesiastical Courts of Ireland until 1783, and the passing of the Act 23 Geo. III. c. 28.

So far for 'Bishop Gibson's misapprehension of the facts.'* It is surely a matter to be much regretted, that such an attack on the veracity or accuracy of a Bishop of London so justly honoured as Gibson—'Clarum et venerabile nomen'— should have received sanction and endorsement from Fulham Palace on such evanescent evidence.

But if this volume fails thus utterly in disproving the assertion that the principle of the Reformation statutes, and the practice of earlier times, committed to ecclesiastical persons the hearing of ecclesiastical appeals, it certainly contains a dreary record of cases which must tend strongly to increase the prevalent disinclination to seek, by legal censures, to preserve the purity of doctrine. It would almost seem that, as if by some hidden law of necessary acting, every such attempt must, in some shape or other, recoil upon the promoter of the suit. Certainly until some great reform has been wrought in the composition and the conduct of these Courts, it must be a most anxious question to every one required by the duties of his office to maintain the legal standard of doctrine, whether he will not rather imperil than protect the truth, by bringing it, even in the last extremity, before such a tribunal. We have already stated† our own desire to see some great reform in this particular. The course of every

---

* 'Ecclesiastical Judgments,' Preface, p. xv.   † Vol. i. p. 275.

such trial since we wrote has, we feel assured, widened the conviction of the necessity of change, and so prepared the way for some reform. But such a time of uncertainty and doubt is the very last in which the old defences of subscription should be abandoned. The counsel, therefore, of the late Commission seems to us to be wise and salutary; for, whilst it maintains in effect the old defences, it removes objectionable phrases, which gave no security, whilst they provoked attack. The Government who issued the Commission, cannot, of course, trifle with the question they have raised, and raised so far with a success greater even than could have been anticipated. They have now a clear course before them. 'To carry,' say the Commissioners, 'these recommendations into effect, some alterations must be made in the Canons of the Church, and some in the Statutes of the realm. We trust that our proposals will be willingly accepted both by the Church and by the State.' There is every reason to believe that, if the subject is properly introduced to Parliament and Convocation, it will meet with the readiest and the most respectful attention. Parliament has already shown itself anxious to obtain such mitigations as are here proposed, and the Convocation of Canterbury has even outstripped Parliament, in having suggested direct alterations of the existing law. Both, we doubt not, will legislate in the same spirit, and with the desire to perfect what both honestly desire to retain.

Upon this question the weighty words of Mr. Burke have been often quoted; but coming as they do amongst our present strifes from the calm repose of that honoured tomb where from Burke's

'sepulchral urn,
To Fancy's eye the lamp of truth shall burn;
Thither late times shall turn their reverent eyes,
Led by *his* light, and by *his* wisdom wise;'

we will once more set them before our readers. In opposing the prayer of the Feathers Tavern petitioners, he says:—

'A church, in any legal sense, is only a certain system of religious doctrines and practices fixed and sanctioned by some law, and the establishment is a tax laid by the same sovereign authority for payment of those who so teach and practise. For no Legislature was ever so absurd as to tax its people to support men for teaching and acting as they please but by some prescribed rule. . . . . The matter does not concern toleration, but establishment. . . . If you will have religion publicly practised and publicly taught, you must have a power to say what that religion shall be which we will protect and encourage. . . . . The petitioners are so sensible of the force of these arguments that they do admit of one subscription, that is, to the Scripture. I shall not consider how forcibly their arguments militate with their whole principle against subscription. . . . The subscription to Scripture is the most astonishing idea I ever heard, and will amount to just nothing at all. Gentlemen so acute have not, that I have heard, even thought of answering a plain obvious question, what is that Scripture to which they are content to subscribe? . . . . Therefore, to ascertain Scripture you must have one article more, and you must define what that Scripture is which you mean to teach. There are I believe very few, when Scripture is so ascertained, who do not see the absolute necessity of knowing what general doctrine a man draws from it, before he is sent down authorised by the State to teach as pure doctrine. . . . If we do not get some security for the doctrine which a man draws from Scripture, we not only permit, but we actually pay for, all the dangerous fanaticism which can be produced to corrupt our people, and to derange the public worship of the country.'*

PARTICULARS of Appeals in Spiritual Causes brought before the Court of Delegates, A.D. 1609-1823, with the names of the persons sitting on each Commission, distinguishing the Judges who were present when the sentence was pronounced, and those who were nominated on each Commission.

The attendance of the general body of delegates was not expected save at the opening of the Appeal, at the hearing of the case, and the delivery of the sentence.

No. 525. BISHOP OF S. DAVID'S *v.* LUCY (2 Appeals).

Office of Judge promoted by Lucy for simoniacally collating his nephew to the Archdeaconry of S. David's.

Delegates named in the Commissions of Appeal:—

I. Dated 13th March, 1699, on the Appeal *a gravamine.*	II. Dated 19th August, 1699, on the Appeal from the *Final Sentence.*
John, Earl of Bridgwater.	John, Earl of Bridgwater.
Thomas, Earl of Stamford.	Thomas, Earl of Stamford.
Charles, Earl of Manchester.	*John, Earl of Marlborough.

---

* 'Speech of Mr. Burke on Act of Uniformity.' vol. x. pp. 11-20, ed. 1818.

CLERICAL SUBSCRIPTION. 39

*John, Earl of Marlborough.
Ford, Earl of Tankerville.
*Humphrey, Bishop of Bangor.
Simon, Bishop of Ely.
John, Bishop of Oxford.
*John, Bishop of Norwich.
Richard, Bishop of Peterborough.

Sir George Treby, C. J. of King's Bench.
*Sir Edward Ward, C. B. of Exchequer.
Sir John Powell, J. of King's Bench.
Sir Littleton Powys, B. of Exchequer.
Sir Henry Hatsell, B. of Exchequer.
Sir Charles Hedges, Judge of High Court of Admiralty.
*John Edisbury, LL.D. Master in Chancery.
William King, LL.D.
John Bridges, LL.D.
Owen Wynne, LL.D.

Ford, Earl of Tankerville.
Lewis, Lord Rockingham.
*Humphrey, Bishop of Bangor.
Simon, Bishop of Ely.
John, Bishop of Norwich.
John, Bishop of Bristol.
James, Bishop of Lincoln.
John, Bishop of Chichester.

Sir George Treby.
Sir Edward Ward.
Sir John Powell.
Sir Littleton Powys
Sir Henry Hatsell, &c.
Sir Charles Hedges.
*John Edisbury.
William King.
*John Bridges.
Owen Wynne, &c.

The names of those Delegates who on either Appeal were not present when Sentence was pronounced, are marked with an asterisk*.

The names of those who were nominated on *one* only of the two Commissions are printed in italics.

No. 626. SALTER v. DAVIS.

Office of Judge promoted by Salter against Davis, Vicar of Penn, for omitting to read the 39 Articles, for preaching in favour of Popery, for neglecting cure of souls, with other offences.

Delegates named in Commission of Appeal, dated 10th December, 1691:—

Henry, Bishop of London; Gilbert, Bishop of Salisbury; Edward, Bishop of Worcester.

Sir William Holben, Justice of Common Pleas; Sir Thomas Rokeby, Justice of King's Bench; Sir John Powell, Baron of Exchequer.

Hedges, Master Edisbury, Littleton, Bramston.—*Civilians.*

None but the Civilian Members of the Commission were present at the Proceedings in this Case; but it did not come on for hearing.

No. 788. PELLING v. DR. BETTESWORTH (Dean of the Arches).
(Dr. Whiston's Case).

I. *Delegates named in the Commission of Appeal, dated 16th May, 1713:—*

Jonathan, Bishop of Winchester; George, Bishop of Bath and Wells; William, Bishop of Chester;* Philip, Bishop of Hereford; Adam, Bishop of St. David's.

Thomas Lord Trevor, C. J. of Common Pleas; Robert Tracy, Esq., Justice of Queen's Bench; Robert Price, Esq., Baron of Exchequer.

Wood, Pinfold, Parke, Phipps, Strahan.—*Civilians.*

On the 1st of July, 1713, when all the above-named Delegates, except the Bishop of Chester, were present, sentence was pronounced in favour of the Appeal, and a Citation decreed for Whiston to appear before the Court, which then proceeded to hear the Cause on the merits.

II. *On the 7th July, 1715, a ' Commission of Adjuncts' issued, which included all the Delegates above-named (amongst whom was now the Archbishop of York, lately Bishop of Chester).*

and *in addition*

 John, Bishop of Bangor; William, Bishop of Lincoln; Charles, Bishop of Norwich.

and

 Sir Peter King, C. J. of Common Pleas (Lord Trevor having been removed on the accession of George I.); Sir Samuel Dodd, C. B. of Exchequer.

Of these Delegates there were present on the first day when the Commission of Adjuncts sat (7th July, 1715).

     The Archbishop of York.
 Bishop of Winchester, Bishop of Bath and Wells, Bishop of St. David's.
  Sir Samuel Dodd, Robert Tracy, Esq., Robert Price, Esq., &c.

and

 Pinfold, Parkes (or Paske), Phipps, Strahan.—*Civilians.*

But the case did not come to a Judgment.

[Appeals from the Ecclesiastical Courts in Ireland came before the High Court of Delegates in England apparently until 1783—in which year the Act 23 Geo. III. c. 28—declared that no Writ of Error or Appeal should be received or adjudged . . . . in any of His Majesty's Courts in this kingdom, in any Action or Suit at Law, or in Equity, instituted in any of His Majesty's Courts in Ireland.

This Court was appointed under 28 Hen. VIII. c. 6.]

 No. 1240. HAVARD (of Tewkesbury) *v.* Rev. EDWARD EVANSON
    (Vicar of Tewkesbury, &c.).
      (Heresy).

Office of Judge promoted *inter alia* for maintaining Doctrines repugnant to the 39 Articles.

 Delegates named in the Commission of Appeal, dated 27th June, 1775.
 Sir William Henry Ashhurst, J. of King's Bench; Sir William Blackstone, J. of Common Pleas; Sir John Burland, B. of Exchequer.
 James Marriott, Andrew Cotton Ducavel, William Macham, Francis Simpson, William Compton.—*Doctors of Law.*

Havard appealed against the decision of the Court of Arches, which refused to admit certain Depositions—the Court of Delegates confirmed their suppression, but instead of confirming the acquittal of Evanson retained the cause for further hearing. Havard finding it impossible to obtain success without these Depositions abandoned the Appeal. The Court did not sit on its merits.

No. 1252.　HARFORD *v.* MORRIS (a Case of Nullity of Marriage).

Delegates named in Commission of Appeal, dated 19th April, 1777 (two years after the preceding case).

Lord Hillsborough and two other Peers; Archbishop of York and two other Bishops; three Common Law Judges; five Civilians.

The last cause in which Bishops were summoned or sat.

THE GALLICAN CHURCH.*
(*October*, 1865.)

A FULL and really philosophical estimate of what have been for centuries the effects on England and France as to character, morals, and religion, of the mutual relations of the two nations to each other would be a work which could scarcely be exceeded in interest. In war it is plain at once that the one has ever been the whetstone of the other's chivalry. Pre-eminently is this true of England, whose insular security and large commerce might by degrees have sunk it into Dutch habits of unwarlikeness, if it had not been for the perpetual stirring by our fiery neighbours of the stagnating streams which are wont to sleep in the level lands of increasing national wealth. Every attack on England, every returning invasion of France, kept alive the martial spirit which might otherwise have slumbered to the death. For the temper which had been bred in those who fought at Agincourt and Cressy spread with the returning army through the island. So Shakespeare describes the return of Henry the Fifth:—

> 'Athwart the sea: behold the English beach
> Pales in the flood with men, with wives and boys,
> Whose shouts and claps out-voice the deep-mouthed sea.'
>   *Act V. Scene* 1.

In manners too, and even in religion, the same influence, though far more subtle in its action, may undoubtedly be traced. And as to all of these England has for the most part in times past, in spite of occasional outbreaks of Anglomania,

---

* 1. 'Le Maudit.' Par L'Abbé * * *. Cinquième Edition. Paris, 1864.
   2. 'La Réligieuse.' Par L'Abbé * * *. Dixième Edition. Paris, 1864.
   3. 'Le Jésuite.' Par L'Abbé * * *. Paris, 1865.

been the receiving and France the imparting people. The history of dress may prove and illustrate this. How invariably has Paris reproduced itself in London. What a confirmation of it would our milliners' shop-windows exhibit; what proofs would be furnished by the confidential communications, if they could possibly be published in a Blue Book, which take place between the leaders of fashion and the accomplished artists who execute and guide their capricious will! And this sparkling foam upon the wave's crest tells accurately enough which way the deeper currents are sweeping.

But though this is true of the past, it seems probable that, except, we trust, so far as regards military rivalry, it will be unspeakably more true of the future. For good or for evil the intercourse which now exists and daily increases between France and England is such as would never have been dreamed of by our fathers. The commercial treaty which has done so much to augment this intercourse is as much a result as a cause of this new unity between the nations. The influence of no single person can for an instant compare with that of the present Emperor in having brought about this result. Having seen with his wonted sagacity that the interests of France would be largely promoted by the upgrowth of kindly offices and increased intercourse between her and ourselves, he has, ever since his reign began, promoted its increase with a steady farsightedness of action possible only in one who combines his deep silent insight into affairs with his resolute and unaltering determination to see at last effected whatever he has once designed.

Every year of his reign has increased, and probably will increase, the straitness of our union; and though at first sight it might seem as if the religious separation of our people from all visible communion with the Church of the West would forbid, as to that subject matter, any influence of France upon us, yet a deeper investigation of the case would show the poverty and lack of insight betrayed in such a conclusion. The lower tier of clouds, which to unenlightened eyes usurp the whole heavens, are themselves acted on and swayed by the higher currents which sweep unseen through the firmament; and tempers of unbelief and of devotion diffuse themselves with a wonderful equality of flow like atmospheric influences, ever present and prevailing, around outward institutions the most various in form and appearance. Separated, therefore, even as we are from others, we cannot safely disregard the ebbs and flows of religious belief on the other side of the Channel. It may be that there is before us the prospect here too of an increased union. Many pregnant signs suggest the possibility of the Empire leading the way to the establishment of a church far more really national than France has ever yet seen; such an one as floated in idea before the eager gaze of the youthful Bossuet; such an one as England's contemporary Archbishop was sanguine enough to believe might one day, when more perfectly reformed, be knit by open bonds of spiritual alliance to the Island Church.

At such a time it must be a matter of more than common interest to English Churchmen, especially, to know the real state and temper of religion in France. This the three notable sets of volumes which we have named at the head of this article are intended to set forth. Their author is a distinguished French Abbé, mixing with the religious and literary society of Paris, and who, though well known as the writer of these obnoxious volumes, has never afforded in his faith or conduct any mark at which the keen eye of religious jealousy could aim, so as to secure his long-coveted suspension from the ministry. For in France it would answer many a page of argument, if the ultramontane scribe could but indite against the reasoner, 'C'est un interdit.' The three works, taken together, explain the whole question; and the briefest way in which it can be set before our readers is by following the lead of the three works themselves, in the order of their appearance. They bear the questionable shape of novels—a reproach repeatedly flung in the face of their author. He has as constantly replied, that he has adopted that form only because the novel is the most popular literature of the day, and his desire is to be read. He quotes, in self-defence, other great ecclesiastics to justify his form of publication. 'Le prêtre' (he says) 'qui a écrit "Le Maudit" a fait comme le Cardinal Wiseman, comme Fénélon, comme Camus.'* He says, and says it with perfect truth, that the story is in his hands the simple thread upon which his facts are strung. No one, indeed, could mistake him for a novelist; for from the merits and the defects of that peculiar form of literature, he is almost equally free. There is no sensational writing in any page of these volumes; and there is, on the other hand, very little story. It is not with him, as it is with Dr. Mason Neale, that the intensity of his religious convictions hardly keeps down the natural genius of a master of fiction; he has no such struggle: he labours with his story to make it hold his facts and reasonings; and it does that, and does no more. From the beginning the most inexpert tyro in novel reading can see what the end is to be, and he is never deceived in the unwinding of the thread. If there is any surprise anywhere, it is evidently quite as great a one to the author, as it is to the reader. All this, which would take utterly away any claim that he might put forth to high place amongst the writers of fiction, only adds to the value of his volumes as a statement of the facts which constitute the spiritual life of which he is recording the history. There is no story the interest of which must be kept alive by humouring these facts; there is no evidence of lively imagination, which might lead unawares to their being invested with a colour of

* 'Le Maudit,' p. 2.

his own. Any careful student of history, who has followed closely Lord Macaulay's treatment of Sir Elijah Impey, or the Duke of Marlborough, will distrust all his other portraits, because he will know that it is the habit of the artist's mind to form for himself the countenance he is about to depict; but the purchaser of the work of the dullest photographer knows that he is at least free from these misleading freaks of the imagination. That security the reader of these volumes possesses.

Not that the Abbé M. is by any means a dull man; but he manifests no such gifts of imagination as would lead us in any degree to distrust his facts. 'Le Maudit,' which first created the author's reputation, and of which many large editions have been sold, opens with the history of a young priest in the south of France, well-born, well-nurtured, and endowed with unusual gifts of intellect—Julio de la Clavière—who, with his (supposed) sister, Louise de la Clavière, had been brought up by an aunt, who had adopted the orphan children and been to them all that a mother could have been.

The opening chapters depict the dealings of the Jesuit Fathers with the ladies of the family. Madame de la Clavière was rich, and her nephew and niece her natural heirs. She had yielded herself to the guidance of a Jesuit confessor, and he, at the bidding of the Company, was bent on securing for it the worldly substance of the devoted trembling aunt. To secure this the niece was to be persuaded to enter a convent, and the nephew to become a priest. In these vocations a small pension would be all that either would require, and the Company might win the inheritance. These plans are first thwarted by the niece's doubts about her vocation, which, under an attachment she forms for a young friend of her brother's, preparing at first with him for the priesthood, but led by doubts and inquiry to abandon that intention and become an advocate, deepen rapidly into an absolute rejection of the state for which she had been designed. This provoking mischance is traced, in great measure by the sharp-sighted Fathers to the influence of her brother, who himself has read, and has encouraged her in reading, many works which have carried her thoughts, and interests, and aspirations, far outside the narrow sphere to which her spiritual guides would have restricted them. Thus he becomes early an object of suspicion and dislike to the ' Reverend Fathers.' They were at this time only feeling their way in the provincial town of T.; and it was esteemed by them essential to their success that they should obtain funds sufficient to enable them to raise buildings commensurate with the importance of the Society. France was the country for the support of which they were by far the most anxious. In their estimate, ' Rome est aujourd'hui dans la décrépitude sénile : la vie ne part pas de là, pas plus pour la religion que pour le reste. La France c'est le pays de vie exubérante.'

To secure the funds needful for erecting these buildings, all their spiritual powers are unscrupulously exerted. We are led by the Abbé into the dark conclave in which business of this delicate kind is conducted :—

'The provincial Father had convoked a secret council. When darkness reigned in every corridor, and the dead silence of the building showed that all the other Fathers had retired into their cells, seven old men entered the convent hall. A single lamp lighted that hall, casting a pale and lurid ray upon the walls. Here and there hung engravings of St. Ignatius, of St. Francis Xavier, of the martyrdom of the brethren in Japan and China, and of the Sacred Heart of Mary. . . . . A table covered with green cloth, and chairs for the assembled Fathers, completed the furniture of the room. . . . . The Reverend Father Provincial, having deposited on the table a large portfolio, knelt down and repeated in a slow and subdued tone the Veni Sancte and Ave Maria, the other Fathers joining. They then rose and seated themselves. All eyes were fixed upon the ground as the Provincial began by opening his portfolio and stating, " I have received from our very Reverend Father General authority to build at T. a house for our order." '

He proceeds to state that three million francs must be raised for the building, and raised from local resources. A subdued smile courses over some of those aged lips, as the question is put from whence the needful funds are to come. It appears that all their means of every kind reach to little more than half what they require, and so the several Fathers who act as confessors are stirred up to use more energetically their power over those whom they direct. Whilst each one details his own failures or successes in the common cause, the Father Briffard, with whom we are specially concerned, called upon by the Provincial Father to state his success, produces with a smile of satisfaction, which plays over his lips, the will of Madame de la Clavière, by which, securing pensions of a thousand francs to her nephew and her niece respectively, and one of three hundred to a favourite servant, she leaves all her estate to a M. Tournichon, the safe creature of the Company. 'And to what,' the Provincial asks, 'does this amount?' 'It is valued,' is the reply, 'at four hundred and fifty thousand francs.' 'And will the donor die soon?' he responds, and receives the gratifying assurance that she has scarcely a breath of life left in her. The Virgin is thanked in concluding prayers for these special favours, and the commencement of the building is determined on.

It had not been without a struggle that the aged aunt had handed over the orphans' fortune to these grasping hands. 'Remorse,' she had avowed to her confessor, 'and deep disquietude possess me! Louise and her brother are directly my heirs. Can I in conscience disinherit these children of my own and of their uncle's fortune?' 'Yes,' is the answer; 'I have certain means of knowing that the uncle's fortune was amassed by usury.' 'But how? his reputation for honesty was perfect.' 'What matters that; for his unjust gains he is now burning in Purgatory, and your only mode of giving peace to his soul, and saving your own, is by thus making restitution.' 'Ah, but those poor children!' The sacrifice is urged upon her as most acceptable to God; the fainting heart of the old devotee yields with difficulty; but the will is extorted from her.

Here is laid the foundation of a lifelong persecution of Julio de la Clavière, who at first suspects, and afterwards opposes to the utmost, though in vain, in the courts of law his own and his sister's spoliation. The Cardinal Archbishop Flamarens, one of the best drawn portraits in the book, touched with a play of humour which is the Abbé's forte, gives the true solution of all the life that is to follow, in the few words with which he replies to the objections taken to the ordination of Julio: 'I understand it all; they have robbed him of his fortune, and now they persecute him.'

The persecution begins with the endeavour to prevent by secret slander his admission to the priesthood: next it seeks to prevent his appointment by the Archbishop, who is captivated with his whole manner and attainments, to the office of diocesan secretary. The Archbishop, however, is firm, and the entrance of the young man on his new office introduces a capitally executed passage describing the daily budget of a French Archbishop's letters from his diocese, and the treatment by a kind and skilful, though perhaps a slightly worldly hand, of the various cases of his clergy. This chapter might be read with great advantage by many besides French Archbishops. It exhibits with the utmost skill how much acute discernment, mixed with hearty kindness, may do to quiet extremes without the scandal of a scene, to forestall coming evils in their bud, and to stir up sleepy respectability to exertions of which it had never dreamed. At this time the young Abbé seems to triumph, and the astute Fathers to have failed. He is called upon to preach in the Cathedral, and acquits himself so admirably, that at the request of the Chapter he is nominated by the Archbishop an honorary canon of the church. But the Jesuits never leave the prey they once have tracked. They stir up a cry of heresy against the young canon's sermon, and they play off against the Archbishop his chaplain, and above all, his sister who lives with him, and on whom he is dependent for his family and social life; a scene of unusual altercation disturbs his dinner-table; he retires to his room, to be followed by a fierce letter of denunciation, which he traces to the Jesuits, and is seized in his overwrought condition with a fit of apoplexy under which he sinks. Before his death he sends for Julio, to receive his confession, and in the clear atmosphere of those last hours, when one by one the busy illusions of life have all but passed away, the spirit of the dying man rises to the perception of the greatness of the Church's vocation and his own, and he delivers to the young Abbé what is appropriately termed his 'spiritual testament':—

'I die in the bosom of the Catholic Church Apostolical and Roman, of which I have been Priest, Bishop, and Cardinal: about to appear before Him who is the immutable truth, I declare that it has been against the dictates of my own heart, and with an extreme repugnance, that for more than forty years of my life as priest and bishop I have followed the perilous crew which now guides the Catholic Church. I have been forced to repress all the holiest instincts of my soul . . . . and to this I have owed my rapid advance in honours. I saw that I must choose between the dignities which flattered my ambition and an agitated, even persecuted, life. I was feeble, and I shrank back from the glory and the sufferings of the new apostolate. I preferred the vain glory of the purple: to reach it I betrayed and slew the truth.'

He sees how the Ultramontane party, directed by the Jesuits, and in everything exalting the Papacy above the Scriptures, the Creeds, and the Church, is destroying all possibility of a religious future for the French people; and he dies penitent for his own share in the mighty evil which has been already wrought. He charges Julio to make his retractations known: gives him as a perpetual pledge his Cardinal's ring, and dies with the adieu of a father leaving his troubled inheritance to a beloved son.

To prevent the publication of this last 'testament' of the Archbishop, which Julio at once sets about preparing, is the first care of the reverend Fathers. All direct threats and cajolery having failed utterly, they turn, according to their wont, to female aid, and bring his aged aunt and his adored sister to persuade him to abandon his intention of making public the revelation to which he had pledged himself to the dying Archbishop. All that can be won from him is that it is published without his name by his friend the advocate M. Verdelon. The sale of the brochure is immense, and the anger of the Jesuits proportionate to the injury they perceive that it will do them. Meanwhile the new Archbishop, Mons. Paul le Cricq, appears on the stage, and Julio soon feels the effect of the loss of his former patron. The new Archbishop, indeed, hates and fears the Jesuits; but fearing even more than he hates, he serves them with the grudged but thorough service which fear can extract from an ignoble spirit. His object is to gain the purple as well as the archiepiscopal mitre of his predecessor. To obtain this he must secure two separate influences which it is not easy for him to combine. He must have the support of the French Government and the nomination of the Pope, and this latter cannot be won unless with the assistance of the Jesuits. Side by side with the lofty throne of the successor of St. Peter is erected the chair of office of the General of the Jesuits.

'There are two kings in the Catholic monarchy. . . . . One is the king in appearance, and is named the Pope: he is enthroned at the Vatican, with cardinals, chamberlains, prelates, guards. . . . The other is the actual king; his seat is at the Gesù; he is styled "the General of the Jesuits." He is at the head of the most compact, active, and powerful association of men which the genius of man has ever framed. You address the first of these great men as " your Holiness," the second as " your Reverence." When you are admitted to an audience with the Pope, you meet, in the antechamber of the hall (not to be reached till after three separate genuflexions) in which the Vicar of Christ will present to you his ring and his slipper to kiss, four or five young prelates in violet cassocks and gently swelling rochets, who relieve with their easy conversation the *ennui* of the ceremonial. When you have passed the vestibule of the Gesù, and approach the presence of the General, you pass through a hall in which forty secretaries are writing in every known language, and you will present yourself to one who is charged with immense interests, and who will make you sit and converse with him. The one is the Richelieu of Catholicism; the other is its Louis XIII.'

Here, as everywhere else, the power is with the worker; and the Supreme Pontiff himself, as well as all his Archbishops and bishops, must bow at last the gemmed tiara before the hard rule of the Iron Sceptre. It was a difficult task for Monsignor Le Cricq, for Julio had influential friends; the story of the spiritual testament of Monsignor Flamarens had obtained a wide circulation; great interest was felt about him, and he was a man whom it was scarcely safe openly to persecute; yet the needful Jesuit support could not be had without the persecution of the obnoxious Abbé. The nomination of the French Government would be lost, if, in gaining that support, he involved himself in a scandal or awakened a cry; on the other hand, the Pope would not venture to act if the Gesù frowned on the proposal. On the whole the difficult problem was dexterously worked out. Julio was first deprived of his office of Secretary. This could cause no reproach, as it was natural for the Archbishop to desire to see a friend in an office of such confidence; and yet it was indicative and intelligible enough. It was an instalment of the sacrifices to be made to the Jesuits, and as an instalment it was received; but as an instalment only. Next Julio is appointed fifth curate to the Vicar of T.,—a terrible descent on the ladder of ecclesiastical promotion. Simply and earnestly the young man sets himself to his work, and he is soon appreciated and beloved. He is most earnest in enforcing Christianity in its creed, its motives, and its conduct; but he has a detestable habit of preferring these to the advancement of any form of priestcraft. He makes the powerful Carmelites his enemies by counselling the postponement of the irrevocable vow for a young child whose feelings and whose vanity had been worked on to give herself up to the austerities of that severe Order. He offends even more grossly the conventional notions of the modern religionists by exalting before the young the ennobling and purifying character of married love. This last offence is appreciated with peculiar sensitiveness by the Archbishop, and Julio is at once subjected to an honourable banishment from the seats of ecclesiastical influence. The cure of St. Aventin, in the valley of l'Arboust, was vacant, and to it the Archbishop sends him to preach ideal love to the shepherds of the mountains.

The news of his intended banishment flew round the town of T., and whilst the Jesuits triumphed, many of the sagest and holiest of the flock mourned for the loss of a pastor who had elevated all their views and lived before them the life of an evangelist. One of the most distinguished professors in the town wrote to 'beseech him, before departing for his mountain exile, to examine seriously whether he ought thus to yield to his mortal enemies; whether this was not a sign from Providence which called him to higher destinies, and summoned him to another sphere, in which, supported by men who yet had faith in the future of Catholicism, he might still labour at his great work of reconciling it with the requirements of the present time. To bury himself in an obscure ministry, amongst a few poor mountaineers, in a region blocked up for eight months of the year with snow, was truly to abandon the mighty task he had so fully contemplated, and the outline of which he had laid down in his sermon at the Cathedral and in all his addresses at T.'

Julio's answer protests that in no degree does he shrink from the hard apostleship to which he has been called; that he is conscious of needing work and study to fit him to fulfil it; moreover, that the time of action is not come for him: that Rome, trusting altogether to its expiring earthly sovereignty, unable to comprehend the march of the human mind, and to fit the instruments by which it conveyed eternal truths to the wants of the present time, would regard as treason all efforts at reform; that for one, therefore, whose calling was not the demolition of the present, but its future reconstruction, when ruder hands had accomplished their vocation of destruction, the present was a time of waiting, not of active labour, and that in such a temper he devoted himself to his mountain cure.

To it he therefore betook himself; and here he read, studied the physical geography of the mountains, acquainted himself intimately with the face of nature round him, and above all laboured with his whole heart to humanise and christianise his mountain flock. In this he is sorely hindered, not only by the grossness of their habits, but even more by the superstitious system of the Church in which he ministers. First, he is withstood by a Pharisaic devotee, introduced under the indicative name of 'La Mère Judas,' whose claims to extreme sanctity and spirituality he judiciously but firmly resists, and who becomes forthwith his enemy; then, by the clerical encouragement of pretended visions and heavenly visitations amongst the young and enthusiastic females of his flock, and at length by the disturbing labours of a Capucin, who is sent to conduct a mission in his parish: a great eater, a deep drinker, and a noisy preacher, described by the Abbé with the most pleasurable humour, who utterly deranges the whole plan of the young Curé's ministry. Here, then, too, in his mountain seclusion as much as in the town, the whole tone of the existing Church is against him.

But he is not left to the isolation and rest of his mountain home. His aunt dies, and he resolves on challenging the iniquitous will which had been the handiwork of the Père Briffard. M. Verdelon the advocate, his own friend in youth, and now the lover of Louise, undertakes the conduct of the suit, and speaks with all the ardour of a lover, and all the force of one maintaining the highest principles. At first it seems that the Jesuits will be foiled. M. Tournichon, to whom, on their behalf, to avoid the laws against captation, the inheritance had been bequeathed, had been so unwary as to allot far less than she conceived to be her share of the prey to the favourite attendant of Madame de la Clavière, whom he had been forced from the influence she possessed over the mind of her mistress to admit into his secret councils. Disappointed of her reward, the inflammable Pyrenneian is at once smitten with horror at the injustice done in disinheriting the niece and nephew, and she makes revelations on which M. Verdelon relies. The aunt had shrunk from the injustice she was being compelled to perpetrate. She had even summoned a notary to alter her will, but had yielded at last in her feebleness to the spiritual terrors brought to bear upon her; had postponed the projected alteration, and died before it was accomplished. Such evidence would have destroyed the validity of the will; but the witness is at length, by flattery and gifts, prevailed upon to declare that her first assertions were the result of irritation, and not warranted by fact. Unsupported by this evidence, M. Verdelon's eloquence fails to convince the court, and the inheritance is given to M. Tournichon, the nominee (and as the Provincial Master complains bitterly when he receives the account of his expenses, the spoiler) of the Jesuits. But Julio will not so yield up his cause, and if he cannot gain the verdict of the court, he resolves to gain that of France to his side. He sets himself accordingly about the preparation of a memoir of the whole transaction. The effect of such a statement from his pen is so greatly dreaded by the reverend Fathers, that every attempt is made to persuade him to suppress it. In the armoury of the Gesù are weapons of every shape and kind, and the one drawn forth on this emergency illustrates some of the chief peculiarities of the Society. A reverend Father, who is supposed to possess the special gift of affecting the female heart rather than any peculiar attribute of sanctity, is sent down into the province to stir up the Marchioness of * * * to undertake the task of preventing, through the influence of Louise, the publication of the dreaded memoir.

The Marchioness had been an early friend of the late mother of Louise, and through the fond remembrances of the daughter's heart, soon won her confidence. Louise was now living with her brother at his remote cure, and they were everything to each other. She had passed through the great trial of finding that with the loss of her dower she had lost her lover, who, with ambitious views filling his mind, could not bring himself to wed the disinherited damsel. On her fears the Marchioness works through the sole earthly avenue remaining open in her heart. She shows her that Julio will certainly incur an interdict, that he will be lost here and hereafter, and that she must be his saviour from the misery before him. But Julio will not yield, and under the crafty guidance of the Marchioness, Louise is to try the effect of withdrawing herself for a time from him, and extorting as the condition of her return, his withdrawal of all future resistance of the reverend Fathers. Meanwhile other influences were brought to bear on Julio. The General of the Jesuits wrote to the Archbishop, in terms which showed that he would endure no longer trifling. Either Julio must be silenced, or the dreaded interdict must issue, or the Cardinal's hat must evaporate in disappointment. So imperative was the summons, that the Archbishop would probably have yielded, had not a most unlooked-for incident protected Julio. A priest named Loubaire, whom, when vicar of a parish near St. Aventin, Julio had saved from death and dishonour, was devoted to him with all the burning ardour of his Southern blood. Of a not unspotted life himself, he had seen and venerated the saintly character of the young Abbé, and now formed the insane resolution of saving the innocent martyr from archiepiscopal persecution by the threat of assassination. He insinuates himself into the palace and presence of the Archbishop in his hour of perfect solitude, and obtains, by the threat of instant death, an oath that Julio shall not be made a victim, and then attempts, and almost executes before the face of the prelate, his own destruction. The effect produced on the Archbishop's mind is terrible, and it is whilst it is at its full that the irresistible Society requires the sacrifice of its victim. To combine a regard to his oath with a performance of the mandate of the General was not easy, but it was effected by the Archbishop. A letter of unwonted kindliness brings Julio to the Prelate, who discourses with him in the most affable terms, laments the hard necessities which surrounded him, and have made him seem unkind to one he so highly values.

'There is so much to manage—all is so far from being rosy around the Episcopate. Oh! how much happier, oh! how much more peaceable is the condition of a good pastor in his parish. Still, one must bear one's cross. But to come to the point. My dear Abbé, you are attacking an Order venerated in the Church; you remember the words of your Breviary —"an Order established by God in the last times for the conflict with heresy . . . ." and how have you attacked it? Terribly, because with such moderation. . . . . Meanwhile, all the world is against you. I hear from Rome that you are in *The Index*. What would you have me do? You have set the Jesuits at my heels; they will give me no repose. Do you know that the good Fathers comprehend no raillery, and that they will abuse an Archbishop of T. quite as readily, and with as little remorse, as a vicar of Aventin! I know them well. . . . . But I would prove to you my love: I will not be the executioner of their hatred: only deal kindly by me. You can live honourably on the annuity secured to you:

abandon the ministry for two or three years. . . . . Alas! my dear Abbé, who knows what in three or four years may have become of Rome or of the Jesuits? Events pass so fast now a days. Do kindly what I ask; resign this vicarage of St. Aventin . . . . take an " Exeat pro quâcumque diœcesi." When calm has been restored, when events are more advanced, when perhaps Garibaldi and his *chemises rouges* have had their way with Rome, and the Index, and the Jesuits, you will come back to some good post in the diocese.'

The Abbé yields to this gentle handling, takes his Exeat, returns to St. Aventin to prepare for his departure, and finds Louise gone, and no trace of her to be discovered.

Then follows what the Abbé M * * * has entitled the Odyssée of Julio. He sets out to find his sister, whom the Marchioness had carried off and got safely conveyed to a remote convent in Italy. Julio's search for her exhibits many other traits of Jesuit power and management. He is perpetually dogged by one who enacts the character of a free thinking and free living Abbé, himself a victim of the Jesuits, but who is in reality their spy, set to watch Julio, and if possible to beguile him to Rome, and the yet remaining prison of the Inquisition. In the course of this search he at last discovers Louise, rescues her by a sudden abduction from the church in the services of which she is taking part, carries her safely to the mountains, there is parted from her, and wounded by banditti, and is rescued by the Jesuit guard, to be consigned safely to the cells of the Holy Office at Rome. Thence all efforts made by the French Government and by private friends, stimulated by the efforts of Louise, who had reached Paris in safety, alike failed to relieve him, until Loubaire reappears on the stage, and, with the aid of some mountaineers, delivers him by force from the prison of the Inquisition. As soon as he had effected this, Loubaire hastens back to his mountain charge. But he is not allowed to resume it. His letters to Louise, whilst at Rome he was seeking to effect the liberation of his friend, had all been intercepted. He had been delated to the Archbishop of Chambéry, as the enemy of the Society of Jesuits and of the Papal Chair. On reaching his cure of Lans-le-Bourg he meets the news: 'You are summoned before the Archbishop at Chambéry; you are no more vicar of Lans-le-Bourg, your successor is appointed.' He obeys the summons to Chambéry, and is told that his powers to execute the functions of the priesthood in that diocese are removed, but that he will be granted an Exeat, but unaccompanied with a recommendation, without which he would in fact be admitted into no other diocese. He breaks away with the natural impetuosity of his character with the last words, 'It is a sentence of death, Monseigneur.' 'It is all that I can do for you,' replies the complacent prelate.

He betakes himself to Paris, where, as he says to his friend, 'If your shoulders will bear them, you may carry burdens, or accustom your hands to break stones for the macadamized streets of Paris.' We will not interrupt here our outline of the story, but we shall have hereafter to return for a little to this subject.

Loubaire finds work at a printing establishment, and to Paris in due time comes the Abbé Julio. Louise had met with noble and distinguished friends of her aunt's, and for a time had been admitted to their society. But even here Jesuit intrigue and influence had followed her, and forced upon her reluctant friends the breaking up of their old alliance. On reaching Paris Julio sought for employment as a priest in that Church which possessed all his affections and his trust, and for the reform of which, in its temper and administration, he longed so ardently. Through all his disasters he had retained the warm affections of one enlightened prelate, the Bishop of A.; and armed with his recommendation, he applied to the Archbishop for employment. The Jesuits at once seek to bar the entrance to all sacerdotal work against the doomed man. At all hazards, with his oratorical powers, every pulpit must be closed against him. But at first they fail. They dared not approach directly the Cardinal Archbishop. It is not every Bishop, especially when the Cardinal's hat has been already won, who will suffer the reverend Fathers to govern his diocese, for him; and his Eminence was known to be rigorously just as well as full of kindness; so they first try to reach him through M. le Promoteur, an official charged with the immediate discipline of the diocese—one who in Paris has need to be of the acutest intelligence, and endued with all the skill of the ablest member of the detective police; one who can deal with all the false Bishops from the East, who with long beards and most doubtful pretensions come to collect in Paris alms for the poor Christians of Lebanon, or for the erection of a Carmel amongst the rocks of Mount Tabor.

This office, so little likely in its administration to breed charity in any spirit, was held at the time by the Abbé Baraminos (known among the young and gay curates of the metropolis by the sobriquet of M. Gare-à-Minos), a priest large in stature, dry and sharp of aspect, and of very uncertain temper. The supplest of the reverend Fathers lodged, during the familiar intercourse of the salon of the Duchess de Chantenay, in the faubourg Saint-Germain, in the mind of M. Baraminos the most violent prejudice against Julio de la Clavière. But the commendation of the Bishop of A. prevailed for the time with the Archbishop against M. le Promoteur; he received the Abbé with kindness and attention, and appointed him at once as second Almoner of the Lycée of St. Louis. But his Eminence lacked the firmness needful to maintain his appointment. The busy tongues of a multitude of well-trained instruments assailed the name of Julio with every conceivable calumny; and at length in full council M. Baraminos ventured to express the general feeling of horror with which the appointment of Julio to so distinguished a post had been received. 'But what am I to do with him?' asked the Cardinal, 'for there is really nothing against him as a priest.' 'Surely,' replies the ready M. le Promoteur, 'he would be well placed as *diacre d'office* in a parish church.'

Now this is an office which the ritual of Rome and the luxurious habits of fashionable life have combined to create as it exists in Paris. You go into St. Roch or the Madeleine and see the gorgeous rites of the high mass proceeding in their splendour. You see the curé officiating between two priests with white hair, clothed with dalmatics as stiff and splendid with their gold lace as the chasuble of the Vicar himself. You suppose that the first pastor of a great Church is there in the exercise of his sublime function, surrounded by two high dignitaries, his clerical equals. But you are mistaken. They are two unhappy priests who are retained for this special office—and who must not eat anything till the late mass—at one perhaps on Sundays, at noon on ordinary days—has been concluded. These men are often poor priests, exiled it may be from Poland for their religious opinions, or hunted down by the hatred of the Jesuits; they are men without a future: the least distinguished candidate for the priesthood may rise to any height in his profession, but the wretched *diacre d'office* can only sink lower as he grows older. From the splendours of the Madeleine or Sainte Clotilde he falls to La Villette, to Grenelle, even to Montrouge, and at last his bones are sent with those of the lowest of the populace to the common trench at Ivry or Clichy la Garenne.

A curt announcement from M. de Baraminos informs Julio that to this hapless office, in the little church of Notre Dame des Champs, he is degraded, and that even from this on the first complaint he might reckon on being removed. Julio received the blow with calmness, Louise with tears. She would have had him refuse the offered post. His reply reveals his heart. 'The house of Christ at Nazareth was less distinguished; Pope, Archbishop, or Diacre d'Office, what matters it in God's eyes? It is to fill a function of His priesthood. . . . Beloved sister, you are a tempter to your brother.' With a suppressed sob she answered, 'You are right, I spoke as a woman: it is great to make yourself little.'

But Julio had still friends with some influence, and through one of these he is appointed to preach a Lenten sermon at St. Eustache. The whole Jesuit class was convulsed by this announcement. It was what above all they dreaded, and what before everything they must prevent. They besiege the Archbishop, but he stands firm in protecting the Vicars of Paris in their right to choose their own Lenten preachers, and it is plain that the pulpit must be open to Julio, and the sect is driven to its last and lowest machinations. The old Jesuit spy who had haunted him as an ever present imp through Italy is employed to assemble a crowd of the charitable dependents of the body to fill the church, and, as Julio mounts the pulpit, to raise a riot within it which shall not only prevent the sermon being preached, but suffice to warn every other Vicar in Paris of the danger of allowing such a firebrand to climb the steps of his pulpit. The plan succeeds perfectly, and the orator's voice is drowned utterly in the disgraceful noise of the rabble.

Julio now turns to the attempt to utter through the press that voice which he is prevented speaking from the pulpit. The most triumphant success attends a religious journal which he edits, and in which contending earnestly for all the truths of the Church Catholic, he temperately combats the extreme views of the ultramontane section. This completes the measure of his crimes. An immediate ostracism of his sister and himself from all religious and from the higher social circles is his first visitation; his next the withdrawal of his powers to officiate in Paris, with a recommendation that he should return to his old diocese. Hardly through the strong influence of powerful patrons is the Archbishop of T. persuaded to restore him to a small country cure. There for a short time he labours with his former success, though haunted by a new and terrible anguish which we purposely pass over. Then he loses his sister, whose delicate frame could no longer support all the exposure, privation and anxiety of the lot which the sharing her brother's sorrows had made her portion. Whilst he is in this last anguish the ambitious views of M. le Cricq approach their highest fulfilment. He had sheltered Julio from the open attack of a certain bigoted prelate in a counsel at Limoux, and this incident had been so well used by his friends at Paris that the French ambassador was instructed to ask for the liberal Archbishop the coveted Cardinal's hat. The application was received with favour, when the Pope was assailed by the head of the Jesuit Society for intending such an honour to one who had sheltered so notorious an offender as Julio. When the Archbishop next saw the Holy Father it was evident that a storm had swept over the heavens of the Vatican. The Archbishop's discerning agent at the Roman Court soon learned the cause, and suggested with admirable dexterity the only remedy. The Archbishop retires into a 'retreat,' to be accomplished at the Gesù, and to perfect his good work consents to place Julio under an interdict. He wins his hat; and Julio, suspended from his ministry, degraded, in fact, from his orders, broken in body, and worn out in spirit, retires to the southern slopes of the mountains to die in the Hospice de Bigorre, ministered to in his last moments by a friendly stranger priest, whom the hand of persevering bigotry strives in vain to banish from his dying chamber.

We have traced the first of these stories thus at length because without doing so it was not possible to display, with any clearness, the lesson it is framed to teach. We need not enter with the same fulness on the remaining volumes. Their plan is the same as that on which 'Le Maudit' is constructed. The first of them relates the story of a woman given up to a life of charity and devotion; in the present state of the Church of France she is passed from religious house to house, and from order to order, to find the same repulsive features perpetually reproduced in every society she joins. Pettiness, intrigue, jealousy, and debasing superstition mar at every turn the fair professions of a 'religious life,' until she is driven from it to spend her fortune and her powers in organising for the girls of France a system of education, which, by setting them free from the present dominant priestcraft, shall fit them to be wives and mothers, instead of breeding them up in ignorance of themselves and of the world round them, to become hereafter either freethinkers or devotees. The third story is intended to reveal, by similar processes, the interior life of those terrible Jesuit priests—the Prætorian Guard of the Papacy, at once its defenders and its dread—of whose work the history of Julio is a specimen.

We should in a great degree repeat what we have already said if we followed out this story in detail, and we shall not, therefore, do so, but we are tempted to lay before our readers one passage from it, because it is pleasantly characteristic of a vein of genuine humour which is continually reappearing amidst the deep convictions, profound sadnesses, and high hopes, which fill the volumes. The hero of these volumes is the younger of two sons of a father of high birth and large fortune, who would himself have given them a liberal education based on the idea of what, as an emigrant to our shores, he had seen as an English education. The mother, under Jesuit directions, opposes with all a woman's power the father's resolution. After incessant conflicts the matter is adjusted by the elder son going to the University, and the younger being handed over to the teaching of the 'Reverend Fathers.' The mother suffers in after years a bitter punishment for this early victory. The elder son dies in consequence of an accident, and she is then bent upon the younger taking his brother's place, and continuing the ancient line of his noble family. But the Jesuit yoke to which she had herself submitted him was not thus to be broken from his neck. As a rule the Jesuits, far less than any other order, seek to make their pupils renounce the active world and choose the 'religious' life. Their long-sightedness enables them to see that their power will be increased by their pupils holding high places in the world, and providing a new generation of youth for them to train. But there are exceptions to this rule. There are some whom they are most anxious to secure; and from three descriptions of men, when they can, they always seek to replenish their numbers: these are the nobly born, through whom they hope to spread their ramifications amidst the higher ranks of society; the rich, because better than any other they know the value of possessing largely the sinews of war; and the men of intellectual power, through whom they can act upon every rank and class of society.

Our hero combined these three advantages, and they early marked him for their own, and held him with an iron grasp in spite of his dying father's sobs and his broken-hearted mother's shrieks. This, however, was at the close of his training. The incident to which we refer belonged to his boyish days in the Jesuit seminary. He is visited in the seminary of Saint-Acheul by his father's friend, the great advocate, M. Dupin. The young Jesuit élève had himself already learned to entertain so doubtful a regard for the distinguished friend of his father as an enemy of the Company, that when he has to tell the Reverend Père who it is that has come to see him, he makes the reluctant confession 'rougissant jusqu'aux oreilles.' But the Jesuit Fathers manifested their wonted discretion. As soon as they had learned who their visitor was, the ordinary Father who was in attendance on the young pupil was at once withdrawn, and the distinguished rector of the seminary substituted for him. Then begins the play between the two men. M. Dupin had recently uttered, in defending the 'Constitutionnel,' the stinging mot, 'l'Institut de Loyola est une épée dont la poignée est à Rome, et dont la pointe est partout.' In the midst of their conversation he is playfully reminded of his mot by the courteous Father, who, when the utterer would apologise for it as the trip of an extemporaneous speaker, defends and justifies it as being no more than a declaration of the universal watchfulness of the Company over the cause of truth. Their converse is followed by a dinner, in which the best seasoned viands and the richest wines are bestowed upon the honoured guest; pleasant and seemingly impromptu honours are paid to his eloquence and fame; until at length, at the close of a religious service in their chapel, he is won to carry a wax taper in their procession, and to utter a complimentary oration.

After the oration in praise of his eloquence he is fairly conquered:

'Ce fut là le bouquet. Or les flatteries du recteur, les vins fins, les chants religieux de la chapelle, le sermon, peut-être les cordons du dais, et l'improvisation du rhétoricien, produisirent un tel effet que M. Dupin, transporté, ému, prit congé des Pères par un petit discours, où lui aussi prodigua l'encens, mais sans le moindre mélange épigrammatique.'

And so the purposes of the wily rector were accomplished.

Perhaps the great advocate had been in some degree taken captive by the Order; perhaps that stinging tongue would be found sweetened when the next great call elicited one of his forensic triumphs; but however that might be, Samson was exhibited to France as just released from the arms of the Philistine idolatress: 'Le lendemain vingt lettres apprenaient à Paris, que M. Dupin avait dîné chez les Jésuites à Saint-Acheul, et porté les cordons du dais; les lettres moqueuses jetèrent un ridicule sur l'avocat.'

This is a fair specimen of one of the humorous descriptions of the Abbé M. But it is not on these lighter traits that the volumes depend for their interest. They are, indeed, full of manifold and curious instruction. They exhibit, we believe, with studied fairness, the strange working of religious opinion and principle, under the perplexing action of the present wide-spread unbelief on the one side, and of a bigoted maintenance of the most extreme tenets of the Papacy on the other.

Their testimony upon one point which has recently been discussed somewhat largely amongst ourselves is not a little curious. When the unhappy Curé Loubaire is driven for his support to undertake some lay pursuit at Paris, he is represented as taking no peculiar or unusual step, but that for which the French clerical mind was thoroughly prepared, and with the sight of which the Parisian world was perfectly familiar. He labours as a journeyman printer, and finds around him a multitude to whom similar causes had prescribed like employments. A recent statement in the Convocation of the Province of Canterbury that such things prevailed in Paris, woke up an angry rejoinder from a certain French Abbé, and appeared to many of our journalists to be probably exaggerated. The Abbé M***'s volumes would prepare us to believe in its entire accuracy, and to think that it probably rather understated than exaggerated the truth; for we see here the absolute dependence of the priests upon the mere will of their bishops: we become acquainted with the many just grounds, and the far more numerous personal and party motives, which must multiply such interdicts. We see, too, that the interdicted priest has commonly no other resource by which to gain a livelihood than Paris and its menial occupations. Drawn as the French priesthood is almost universally at the present time from the lowest grade of social life, there is in it nothing so terrible as there would be in such a descent amongst ourselves. The French priest is almost always the child of some labouring man. If not raised by the school and the seminary to the priesthood, he would, like his father, have supported himself by the labour of his hands. When he falls from the priesthood there is no intermediate point at which he can stop. He is again, and naturally, an *ouvrier;* and as naturally it is in the great city that he seeks his bread. There he is unknown, and escapes the shame of being seen to fall; there he escapes the enforced celibacy which, wherever he is known, the law of France binds upon him as the remaining burden of his priesthood; there he is sure to find a company of like spiritual lepers, to receive him gladly into their disowned sodality of priestly Bohemians. We should therefore be prepared to expect what we think this recent controversy has proved even to demonstration. The matter socially and religiously is of so much moment that we will place on our pages a concise statement of the question, abridged from a long résumé written by one thoroughly acquainted with the subject.

The discussion originated in a statement made by the Bishop of Oxford, on the authority of a friend, at a meeting of Convocation, with reference to the number of interdicted priests living in Paris, and pursuing all sorts of manual and menial occupations. The Bishop's statement was however misreported in the 'Times.' He was made to say that there were 800 interdicted priests in Paris employed in driving cabs, whereas what he really did say was that there were 800 priests so interdicted in Paris, and pursuing secular and menial occupations, *some* of whom were engaged in cab-driving. The mistake afforded Abbé Rogerson, who calls himself 'Chaplain to the English Catholics at Paris,' an opportunity to step forward and engage in a little controversy with the Bishop of Oxford, who contented himself by informing Mr. Rogerson that the statement actually made in Convocation, or something very much like it, had already appeared in print, and by referring him to an article published in the 'Christian Remembrancer,' a year and a half previously. In this article it was alleged, on high Roman Catholic and Parisian authority, that there were no less than '600 priests serving as coachmen, or connected with the public conveyances, or playing street organs, or serving as porters, or begging.' The Bishop however added that the estimate supplied to him, apparently by the reviewer in the 'Christian Remembrancer,' made these amount to some 750. The Abbé was not however yet satisfied, and he went on writing. In the mean time an able Parisian Roman Catholic periodical, the 'Observateur Catholique,' edited by a committee of learned clergymen and laymen of the Gallican school, published a short article on the controversy, charging Mr. Rogerson with slandering the Bishop of Oxford, and terminating thus:—

'Il est bien certain que les prêtres interdits se refugient en grand nombre à Paris de tous les diocèses de France. Le nombre fixé par l'Évêque d'Oxford est *plutôt affaibli qu'exagéré*. Tous ces prêtres sont cochers de fiacre, cochers ou conducteurs d'omnibus, cabaretiers, vitriers ambulants, &c. Si l'Abbé Rogerson connaissait un peu mieux l'état où se trouvent les malheureux prêtres interdits et leur nombre, il ne lui aurait pas pris fantaisie de contredire M. l'Évêque d'Oxford.'

Forth again came Mr. Rogerson, as well as 'the knightly

papal champion of all England,' Sir George Bowyer, both of whom addressed letters to the 'Times.' Sir George described the 'Observateur Catholique' as a 'newspaper,' and its editor, the learned Abbé Guettée, as himself an interdicted priest, and as one who had 'joined the schismatical Greek Church,' and whose testimony was therefore unworthy of credit. He also stated that he had been 'informed by a dignitary of the French church that the whole number of interdicted priests in France is under 100.'

But Sir George Bowyer and the Abbé Rogerson called forth a formidable opponent in the person of the Abbé Guettée himself. In a memorable article in the 'Observateur Catholique, which is reprinted in full in the 'Christian Remembrancer,' he answers his assailants for himself, and inflicts a well-deserved castigation upon these 'néophytes anglais de fraîche date.' He denies having ever been interdicted, and says with reference to his own theological principles:—

'Si le Sieur Bowyer avait lu nos ouvrages, il saurait que nous avons été constamment et que nous sommes encore Catholique, et que nous ne faisons la guerre à la papauté qu'en nous plaçant sur le terrain catholique, c'est-à-dire, en enseignant la doctrine formulée dans les actes des conseils œcuméniques et dans les écrits des Saints Pères. Il paraît qu'en bon papiste, le Sieur Bowyer met la parole du Pape au-dessus de la voix traditionnelle de l'Église. Ceci le regarde, mais du moins qu'il ne traite pas de *schismatiques* ceux qui sont avec la *tradition catholique*, et qu'il garde cette qualification pour le Pape et ses fidèles qui bouleversent toute la doctrine de l'Église, qui fabriquent de nouveaux dogmes, et qui sont assez impies pour attribuer à DIEU les fantaisies de leur pauvre intelligence.'

The committee of the 'Observateur Catholique,' so far from considering the number given by the Anglican Prelate exaggerated, affirm that it is *under* the mark. Cavour, in a speech in the Italian Parliament, estimated the number of the Paris 'unfortunates' at 800; and so do other authorities given by the 'Christian Remembrancer.' The learned Abbé Guettée, who has resided many years in Paris, and who must be well informed, estimates them at some 1400: 'Nous savons de *source certaine* que le nombre des prêtres interdits, exerçant d'infimes professions à Paris, s'élève à environ 1400. Les Bowyer et les Rogerson pourront nier, tant qu'ils voudront, et tout ce qu'ils voudront; notre affirmation n'en sera pas moins d'une parfaite exactitude.' The celebrated Abbé Migne, who is at the head of an immense printing establishment in Paris, and who publishes for a large number of French Bishops, calculates that there are at least 800 of the fallen priests in Paris, and he affirms that many hundreds have applied to him at different times for work. The Abbé Rogerson asserted that he had been informed by ' the chief of the bureau which charges itself with what concerns street conveyances,' that 'for the last eight years he had not known more than three cabmen that were in priest's orders.' We now have it from an official source that not fewer than eighty-one have acknowledged that they belonged to the priesthood; but how many more are there who have not acknowledged?

It would, indeed, be easy to quote a whole list of distinguished names which would establish the unsparing tyranny with which priests of even the highest character and standing are at once placed under interdict if they resist the dominant superstition which is defacing their Church. All the priests who exposed the miserable imposture of Salette were marked out for persecution. The Abbé Guettée has shared it with the most ignorant member of the priesthood; the Abbé Prompsault and a host of others are witnesses to the same evil. 'We ourselves,' writes a well-known clergyman in a recent article, ' are personally acquainted with an excellent clergyman, formerly a vicaire of one of the most important churches of Paris, who was *suspected* by the last Archbishop of reading the "Observateur Catholique," and who was interdicted in consequence, and is now living on the alms of his friends in a wretched garret.' *

* 'Christian Remembrancer,' No. cxxii. p. 336.

It is only as one of the signs of the whole state of religion in France that this particular question is of much moment. But it is important as being one amongst a multitude of symptoms that the deadly influence of ultramontane poison is everywhere threatening the very life of the faith. The same insane jealousy of all freedom has prevented any attempt to give a really liberal education to the French clergy. The spirit which has shown itself amongst ourselves when it was proposed to give our Roman Catholics access to a college of their own in our University of Oxford—the spirit which has succeeded hitherto in thwarting every such attempt, even when advocated by Dr. Newman, which suppressed, by Papal command, the one periodical organ of Roman Catholicism in England which possessed any claim to intellectual merit—'The Home and Foreign Review'—and which we fear will only be strengthened by the appointment of Dr. Wiseman's successor, has triumphed absolutely in France. What has been the consequence may be read in the calm words of Döllinger, certainly no willing witness against, if not a biassed witness in favour of Romanism.

In his speech on 'The Past and Present of Catholic Theology,' he says:—

'Better things, much better things may fortunately be said of France [than of Italy]. There we find above all what is entirely wanting in Italy, a courageous, vigorous, and well chosen band of learned laymen who defend the cause of the faith and the Church in literature with emphasis, dignity, spirit, and ability. And as for the clergy, I need only pronounce the names of Gerbet, Maret, Lacordaire, Gratry, Bantain, Dupanloup, Ravignan, Félix, and it will be admitted that there are men in the ranks of the French clergy who understand the wants of their age and nation, who know how to animate intellectually and to penetrate into the spirit of the doctrine which has been delivered to them by their school, and by that means to act mightily and successfully on the religious and moral feelings of their fellow countrymen. But if we ask, is there no Dalberg there? where are there in France the true theologians, the equals and followers of Petau and Bossuet and Arnauld? where the men of fundamental and comprehensive learning? There is no answer. *France has no theologians* because she has no high school of thelogy, not one school even which teaches the theological sciences. She has only eighty or eighty-five seminaries, which may be very good, even excellent, as pastoral educational establishments, but which, to German ideas, at least, can scarcely count as scientific institutes, and which furnish such scanty primary instruction that for the greater majority of their pupils it is quite impossible at a later time to rear the solid edifice of thorough and comprehensive theological learning on such a frail and faulty foundation. I do not know what reasons have deterred the French Church during the last fifty years from making any attempt at founding a common and central school for theology and the kindred branches of science. One main difficulty, which no means have been found for obviating, may be the state of the institutions for the education of the lower and middle classes, as indeed it was lately found when the Catholic University of Dublin was established that in the absence of good intermediate schools a University is like a ship without water. But things will not remain thus much longer. There is increasing anxiety that the French clergy will be driven more and more out of the bosom of society and national life, will be forced more and more into an isolated and caste-like position, and will forfeit more and more its influence on the male parts of the population which has already been so much weakened. Looking at such a state of things, we Germans have every reason to be thankful that Universities still exist among us, and that theology is represented at them.'

This is the terrible alternative, we believe, before that nation. The great Church of France is being so weakened by the spread of this subtle poison of ultramontane principles that she can no longer witness for the truth of Revelation with her ancient power, before her sharp-witted and busy people. It needs long and careful thought to estimate the wonderful change which has passed over her before those spiritual heavens in which the Eagle of Meaux soared with so majestic a flight could be overshadowed by such dark clouds as those which hang so thick around us everywhere now. We have ourselves, when arguing with a distinguished French ecclesiastic, been met, when we quoted Bossuet, by a shrug of the shoulders, and an assurance that the great champion of their faith himself was 'Vraiment presque hérétique.' At such a time it is well to be reminded what those Gallican Liberties were for which he strove.

He had just been promoted after the termination of the Dauphin's education to the see of Meaux when he preached the opening sermon at the assembly of the clergy of France in 1682. The sermon was an omen of what followed, for it claimed the primacy for St. Peter, with an accompanying caution as to the humility with which the exercise of such a power should be accompanied. Under Bossuet's influence the assembly of the clergy passed the four celebrated propositions which are the basis of that claim for limiting the assumptions of Rome, which is so well known under the name of the Gallican Liberties. The first declares that the Papal power extends only to things spiritual which concern eternal salvation. The second, that it in no way derogates from the authority of the decisions of the Council of Constance, in its fourth and fifth Decrees on the authority of General Councils. The third, that it should be limited by the Canon, and by the rules and usages adopted by different National Churches, and so amongst others by the Church of France. The fourth, that though the Pope is expected to decide questions of the faith for all Churches, yet that his decisions can be revoked so long as they have not been sanctioned by the consent of the Church.

Innocent XI. utterly repudiated these propositions, and demanded of Louis XIV. their formal disavowal. His response, characteristic of the man, was to order by an edict that they should be registered by all the Parliaments and Universities and theological faculties, and that none should be made licentiate or doctor till he had maintained a thesis in support of them.*

Throughout the Pontificate of Innocent XI. there was no adjustment of the conflict. The short Pontificate of Alexander succeeded. On the 4th of August, 1690, he passed a Constitution, annulling all that had been done in the

* Sismondi, 'Histoire de la France,' xviii. 25-28. (1842.)

assembly of 1682. But he did not venture to publish the bull till the 30th of January, 1691, the eve of his death. The informal bull was simply overlooked by Louis. Cardinal Pignatelli, who succeeded as Innocent XII., was supposed to be far more favourable to France. But the conflict between the Régale and the Pontificale still continued. The new Pope, like his predecessors, refused bulls for the consecration of thirty-seven Bishops unless the king yielded. The necessities of Louis forced him to a certain amount of concession in the year 1693. Bossuet, the great author of the propositions, repaired to Rome, and, after three successive attempts, a form of so-called retractation was adopted, with which the Pope was satisfied. Each one of the Bishops-designate wrote severally to the Pope the stipulated letter, in which he declared that he regarded all that was determined or ordered in the proscribed assembly with regard to the ecclesiastical power or action of the Pontiff as if it had not been ordered, and they bound themselves to deliberate no more on what had been by him held to be contrary to the interest of the Church.* The King suspended his order. With this Rome professed itself satisfied; though the claims to liberty which the French Church had always maintained, and which the four celebrated propositions only embody with greater distinctness, were never really disavowed, and were energetically repeated in the letter of Louis to the Cardinal de la Tremoil, in 1713.†

How different is this aspect of the great French Church from that which it exhibits now. Then the Episcopate, headed by Bossuet as its chosen chief, was doing noble battle for the freedom of their own communion. The same body is now seen bowing abjectly before the whisper of the Vatican, trembling before the secret threats of the General

* Sismondi, 'Histoire de la France,' xviii. 183.
† See 'Histoire de Bossuet,' par le Cardinal de Bousset, 298-302.

of the Jesuits, or flocking obediently to Rome to take their humble part in registering the infallible decrees of the occupant of the Chair of St. Peter in favour of the Immaculate Conception in 1854; submitting to have, by simple Papal power, a disputed opinion—against which none had stood more firmly than their own fathers—turned into an article of the faith; or declaring, in 1862, the absolute necessity of the temporal sovereignty of the Supreme Pontiff.

All this, moreover, is in exact accordance with every other change in this once famous Church; with the surrender of its ancient liturgy and the adoption of the Roman in its place; and lastly—though not least—with the new extravagance of its Mariolatry. It is most painful to see the growth of this terrible development. It possesses not only the frivolous and weak, but seems to subdue to itself all the most robust spirits of the existing French Church. How fearful is it to read that almost the last words of such a man as the Abbé Desgenettes were, 'La dévotion au saint et immaculé Cœur de Marie est le principe et le centre de toute dévotion!'* But so it is: this is the natural development of the doctrine of the Immaculate Conception, and it is stamping its revolting features on the literature, the devotion, and the art of Roman Catholic France. Dr. Wordsworth, in his 'Tour in Italy'† notes one instance of this which is too remarkable not to be repeated. The favourite Roman defence for the whole system of Mariolatry is, that it is nothing more than a high honour paid to the great doctrine of the Incarnation; that the Blessed Virgin is, as it were, the nimbus surrounding the humanity of the Eternal Son; that she is never contemplated in the acts which we condemn as separate from Him, but always as the shrine wherein HE

---

* 'Vie de l'Abbé Desgenettes,' par M. Desfossés.
† Vol. ii. pp. 286, 287.

dwelt when He deigned for our sakes to become man; that in this sense 'the Glories of Mary' and such offices, with which we reproach the present Church, would, if our minds were duly filled as theirs are with the great mystery of the Incarnation, be more fitly termed the Glories of her Incarnate Son. All men whose minds are properly endued with Christian charity will delight to believe that so indeed it has been with many devout souls who seem to those without to have drawn perilously near to creature-worship. Such an idea seems to be stamped upon many of the great creations of the ancient painters' genius. In these the Virgin—beautiful and royal as she is in her simplicity—is felt to be the adjunct of the Divine Babe. Wonderfully is this expressed in Raphael's noble picture in the Dresden Gallery. Even in that blaze of glory, the countenance of the Infant speaks of commanding majesty, that of the Virgin of faith and supplication. But it is not only in such vast creations of matchless genius that this subordination of the Mother to the Child is expressed: it is the traditional rule of all the earlier Christian painters. Let any one cast his eye over the walls of our own National Gallery, and he will mark everywhere the same feature, running through every school, and more or less distinctly impressed on every picture. He will find it preeminent in Pietro Perugino, Francia, and Domenico Ghirlandajo; but he may trace it as essentially present in the Madonnas of Filippo and Filippino Lippi, of Pinturicchio, of Marco Basante, of Battista Cima, of Mantegna of Padua, and of Garofalo. It was, in short, then the rule which religion had imprinted upon art. 'But now,' Dr. Wordsworth tells us, his friend, 'a distinguished French layman, a member of the *Institut*,' said to him, 'now, you see, they have taken away the Divine Child from His mother's arms, and they exhibit the Blessed Virgin *standing as a goddess* on the altars of our churches, with her hands outstretched towards the people, as if she alone were the Arbitress or the Dispenser of all graces and favour to man,"—" comme dispensatrice de toutes les graces," were his words. 'I observed this attitude,' says Dr. Wordsworth, 'also in the *Maison Mère* of the "Sisters of Charity," in the Rue du Bac, No. 140. This change has been introduced since my former visit in 1854.*

What will be the end of this new course on which the Gallican Church has entered it is most difficult to forecast. Its immediate effect, beyond all question, has been to alienate from her, to a fearful degree, the whole educated and masculine mind of the nation. Who can calculate what might not have been the return to faith and worship in that people, on whose whole character of old the lines of religious belief and devout action were so deeply marked, if, in the first great reaction from the horrors of their infidel Revolution, the Church of their fathers had stood before them in the simplicity and love of the Gospel; if she, with God's words and the ancient creeds on her lips, had shown them how to reconcile reason and Revelation, true liberty and ardent Faith? That opportunity has been let slip; and let slip in spite of all the efforts of some of her noblest sons. Even of her Bishops, some foresaw the evils which this blind exaltation of the Papacy was bringing on her; none, perhaps, with greater clearness than Monseigneur Claude-Hippolyte Clausel de Montals, the able and venerable Bishop of Chartres, and cousin of the eloquent and noble-hearted Frayssinous, Bishop of Hermopolis. It is touching to find the old man in almost his latest publication mourning over the depressed and divided condition of the Church which he had done so much to restore from its ruins; whilst it is not a little instructive to find him attribute all these evils to the spread of the ultramontane cabal, 'cabale,' as he calls it, 'nombreuse,

* Dr. Wordsworth's 'Tour in Italy,' vol. ii. p. 287.

pleine d'âpreté et de violence, qui s'est établie à Rome et qui a un grand nombre d'associés résidant en France et en Italie.'* Such words may seem strong, but in his long life he had seen enough to justify their use. Who can say how far even the overthrow of the throne of Louis Philippe was not, in a great measure, to be traced to the intrigues of that ultra section? We cannot forget the strange sight exhibited by so many of the high French ecclesiastics at that troubled time. Amongst the turbulent utterances of these friends of revolution, no voice was clearer in its note than that of the then Archbishop of Lyons (De Bonald), himself intimately connected with the Jesuits, who promised to the clergy, as the result of the Revolution, the liberty for which they had so often thirsted when they contemplated its enjoyment by their North American brethren. Surely burning words may be excused from one who had seen the acting of the 'cabale' under so many phrases. And how sadly are all his auguries of evil being even now fulfilled! The men of France—and especially the thinking men, who ultimately set the general tone of opinion—are, as a rule, severed from, if not hostile to the Church. If any one doubts this, let him go, as we have gone, in the early Sunday morning to the Churches of the Madeleine or St. Roch in Paris, and stay there till the midday mass, and note the proportion between the men and the women who have attended the various services. With all our own dangers—and we have shown repeatedly that we are not disposed to undervalue them—the difference in this respect between the congregations in the great Parisian churches we have named and those which assemble every Sunday morning in St. James's and St. George's, London, is most marked. Everywhere are tokens of the same fact. The whole tone of French literature exhibits a like divorce

* 'Coup d'œil sur la Constitution de la Religion Catholique, et sur l'état présent de cette Religion dans notre France,' p. 5.

between literature and religion. As a rule, all that is fresh, vigorous, and powerful is unchristian; that which professes to be religious is trashy, meretricious, and effeminate. Here again the difference between the two countries is remarkable. There is, as we sadly know, sweeping over us too a wave of unbelief; the vial poured upon the air has tainted our own atmosphere; we have philosophers who sneer and even divines who cavil at eternal truths. But, with all this, there never was a time in our literary history when the best and strongest writers were more honestly pervaded by an outspoken faith in the Christian revelation. Only let any one compare the answers which have been drawn forth in the two countries by the recent assaults upon the Faith, and he will be able to estimate the marvellous difference which exists between them.

What then is to be the future of the Church so circumstanced? More and more alienated from all the commanding thought of the nation; more and more leaning, first upon the immediate physical support of the Imperial Government (which, however, is now markedly averse to her ultramontane tendencies), and secondly upon Rome, which is carrying on daily her favourite work of denationalising the vassal communion; becoming more and more a mere parasite of the Papacy—that Papacy itself to all appearance in the spasms which, whilst they lend it for the moment a preternatural and shocking strength, show like the surest tokens and the most immediate forerunner of a coming dissolution—what, we ask, is to be its end? Will it once again be swept away by some terrible storm of unbelief? Are all these evil symptoms signs of the approach of that day of which it is written, 'When the Son of Man cometh shall He find faith on the earth?' Or is there yet before it the possibility of a mighty reaction? May it be, as we have hinted above, that Imperialism will yet restore the nationality of this once noble Church? If Dr. Wordsworth be right, Imperialism owes to it this retribution. He traces much of the ultra-Roman tendency of the present Gallican Communion to—

'the inquisitorial interference of the State in religious matters, such as the erection of churches, which are dealt with in the same way as hôtels de ville, bridges, prisons, and railway-stations. . . . . . This *patronage* of the Government, which dates from the days of the Organic Articles and Laws of 1802, has estranged the affections of the Church from the Government, and has placed the Church in an *extra-national* and *anti-national* attitude. It has made it anti-Gallican and *ultramontane.* It has produced a result which was never anticipated by Napoleon I., who framed the Organic Articles, nor by Louis Philippe, whose policy in Church matters was in accordance with their spirit. It has given a predominant influence to the *Papacy* over the *French Church.* It has done more for the extension and triumph of Ultramontanism than could have been effected by Hildebrand himself.' *

There are not lacking signs which seem to show that amongst the deep purposes revolving in the mind of the present Emperor have been some which would indeed redress this wrong by reanimating the national character of the Gallican Communion. But we anxiously ask, Can even he effect this mighty change? Can he roll back the wrongs of years? Can he arouse the French clergy to see that such a course would indeed secure, not as they now speak, their 'servitudes,' but their truest liberties? Can it be that future Bossuets shall arise within her, not as now to be frowned coldly down or persecuted even to the death, but to form, and guide, and enlighten the mind of her own people; to reform her developments and abuses; to give back, as he would fain have done, the communion in both kinds to the worshipper, and a reasonable Faith to the inquirer; and to stretch out the hand of welcome to every effort for the re-union of Christendom? Is there such a day in store for her? God grant that it may be so, and that we may share the benefit: that with the two Reformed Churches, linked in loving alliance, France

* Dr. Wordworth's 'Tour,' vol. ii. p. 294.

and England, the great twin arbiters of the world's destinies, may contend together against the Common Enemy, and maintain the Common Truth.

One conclusion, where so much is doubtful, seems, however, inevitable, and it is this: that those amongst ourselves who are lured away from their Fathers' Church by the boasted profession that they will thus leave discord for unity, are the victims of the very shallowest of impositions. The differences which exist within the English Church, and which all wise and good men will ever seek to reduce in their proportions and to clear of their bitterness, are the expression of differences in the mind of man, and must be found wherever all liberty of thought is not absolutely stamped out by the foot of arrogant assumption. The deep policy of Rome may throw around these differences such a veil of authority, and such a halo of devotion, that they seem to have disappeared; but they are just as certainly present beneath the veil, and the stumbling steps of him who enters ignorantly into the folds of that mist will soon strike heavily against them. He who quits the liberty of the English communion in order to find in that of Rome a perfect and unquestioning rest for his weary spirit will, unless he is essentially servile in his nature, meet undoubtedly with the heaviest disappointment. He will find that the concealed acting of old perplexities is more entangling than ever was their avowed presence, and that he has but increased the difficulties of believing when he has substituted for the Scriptures and the Creeds of the Universal Church the voice of an ultramontane director, requiring him to view with equal faith the impostures of La Salette and the Miracles of Christ; or the Immaculate Conception of the Virgin and the Incarnation of the Lord. He will have sheltered himself from the wind, but he will have fallen into the jaws of the whirlwind; or rather, to express it in the Prophet's words, it will be to him 'as if a man did flee from a lion, and a bear met him, or went into the house and leaned his hand on the wall, and a serpent bit him;' the end, we fear, of many a wearied spirit, which for very hopeless weariness stays in the disappointing shelter it chose so blindly from its own perplexities.

THE CHURCH AND HER CURATES.*
(*July*, 1867.)

WHATEVER other results may follow from the important change now passing over our great National Representative Assembly, one, if we may judge from the experience of the past, is sure to follow—that many, if not all, of our noblest institutions will be tested anew by searching popular inquiry. The waves drive inward from the ocean storm, and as their swell reaches the shallows, it is lifted into more threatening crests, and runs in among the creeks and gullies of the coast with whitening breakers and thundering voices. Whether the old cliffs will stand unmoved, and rampart-like beat back the billows, must depend upon the state in which the attack finds them. If their foundations are solid and their front compact, the heaviest surf will play idly round them, and they will hold their own amidst 'the Hell of waters.' But if there be rifts and cracks along their line, and over-toppling crags weighing unequally their brow, there may be many falls and much loss of precious ground.

At such a breathing time then as the present, it is well to look to our state of preparation, and guard by groins and jetties the line of coast which is sure ere long to be tested by the wild break of the untamable waters.

Now amongst the institutions which must be thus tried,

---

* 1. 'The Position and Prospects of Stipendiary Curates: a Paper published by order of the Provisional Council of the Curates' Augmentation Fund, setting forth a Plan for the Improvement of the Position and Prospects of Stipendiary Curates, with certain Objections to the Fund considered.' Third Edition. London, Oxford, and Cambridge, 1867.

2. 'Report of the Society for Promoting the Employment of Additional Curates in populous Places.' 1866.

3. 'Report of the Church Pastoral Aid Society.' 1866.

4. 'Sons of the Clergy Report.' 1867.

5. 'Report of the Bishop of London's Fund.' 1866-67.

our Established Church stands perhaps in the fore-front. Our readers know that we look with anxiety on some of the conditions of its internal state, and are not altogether satisfied that the best of all defences against any external violence, a thorough well compacted inward coherence, is as fully maintained amongst us as it might be. But to that subject we have no intention of returning at present. It is to other aspects of our great Established Church that we wish in a few words to call the serious attention of our readers.

It is then against our Church as an establishment that we expect this first storm to break. So it was after the passing of the first Reform Bill. Hardly had the passionate cries amidst which that bloodless revolution was accomplished died upon the ear, when new voices awoke on every side clamouring, some for the reform, some for the remodelling, some for the abolition, of our National Church Establishment.

It argues surely not a little for the strength of the old walls, and on the whole for the instinctive prudence with which their defence was conducted, that in those turbulent times they were not dismantled but restored, and that the too eager utterers of the opprobrious invective 'Down with the old hag,' awoke in the public mind not the Divine Rage they hoped to excite against their victim, but a deep disgust against themselves and a settled opposition to their attempts.

Something of the same sort is pretty sure to follow our new political reformation. An electric condition of the air quickens into a very troublesome activity all the lower forms of animal life; and speculators, and nostrum-mongers, and men of one idea, are always excited by a thundery state of the political and social atmosphere. Societies for the Revision of the Prayer Book, and Anti-State Church

Societies, and Liberation Societies, and the like, feel that their time is come, and begin buzzing about amidst the larger and more highly animated organisations which they so pertinaciously infest, and stinging or irritating all whom they can reach. Any one who has noted the degree to which the scarcely visible insects which haunt the gem-like islands of the Lake of Killarney can at such time madden the old boat-men, whose tawny skins look utterly midge proof, can in some degree understand the annoyance which these congeneric swarms are ready to inflict in such paroxysms of their vitality on the defenders of our great institutions.

The first attack will probably, for many reasons, be made upon the Irish Establishment, and if that was our subject we could be somewhat largely if not always very pleasantly didactic as to what it should do to prepare itself for the evil day. It is not improbable that the assailants of the English Establishment may postpone their more open assaults on its existence till they have played out their Irish game. This is at the present moment the plan of their campaign. There is, we have every reason to believe, very little genuine Irish hostility to the Irish Church Establishment. There is indeed a band of Irish patriots who hate it in common with the Imperial Parliament and the Imperial Crown, as a badge of the long-continued servitude of Erin. But though on occasion a somewhat noisy, these are not a very powerful body. They are indeed always ready to break a few heads at a fair, but they have no serious thoughts even of capturing Chester Castle, still less of demolishing the Tower of London, or destroying the Irish Church Establishment. The lecturers and speakers against it are, for the most part, paid agents of the English Liberation Society, who on Irish soil are opening their first trenches, and constructing their earliest parallels for the breaching of what they think the most assailable point of the common fortifications of the two conjoined establishments. The 'centres' who direct these secret movements are likely to delay their assault upon the home-camp till they are reinforced by the strength which any successful action against these more distant bands would assuredly give them.

But though the main attack may be delayed, there will probably be a good deal of useless preliminary firing. As we run our eye over the not very enticing bill of literary fare which the 'Liberation Society' now hangs out to tempt us, we can anticipate tolerably well of what the banquet will consist. Thus we are invited to hear 'The Rev. Daniel Kattern refute the objections to organisation for Anti-State Church purposes.' We are bidden 'to examine' with Mr. Miall, 'the title-deeds of the Church of England to her parochial endowments;' to accept Mr. Hinton's view of the question, 'Church property, whose is it?' or to receive the dictum of Mr. Eagle, '*Barrister-at-law*' (a vulturine appellation very strange to us in the reports of our Law Courts), that 'Tithes are the property of the public and the poor.' These are the heavy joints; but more appetising fare in the way of entremets are not excluded from the feast, and so we are treated to a set of two dozen tracts on 'Bishops and their *Salaries*,' showing the sums 'squandered on the wearers of lawn-sleeves.' 'Archdeacons and their *Incomes*,'—how nice and delicate the distinction!—as to whom we are told that 'no class of dignitaries exhibit the mal-administration of the Church in a stronger light;'—perhaps because they work harder and for less pay than almost any other operatives. We have again 'Our Cathedral Bodies, and what they Cost,' wherein we learn that their revenues are worse than lost; that the Cathedral towns are nests of immorality, the worshippers petrifactions, the Cathedral Close 'the valley of the shadow of death;' and we wind up all with the 'incomes of the working classes:' and 'The Curate's complaint.' We have no doubt that 'tears of compassion tremble on the eyelids' of the writer of this jeremiad 'ready to fall when he has told his pitiful story.' How near also may be the 'kicking of the spiritless outcast,' who will not join in overturning the Church of which he is a minister it might be rash to prognosticate. These straws show which way the wind is setting, and where the storm is likely to burst, and we think it well that before its arrival every possible provision should have been made to prevent mischief.

Now, all attacks of this character rest for their basis on two propositions; one of which is absolutely false, and the other most exactly and painfully true. The first proposition, repeated over and over again under every form of false statement, is 'that the Established Church is immensely rich, by far the most richly endowed Church in Christendom, with a vast revenue; it may be stated at ten millions sterling per annum,' &c.*

We shall not waste time and words in confuting these monstrous assertions. They are made in the very teeth of statistical inquiries most wide in their extent and most searching in their minuteness, the result of which shows that the Church of England, instead of suffering under this plethora of means, could not secure a moderate competence for all her working clergy if every reservoir were broken down and all her resources poured into a common fund for after subdivision.

It may suffice for our purpose to quote the general result to be extracted from the Tables compiled in 1835 by the Commissioners appointed by His then Majesty to inquire into the Ecclesiastical revenues of England and Wales. From these it appears that the whole net income of the Established Church, including the revenues of the archiepiscopal and

* 'Church Property, Whose is it?' By the Rev. J. H. Hinton.

episcopal sees, the cathedral and collegiate churches, the several dignities and benefices, amounts to 6,495,218*l*.; which if divided amongst the 25,000 clergy of England and Wales, would give to each about 259*l*. a year.

But false as is the first of these propositions, the second is unhappily too true, and that is that the great body of the English clergy are shamefully underpaid. Without committing ourselves to such highly-coloured statements as those put forth by the 'Poor Clergy Relief Society,' which represent 'hundreds, literally hundreds,' of the clergy 'with their families as struggling in rags and penury, and many actually dying of cold and hunger,' and allowing for the great increase in the income of the poorest benefices which the judicious management of their resources have enabled, and are year by year enabling, the Ecclesiastical Commission to effect, it still remains true that the great bulk of the English clergy are most meanly remunerated for their labours. By whatever test we try the amount of the remuneration they receive, the conclusion is the same. If, for instance, we estimate the capital laid out in fitting an ordinary English clergyman for his work and compare it with what he can hope to earn in his profession, the result is most startling. We say nothing of the 'literates,'—who are still in well-regulated dioceses received as candidates for Orders only in rare and exceptional cases, and with regard to whom it is almost as impossible to calculate the cost of production as it is that of the wares of the 'cheap Johns' of other trades;—but as to those who have passed through the regular school and academic courses, we cannot estimate the outlay of capital under the most favourable circumstances at less than a thousand pounds sterling. How many parents, and those not rich ones, would gladly compound the actual expense incurred for that sum! And what, so far as this world's goods are concerned, is the return? There is, first, what may be called the apprenticeship time of the young curate, when he receives any sum for his labours varying from nothing to 50*l.* a year. How long this period may be extended in any given case it is impossible to say. But when it is passed, and the young man has learned his business, and too often married a wife and begun to furnish a nursery, it is no great increase to which he can look forward. His salary may be raised perhaps to 100*l.* or 120*l.* a year; it is but seldom, since pluralities were happily abolished, that a house is provided for him; or if it is, the estimated rent is deducted from his small salary, and on that miserable pittance he may continue to exist for an unlimited time, possibly for his whole life, though his labours may be honestly and ungrudgingly given to the work of his high office. Many are those to whom preferment never does nor can come. That to which the poor hardworking curate may most hopefully look, the preferment administered by his bishop, is utterly insufficient to supply such claims; for the benefices in England, to which the Bishops appoint, form but a very small number in the list of livings. Whether, on the whole, this is an advantage or a disadvantage to the Church is a question on which we will not enter here. Its settlement would involve many most conflicting considerations, but this inevitably results from it, that, even where the Episcopal patronage is most fairly administered (and we know cases in which none but curates of the diocese are admitted to share in it), a very small proportion of the curates can ever obtain preferment from its resources. Many, therefore, unless they have claims on private or political patrons, must, in spite of the real service of years, live and die as curates.

But this is not all. Even if they do obtain after years of work a benefice, they are often little better, and not unfrequently are worse off than they were before. Even the better endowed livings commonly do little more than pay their expenses, and by far the greater proportion of English benefices fall far beyond this level. Perhaps the curate of twenty years' service succeeds at last to a living of 300*l.* or even 400*l.* a year. But with it come a multitude of new expenses which often make the poor man wish himself back again in his less dignified position. The direct claims of charity multiply upon him. The maintenance of the parish-school rests in ordinary cases mainly upon him; the parsonage is to be kept, too often to be put, in decent repair, whilst it may be (for the entail of such poverty is very widely spread) there are no assets in the hands of the widow of the dead incumbent, to meet that most sickening of all charges under such circumstances, the claim for dilapidations. Then for the rector there are new social claims and new contingencies. He has now a certain position to maintain; he cannot wholly abdicate it without greatly diminishing his usefulness and probably incurring reproach. He finds himself commonly in that poorest of all positions in a very wealthy society,—that of a poor gentleman. He mixes in society, bound to conceal the secret grief which is preying on him and to wear a look of complacency over a heart heavy with anxiety.

How, under such difficulties, the English clergy live, bring up their children, give, as they do give, largely to all calls of charity, and still retain their position as members of the gentler classes of society, is at first sight a matter of marvel. We believe the true solution to be this, that as a body they bring to their profession very far more than they receive from it. Here, then, undoubtedly, is a miserable earthly return for the money laid out in the training of the English clergymen.

But to estimate the whole question fully we must weigh the relative as well as the positive returns of their calling as a profession. How utterly insignificant these are when compared, to name no other, with what business, commerce, or the bar yield to the manufacturer, the banker, the merchant, or the lawyer, any one who has the smallest knowledge of the subject can settle for himself. Suppose for a moment that the number of failures in the three pursuits were equal, what possible approach to equality exists between their successes? The small successes of trade, or of the bar, would be absolute wealth to the poor incumbent, and these small successes abound and multiply. Every movement of the social machine creates a new set of profitable places for the barrister of six years' standing, whilst the salaries of the leading clerkships in the house of the successful man of business might endow a dozen archdeaconries. Yet these are but the rank and file of the worldly professions. All professions are more or less filled upon the lottery principle, but the inducements which a lottery parades to lead men to venture with it depend far more on the number of the substantial prizes than upon the compensation given to the multitude of blank ticket-holders. Now the great prizes of the clerical profession are at the present time so few as to be almost beyond hope, except to the very sanguine mother, who expects, as a matter of course, that her young offspring will become Archbishop of Canterbury; whilst the magnificence of the prizes of the other professions rises with the increase of wealth, of property, and of commercial activity. Only let any man run his eye over the column in the 'Illustrated London News' which delights to record the bequests of the wealthy, and he may see what are in number and amount the prizes now obtainable with any moderate share of ability, character, and good fortune, in the fertile fields of English business and merchandise. And yet these tens and hundreds of thousands of bequeathed pounds sterling, which make so many mouths water, themselves represent but a small part of the whole accumulations of our successful traders. For it is distinctively an English habit that the prosperous merchant or man of business seeks at once to become a landowner, so that his money capital represents rather the stock-in-trade with which he works his business than his whole fortune.

Nor is even this all. The vast increase of wealth and, as its sure accompaniment, the growth of more expensive habits, tends continually to lower relatively the social position of the clergy. For whilst the incomes of others increase, theirs, in the great number of instances, must stand still, if not decrease. The commutation of tithes, however necessary it may have been, tends strongly in this direction. Of old the clergy had, through the tithes, their share in all the increased productiveness of the land. But not only is this share absolutely given up under the commutation system, but the increase of productiveness, as it tends directly to augment the supply of the different kinds of grain (on the price of which the clergyman's income depends), and so to lower their market value, tends also to lower the standard measure of clerical remuneration.

The evil of this low standard of clerical remuneration extends far beyond the class which is directly affected by it. It is a matter of the gravest concern to every Christian people that the payment of its clergy should be large and liberal, and to none, from various causes, is this more important than to the English people. Hitherto England has drawn her clergy from all classes of society. There have been paths open through which the child of the poor man, if he had character and talents, might rise to the very highest places in the Establishment. But at the same time the ranks have been equally filled by the sons not only of her ancient gentry but of her highest nobles. The Army, the Navy, and the Church, as it was called, were indeed the only professions entirely open, until within these few years, to these last.

Any change in the social position of the clergy, which altered largely this state of things, would be most injurious to the nation. Even if it were possible to give the very best and highest clerical education to the children of the lower orders, and then to invest them with the ministerial office, the loss incurred by drawing the clergy from them alone would be incalculable. The injury to the higher classes of society would be immediate. It would not be easy to estimate the degree in which, in that rank of society, the presence of the clerical son or brother, or even equal, tends to keep evil out and to bring in good. The whole tone of white society in our West India islands was, we are told, in a short time altered by the sending out of bishops who took an equal social standing with the highest members of the community. The real object of maintaining the equal place of the mitre with the coronet is not thereby to exalt the spirituality but to leaven the temporalty. Nor would the loss of any change in this condition of the clergy be confined to these classes. The poor would suffer perhaps more than the rich. It is sometimes asserted that the poorer classes supply the best clergy for the poor. But all experience proves the contrary. There is under a rough exterior a vast deal of high sensitiveness in the English poor; and, after truth and reality in the directly religious and moral character, there is nothing which they more appreciate in their pastor than the character of an English gentlemen. They feel safe with such an one. There is no fear of his prying into their family secrets, or revealing the whereabouts of the skeleton which is as often hid away in the house of the poor man as of the rich. There is a natural sympathy and kindness in a well-bred clergyman which the poor instantly appreciate, and which wins to him their confidence. As a class, a clergy drawn mainly from the gentler classes are naturally removed further from that terrible picture drawn by the wise man of one of the chiefest evils of the earth—' A poor man that oppresseth the poor is like a sweeping rain which leaveth no food.' *

It is one of the main impediments to the working of the French clergy at this time that this social change has been entailed on them by the Revolution, and that they are almost universally drawn from the lower orders of the nation. This has thrown them out from literature and society, and more than anything else has tended to lower the tone and influence of the great Church of Bossuet and of Tillemont. Yet the French people are far from being as aristocratic in their temper as the English; and the injury, therefore, which would be done to us would be far greater than that which this change has inflicted upon them.

This tendency to deterioration in the social standing of the clergy has moreover developed itself at the very time when it was most desirable to raise, instead of reducing, their position. Never was there a crisis when it was more needful in the interests of this people to take every lawful means to strengthen and develope *the social power* of its clergy. On the one hand the wide-spread intellectual activity of the day, and its habit of questioning everything; with the ready tendency of activity to become restlessness, and of questioning to lapse into scepticism, call for a thoughtful, highly educated, intellectual clergy. If the clergy do not continue to be, as hitherto to so great a degree they have been, the guides of thought; if they lag behind their age, degenerate in scholarship, eschew science, grow meagre in philosophy, and unfurnished in historical lore, the defence of Christianity against its strengthening enemies will have passed into hands fearfully inadequate for the strife. On another side, too, the circumstances of the present time make this need equally pressing. The accumulation of a multitude of men into a confined and insufficient compass, tends as much as desert

* Proverbs xxviii. 3.

loneliness to produce amongst them a fierce and dangerous barbarousness. This overcrowding produces a more intense form of separation between each one and his fellows in all the deeper interchanges of human communion than the mere physical difficulties of distance can do. There is, too, the same difficulty of enforcing law amidst the dense crowd as in the dangerous desert; there is the same power of concealment amongst numbers as there would be in the forest or the waste; there is the same Arab-like freemasonry of offenders and marauders against the laws and usages of civilised society. It is a pregnant sentence in which a most intelligent American witness before the Royal Commission now inquiring into Trades Unions, states one cause which has kept from such associations in the United States some of the evils which have beset them here, 'You know that we have no such dense population as you have here.'*

Nothing but a vigorous spirit of Christianity can thoroughly leaven such masses as these. How little, even as things are, we have succeeded in so leavening these populations, the terrible revelations of this Commission may teach us. Such a state of feeling as they bring to light with regard to destroying property, maiming limbs, breaking hearts and violently taking away life, could not possibly exist where there was any dominant belief in a God or a future judgment.

Now, there never was a time when our clergy as a body were for their numbers as thoroughly efficient as they are now. There is a far higher standard both of personal life and of official labour than was ever common heretofore. Any marked lack of zeal, piety, laboriousness, and intelligence, are the exceptions, and not the rule. The prevalence of these great social evils and national dangers is the result not of the negligence of the clergy, but of their absolute

---

* *Minutes of Evidence*, answer of Mr. Abram S. Hewitt.—Ques. 3743.

insufficiency in number to deal with them. A handful of heroes could not long occupy a plain against a host of enemies. Briareus himself could not with his hundred hands weed out the noxious growth of a million of acres. The clergy are utterly underhanded. They cannot reach the multitude who are nominally committed to them. How can one pastor really deal with the spiritual necessities of ten thousand souls? And yet, at the rate at which our population multiplies, this evil must increase a thousandfold, unless some efficient measures be adopted to increase the number of our clergy, whilst, as we have seen, the whole present tendency of existing influences is to lower their social position, and so to reduce their actual numbers and degrade the sources from which hitherto they have been drawn. That this must in the long run be the consequence of underpaying the clergy, a very little thought may convince any one. For there are few fallacies more transparent than the argument that, as no clergyman is really worth having who works for the temporal rewards of his profession, we may safely lower down those rewards, trusting that we shall thus secure the services of the more earnest-minded, and only bolt, through the shaking of our sieve of misery, the worldly-minded, the ambitious, and the secular. It is, indeed, true that men who become and continue clergymen for the sake of these temporal provisions are, as to their highest function, little worth having: but it is not the less true that without the temporal provision you will get few of the better men. After all, the clergy are men, and must, if they are to live, have the means of living. Then in this country we very wisely encourage a married clergy; and this entails the further necessity of having that on which the wife and family (for where he is poor there always is a family) of the clergyman, as well as the clergyman himself, can live. Then, again, though an overwhelming love for the highest duties of his spiritual office may lead many a clergyman to labour on in poverty with unrewarded zeal and unacknowledged devotion, and though these are the very kernels and living centres of the clerical body, yet we must not reckon on securing these unless we make a suitable provision for our clergy. For fathers and mothers will not bring up their children for the ministry, unless they see before them a reasonable hope of that ministry duly supporting its members: and how commonly is the ultimate choice of a profession biassed by these early and imperceptible influences of the parents' will!

This is then a great national question. So long, indeed, ago as in the time of Lord Bacon distant threatenings of the future evil presented themselves to the long presages of his sagacious mind. He lamented the poverty which even then was in some cases pressing on the clergy.

'As for the benefices and pastors' places,' he says, 'it is manifest that very many of them are very weak and penurious. They who gave away impropriations from the Church seem to me to stand in a sort obnoxious and obliged to God in conscience to do somewhat for the Church, to reduce the patrimony thereof to a competency. For since they have debarred Christ's wife of a great part of her dowry, it were reason they made her a competent jointure.' *

There is little hope of much redress from the remedy to which he points. Well as every patriot must wish it, no great results we fear will be obtained from the labours of the society which seeks to regain for the ministry the tithes which lay impropriators have abstracted.

The temper of the times is decidedly, and not altogether unreasonably, against any general or large increase of endowments. This is one evil which has waited upon the startling interference, whether necessary or not, with the intention of founders which the present age has witnessed. Men do not feel anything like the confidence of other days that there will be any very long-continued respect for their desires if

* Lord Bacon's 'Works,' vol. ii. 549. Ed. 1803.

they found institutions or endow livings. And beyond this there is far too much in the present day of the spirit embodied in the well-known adage, 'Why should I do anything for posterity when posterity has done nothing for me?' Such a temper is altogether hostile to the creation of endowments. They are indeed a growth which, as a general rule, seems to belong far more to the youth than to the maturity of states. From this source, therefore, comparatively speaking, but little is to be obtained.

The temper of charity at present is far more to relieve present wants and supply immediately pressing necessities. This has given birth to various Societies which seek to do what they can to supply the lack of endowments. These are principally connected with diocesan exertions. Something they have done and are doing, aided as they have most materially been by the excellent measures of the ecclesiastical commissioners, both for the management of the estates which have come into their hands and for drawing forth private charity to meet their grants. Two other Societies, both inadequately supported, collect funds for relieving in a different way the pressure of this great necessity. The 'Additional Curates' Society' supplies to the incumbents of poor parishes, and mainly those which contain large populations, funds to enable them to secure the added labours of a curate. This Society has the high merit of being colourless as to any peculiarity of doctrine within the Church of England. For it leaves the incumbents to select and the bishops of the dioceses to approve of the curates whom it maintains, without endeavouring to enforce upon the holders of benefices whom it assists any peculiar shade of religious opinion in their fellow-workers.

The 'Church Pastoral Aid Society,' on the contrary, which arose in what is termed the 'Evangelical' School, watches jealously over the party character of every curate which it pays, and subjects them to the investigation of a Board of 'Tryers,' who, if half that is reported of them be true, would not be unworthy of the most palmy days of Puritanism under Cromwell and Barebones.

Another and a still younger Society—the 'Curates' Augmentation Fund'—working in a kindred field of labour, has undertaken more immediately the Christian task of raising the condition of the curates and supplying a sort of endowment for these unendowed labourers in the vineyard. The design is altogether excellent, and none deserve more richly such assistance than those on behalf of whom it has entered on its wide field of charity.

There are at this time about five thousand curates in active employment in the Church of England. The position of such men is not too darkly coloured in 'The Position and Prospects of Stipendiary Curates,' as stated in the prospectus of this new Society:—

'In the diocese of Exeter,* from exact returns kindly furnished by Archdeacon Freeman, it appears that there are no less than sixty-eight clergymen who, after from fifteen to fifty years' service, remain assistant-curates, with professional incomes scarcely averaging 100*l.* a year, being less than is earned by a skilled artisan, or by a junior clerk in a bank.

'It has been argued that a clergyman is both able and willing to live on a smaller income than his contemporaries in any other profession, and that, as a rule, to "live of the gospel" implies to him, not affluence, but an adequate sufficiency for the requirements of his position. Be that so: but the real question now raised is, whether for a large body of her ministers, the Church does provide even this sufficiency? Let us see how far 100*l.* a year will go. Call it 2*l.* a week. Out of this the curate has to provide a home, the cost of which, under the most favourable circumstances, cannot, considering the position which he has to keep up, fall much below 50*l.* a year, leaving him 1*l.* per week for clothing, maintenance, medical attendance, personal expenses, books, parochial and other claims. In populous districts, where rent and taxes are high, and all the

---

* It is a significant fact, and one which should appeal strongly to the laity of England, that in the same diocese the tithes held by lay impropriators amount to upwards of 160,000*l.* a year.—See 'Exeter Diocesan Calendar.'

necessaries of life dear, it is very difficult for a single man, and *impossible* for a married man, even with the greatest economy and self-denial, to live on this income.

'Compare the curate's stipend in the manufacturing districts, where the services of our ablest men are most needed, with the labourer's wages. A skilled artisan will earn from 6s. 6d. to 8s. 6d., and an under-agent from 12s. 6d. to 21s. per day, and yet the curate, with a stipend equal to only *five shillings and sixpence* per diem, is expected, and justly so, from his sacred office, to make a better appearance, and to give more liberally towards the support of every charitable work, than either of these.

'It would cheer many an anxious heart, even in prospect, and eventually fill many a poverty-stricken home with thankful gladness, could such a provision by any possibility be made a thing that could be fairly reckoned on. It would meet, *pro tanto*, the exact difficulty of an unbeneficed clergy, which is to hold, in matters temporal and social, the social status which the Church assumes that they do maintain; the Ordination Service assumes that they are, as a rule, householders. The world expects them to keep for themselves and others the rank and the education of gentlemen.'

Nor can the often sinking hearts of men of education and sensibility, tried often, how severely God only knows, by the various difficulties of such a position, be upheld by the last comfort of the desolate; for Hope visits them rarely, and with the slenderest imaginings of better days. Again we quote from the 'Position and Prospects':—

'The prospect of preferment open to curates may be thus estimated:

'Out of about 12,870 livings, there are only 7010 of 200*l.* a year and upwards. To supply the vacancies for promotion which occur in these 7010 livings, the selection must be made among the following, viz., 5860 incumbents of smaller livings, 5000 curates, and about 4000 clergy, who, though not engaged in parochial work, are for the most part seeking preferment. It will be seen at once that, even if Church patronage were administered solely with regard to meritorious service, the chances of a man obtaining a fair income, in early or middle life, would be much less than in any other profession. But when it is remembered that perhaps the majority of those who are promoted are young men, *and so hold their livings for a lifetime,* and that they often owe their promotion either to their having a "family living," or to influential friends, or to their possessing the means of purchasing preferment, it is evident that the chances of a man without interest are infinitesimally small. It is arithmetically impossible that the existing incumbencies can afford maintenance within a reasonable time for more than one-third of the clergy ordained, there being 21,000 clergy, and only 7010 livings of 200*l.* a year and upwards.

'With such a remote probability of preferment, even after many years' service, a prudent man, without interest, must necessarily, on entering Holy Orders, contemplate the possibility of remaining a curate all his life, and if possessed of average abilities, may fairly require some guarantee that in that case he will be able to reckon upon his income ultimately increasing to at least 200*l.* a year. It is simply impossible for incumbents to comply with this just requirement; they cannot, that is, *unless assisted by the laity,* comply with the law of supply and demand.'

It is, moreover, well worthy of notice, that this hopeless view of preferment is to a very great degree a recent aggravation of the evils of the curate's position:—

'Formerly every curate looked forward to obtain, and generally did obtain from a very early period of his ministry, a sole charge. He lived in the parsonage house, and, if possessed of even very limited private means, held an independent and fairly good position. From many circumstances he was much less liable to be displaced, often serving in the same Cure for a lifetime, generally for a much longer period than is usual now; whilst in the event of his being obliged, after some years' service, to seek a new sphere of duty, his advanced age was no disqualification in the eyes of an incumbent who was himself permanently non-resident. The curate of former days was, therefore, comparatively free from the disappointments, anxieties, and expenses which are inseparable from the wandering and unsettled life of the curate of the present day.'

To understand fully the extent of this aggravation of the curate's difficulties, the actual statistics of residence and nonresidence, as they represent the present and the past, must be before us:—

'In the year 1810, it appears from Parliamentary returns that the clergy who were non-resident actually constituted a majority of the incumbents in England and Wales. The figures are thus given:—There were 10,159 livings, held by 9754 incumbents; of the latter number 4359 only resided in their own parishes, 5395 being non-resident, and for the most part leaving a curate in sole charge. There is no return showing the exact number of curates serving in this way as quasi-incumbents, but there were certainly as many as 5000.

'After the passing of the Pluralities Act in the year 1810, owing partly to the removal of incumbents who, before that time, had held two or more livings together, and partly to increased power being given to the bishops to enforce residence, this state of things gradually changed; until, in the year 1838, only 3078 curates acted for non-resident incumbents; and in 1864, only 955 were so employed.'

The immediate design of the Society is to relieve the amount of distress which is of necessity involved in these conditions of the curate's office, by a plan which is thus briefly described:—

'At a meeting recently held at Lambeth Palace a Provisional Council was appointed to carry forward the work of establishing a Curates' Augmentation Fund. The object of the fund is briefly this—to give to the working curate, while at work, an augmentation or additional stipend of, if possible, 100*l.* per annum over and above the stipend which he receives from other sources. This augmentation *will not be given as an eleemosynary payment, but in recognition of services, for which the present scale of curates' stipends, taken together with the insufficient prospect of preferment, is acknowledged on all hands to be utterly inadequate compensation.* It is proposed, in the first instance, that every curate of fifteen years' standing or upwards, being in the *bonâ fide* receipt of a clerical income of at least 100*l.* a year, or 80*l.* a year and a house, shall be eligible for a grant.'

The special feature of the plan is its non-eleemosynary character. The grants of the Society are to be good-service pensions, fairly won in the field and earned by long service, not the doles of charity. This is of the utmost moment. We have already too many charitable institutions for the clergy, with all their degrading accidents of canvassing cards and the laying bare of family necessities. It is impossible that such Societies should not lower the clerical character in the eyes of others, whilst they must infallibly injure still more deeply the unhappy men who, bred to better things, are thus thrust into habits of mendicancy. As avoiding this great stumbling-block especially, the path marked out by this new Society is safe and honourable.

The various objections which ingenuity can urge against other parts of the plan are convincingly met in the pages of this pamphlet, which will well repay a careful perusal. It is greatly to be desired that the scheme it sets forth, and which has met at its commencement with much valuable support, should enlist on its behalf the general interest of the laity. It is, in fact, in no common degree a layman's question. The proposal is, practically, that our generation, the laity especially, should do in their day, for the assistant-curates, what our fathers did for the clergy in theirs, when they endowed them with the tithes of the land. It will be a fund for the quasi-endowment of assistant-curates. That the creating such an endowment belongs to the laity and not to the clergy follows from the present status of the curates as a body. They it will be seen from what has been said above are not now a luxury for idle, or even a substitute for infirm, incumbents. If they were, there might be some justice in leaving the better supply of their necessities to those by whom they are employed. But there can be no such justice now, when for the most part the curate exists not for the assistance of the incumbent, but to supply those spiritual services to the population at large which the endowments of the Church, reduced by the drain of impropriations, are wholly unable to supply. The majority of curates at present are engaged in discharging duties and supplying services which cannot legally be demanded of the incumbent, but which the great increase of the population requires, and which the vastly-increased zeal of the clergy leads them, at every personal sacrifice, to seek to supply. It is well urged that—

'As a general rule, it is only a conscientious feeling on the part of the incumbent which induces him to pay any part of his curate's stipend, supposing, of course, that he is able and willing to perform the duties himself for which the endowment was originally intended to provide. And yet the beneficed clergy, whose average income is only 246*l*. a year, contribute no less than 500,000*l*. a year, or, deducting the amount they receive from societies and other sources, 400,000*l*. a year, for the maintenance of assistant-curates. On every principle of justice the laity, as representing the increased population, ought to bear the greater part of this burden. They could certainly better afford to bear the whole of it; and yet how few even of our leading laymen are there who, out of their vast incomse, contribute 100*l.*, or 50*l.*, or even 10*l.* a year towards the support of an assistant-curate! How many of the clergy, with no more legal liability in the matter than the laity, out of their straitened means pay a curate's whole stipend themselves!'

Such a claim as this cannot be neglected in an Established Church such as that of this land without causing great injury to all. The first effect of such neglect must be to diminish the number and lower the character of those who give themselves to this most necessary work.

'If, under the old system of pluralities, the stipends given by incumbents, coupled with the prospect of advancement which the ministry of the Church, regarded in a professional point of view, held out, had not been sufficient, incumbents would have been obliged to give more, or accept the alternative of performing their own duties. In the present day, however, if incumbents, after taxing themselves to the utmost, cannot afford to give stipends which, *taken together with the existing prospect of preferment*, adequately represent, by comparison with the emoluments of other professions, the value of services rendered, the action of the law of supply and demand is virtually suspended, and the consequence is that the work which the curate should do must be left undone, or be done by inferior men, to whom other professions do not present a better prospect. In other words, *there must ensue a deficiency in the supply of candidates for Holy Orders, and the proportion of men of high attainments entering the ministry with a view to engaging in parochial work must decrease.*'

That this great evil has already appeared amongst us is asserted upon very high authority.

'Parents, especially professional men and others who cannot give to their sons an independent income, feel a growing disinclination to incur the great expense requisite to give them a suitable education to enable them to take Holy Orders. Even the clergy themselves take this view of the matter in the case of their own sons. Though they feel that they can themselves bear hardships, privations, and disappointments, they shrink from subjecting their children to trials of such severity.

'That these results of the suspension of the law of supply and demand are already being experienced to a very great extent, there is unhappily abundant evidence. The Archbishop of Canterbury, in his primary charge (1864), says, "It is certain, from correct statistical returns, that the number of candidates ordained as deacons has diminished in the last ten years on an average of sixty-five per year."*

'In a pamphlet entitled "Promotion by Merit Essential to the Progress of the Church," the author, the Rev. E. Bartrum, after entering very fully into the statistics of the subject, and carrying them on from the date of the archbishop's charge, thus states the conclusion at which he arrives:—" It appears, then, that the number of clergymen ordained is not only decreasing, but in *an increasing ratio,* while the proportion of University men is declining and of literates increasing. . . . . The calibre of those entering the ministry of late years has been gradually deteriorating, and we are threatened with one of the greatest misfortunes that can befall a nation —a clergy who in intellect are not superior to the people they profess to teach."'

If this be true, and there is no reason to doubt that it is, the matter is indeed of most serious moment. The evidence taken before the Commission now inquiring into Trades Unions, to which we have already referred, shows the danger to which not morals only, or individual life, but even all skilled industry in this land, and with it her wealth and greatness amongst the nations, are at this time exposed, mainly from the degree to which those working classes who are the very bone and muscle of our population have been left untrained in all religious habits. In the great centres of population this evil exists and spreads. All the efforts of Christian charity have failed as yet to keep pace with the increase of the population. Especially is this the case in London itself, the very head and centre of this land, with its court, and its aristocracy, and its great merchant princes, and its vast hives of hoarded wealth. The estimate of deficiency of spiritual supply given in the statistics ascertained by inquiry in connection with the Bishop of London's Fund is really appalling. Here are one or two extracts from it :—

'Two standards have been adopted as necessary for the efficient working of the parochial system.

---

* The falling off in the number of candidates from the Universities of Oxford and Cambridge during the same decade, appears, from the tables given by the Archbishop, to have been of above eighty a year.

'In the first place, we assume that one clergyman cannot efficiently minister to a population of more than 2000 souls, and in this number we suppose to be included an average proportion of Dissenters, Roman Catholics, and others.

'In the second place we assume, as a basis of calculation, that if the population generally were in the habit of attending public worship, the Church of England would be responsible for providing accommodation for at least 25 per cent., or one in four of the population, after making allowance for the efforts of all other religious bodies.

'This second standard we have adopted in accordance with the principles laid down in the Report on the Religious Condition of the Population, prepared by Mr. Horace Mann for the Registrar-General, in connection with the Census of 1851. Mr. Mann there assumes, and apparently with good reason, after making due allowance for the aged, the infirm, and the young, as well as for those who from various causes might be unable to attend divine worship, that about 58 per cent. of the whole population might attend if they were willing, either in churches or chapels, according to the religious bodies to which they belonged, and that therefore accommodation ought to be provided by the Church and by Dissenters for this number. It appears, however, that in the diocese of London little more than half this provision is made, or about 29 per cent. being furnished by the Church, and 11 per cent. by Dissenters of various denominations. Supposing, then, that the whole required accommodation, that is for 58 per cent. of the population, were to be furnished in the same proportion, it is evident that about 36 per cent. ought to be provided by the Church of England, and about 22 per cent. by Dissenters of all kinds. Instead of 36 per cent., we have adopted the standard of 25 per cent. or 1 in 4; that is, nearly a third less than the proportion calculated by Mr. Mann as the minimum amount of Church accommodation which ought in due time to be provided by the Church of England. In making this deduction we have been influenced by the desire to put forward as moderate and practical a view as possible of the wants of the diocese; and we would again repeat that it is adopted, after due allowance has been made for the estimated proportion of Dissenters, Roman Catholics, Jews, &c., as well as for the aged, the infirm, and the young.

'These standards then being adopted, we have now to state the result of our inquiries into the present religious condition of the diocese of London.

'From the returns obtained at this time, and from other sources, it appears that out of all the parishes and districts included in the diocese (amounting to about 450), about 239 are already provided up to the measure of the standards here adopted. They will, therefore, for the present be left out of consideration in estimating the wants of the diocese. The remaining 211 parishes have been classed as follows, according to the amount of their deficiency:—

'1. As regards Deficiency of Clergy :

Class	One Clergyman only				Gross Population.
I. for	8,000 and upwards	..	11 parishes	..	228,000
II. „ from	6,000 to 8,000	..	14 „	..	171,400
III. „ „	4,000 to 6,000	..	59 „	..	757,500
IV. „ „	2,000 to 4,000	..	110 „	..	919,300
			194		
Not deficient in clergy, but in church room			17 „	..	73,800
			211 Total	..	2,150,000

'2. As regards Deficiency of Church-room :

Class	Accommodation for less than				Gross Population.
I.	.. ..	1 in 10	.. .. .. 58 parishes	..	744,000
II.	.. ..	1 in 8	.. .. .. 27 „	..	324,400
III.	.. ..	1 in 6	.. .. .. 42 „	..	412,900
IV.	.. ..	1 in 4	.. .. .. 71 „	..	609,800
			198		
Not deficient in church-room, but in clergy			13 „	..	58,900
			211 Total	..	2,150,000

' The total population of these 211 deficient parishes is about 2,150,000, the number of clergy is 582. But this number of clergy on the standard assumed is sufficient for the supervision of 1,164,000 only (making allowance, as we have done, for the labours of other religious bodies); there remains, therefore, a population of very nearly 1,000,000 persons for whom a further provision of 500 clergy would be required according to the standard assumed of one clergyman for every 2000 of the population. We would again call attention to the extreme importance of maintaining this standard, especially with a view to the necessity for personal visitation as the chief means by which it can be hoped to make any impression upon those who are careless about spiritual things.

' Again, in these 211 parishes, with their population of 2,150,000, there is accommodation of all kinds provided by the Church of England for 298,000. Of this accommodation about 155,000 sittings, or about one-half, are described as free, besides about 19,000, or more than six per cent. of the whole, provided in school-rooms, mission-chapels, &c. But, according to the standard of 1 in 4, this total provision is no more than the Church of England ought to make for 1,192,000, leaving therefore about 960,000, or nearly 1,000,000 persons in those 211 parishes, for whom, upon the standard assumed, the Church of England ought eventually to provide, either in churches or mission-rooms, 250,000 additional sittings.

In these estimates a large margin is left for the efforts made by bodies not connected with the Established Church to supply these spiritual necessities. We have another statement which appears to have been carefully prepared, and which, dealing more exactly with these extraneous supplies, gives a picture of the spiritual provision, which does not materially differ from the estimate already given:—

PLACES OF WORSHIP IN LONDON AND THEIR ACCOMMODATION.

	Number of Places of Worship.	Sittings.	Population.	Proportion per cent of Population accommodated.
1851	1,097	698,549	2,362,236	30·2
1865	1,316	917,895	3,015,494	30·4
Increase	219	219,346	653,258	·2

'There has thus been an increase of accommodation in fourteen years of about 31 per cent. Had the increase been threefold, it would only have sufficed to meet the increase of population. Taking 52 per cent., Mr. Mann's estimate, as the maximum number to be provided for, the following result is obtained:—

DEFICIENCY OF ACCOMMODATION.

Number of persons unprovided for in London in 1851 .. 669,514
Ditto in 1865 831,387

Increased deficiency 161,873

'It would thus appear, that if all the persons in London who are not physically disqualified, or for any legitimate reasons, were to attend church or chapel at the same time, 52 per cent., or more than one-half the population, would be shut out for want of room. But a worse feature of the case is, that 161,873 more persons would now be excluded, notwithstanding the considerable augmentation of places of worship, than in 1851. Therefore, although the percentage of sittings as compared with population has slightly improved, the actual deficiency has increased. It is estimated, as we have already said, that 45,000 souls are annually added to the population of London. To meet only this increase would require some forty-five new and commodious churches every year; whilst the average accretion yearly since 1851 of places of worship of all sizes has been no more than sixteen.' *

* 'Religion in London,' p. 13.

To conscientious members of the Church by law established the case is of course far stronger than this. In the estimate just quoted every conceivable form of imperfect or mischievous teaching is included under the head of provision for the spiritual necessities of the population. The wide meshes here spread of what by established courtesy are called 'religious denominations,' include Church of England, Church of Scotland, English Presbyterians, Congregationalists, Baptists, Wesleyans, United Methodist Free Churches, Primitive Methodists, Plymouth Brethren, Friends, Countess of Huntingdon's Connexion, Calvinistic Methodists, Mixed and Undefined, Roman Catholics, Latter Day Saints, Jews, Bible Christians, Methodist New Connexion, Unitarians, German Protestants, Catholic and Apostolic Church, Swedish Lutherans, Moravians, Greek Church, French Protestants, Dutch Reformed, German Catholics, Sandemanians, Southcottians, Freethinking Christians, Italian Roman Catholics, Welsh Calvinistic Methodists, Free Church of England, New Church, and Christian Disciples. Now, admitting fully that any form whatever of religious faith raises the man whom it possesses above him who has none, yet who that believes in the mission of our Church, or knows what her work is upon any population on which she has really taken hold, would be willing to substitute for her spiritual guidance of the people these discordant voices of a mixed multitude of sects, some old, some middle-aged, some so young as hardly yet to have assumed a distinctive appellation ? Yet if all these together fall far below the number necessary for grappling with the annual increase of our people, how far more must the clergy of the Church of England alone be inadequate to deal with them. And yet if the clergy are to be increased in number, and the endowments or quasi-endowments of the Church are to remain stationary, the clerical order will be still more depressed, and the augmented number more and more recruited from the lower classes of the community. This is well put forward by the founders of the new association:—

'One more strong incentive to hearty and united action in the matter must be mentioned. A large increase in the existing number of the parochial clergy is imperatively called for. Assuming that ten years ago the supply of the clergy was adequate to the spiritual wants of the country—and the assumption is wholly unwarrantable—we have still to make up the deficiency in the supply of candidates for Holy Orders which has taken place during this period, and to overtake the increase of the population during the same time—an increase which cannot be computed at less than 2,500,000—before we begin to make provision for a prospective increase, estimated at 245,000 a year.

'It will not require an abstruse calculation to enable us to compute the additional number of clergy which will thus be required, if the Church of England is to continue to do her proper work as the Established Church of the land. Allowing one clergyman for every 2000 of increased population, according to the scale adopted by the Bishop of London, and granting that the influence of the Church at different times will vary, other conditions being the same, according to the proportion which the numbers of the clergy bear to the sum total of the population, we see that, to enable the Church to exercise the same influence in 1876 which she did in 1856, no fewer than 4950 more clergy must be ordained in the next ten years than were ordained in the last. The most sanguine will hardly venture to anticipate that this increase can really take place; *but it is impossible that any increase at all can take place without making the prospect open to stipendiary curates more discouraging,* and the necessity for the present movement even greater than at present. Looked at from this point of view it will be seen that the present movement is not merely a measure of justice to stipendiary curates, but is an effort imperatively required for the good of the Church at large. So universal is the application of the principle, "if one member suffer, all the members suffer with it." ' *

These are, indeed, weighty words. Never had the Church of England a greater work to do than at the present time. Never was she more thoroughly bent on doing it, or better equipped for its performance. It is not merely against the weight of numbers such as our forefathers never strove with, that she has now to labour. The wide spread of superficial education leads all men to talk about religion, and numbers to believe most unreasonably that they think about

* 'Religion in London,' p. 9.

it also. Opinions are formed rapidly, and disseminated also miraculously. Every man reads his newspaper; and, however unconsciously, most men, to avoid the trouble of thinking, take up with what is therein day by day repeated to them and asserted for them. Every stratum of the population has its own purveyors of this daily literature. The time is passed even for 'the leading journal' to pervade all classes of society. Almost all are able to read, and all are supplied on the cheapest terms with materials for reading of some quality or other. At the top of almost every Hansom-cab, when our fickle weather permits it, you may see the newspaper spread out for study in the intervals of business; even the half-naked figures stretched at their length on the grass in our Parks often hold in their soiled hands some utterances from the all-pervading printing-office. The influences which spring from such a state of things are strengthened by a multitude of other circumstances. The unmistakable descent of political power from the more educated and better furnished to the less educated and poorer classes; the weakening of parental—that real source of all secondary—authority; the carrying out of this principle to the old sway of masters and employers; the claim of all to think and to act for themselves; all mark the onward progress of a vast ἀνομία. The sanguine see in this lawlessness the bright morning of a day of perfect liberty of recognised opinions, and of a peaceful contentedness, which shall be a law unto itself. Less hopeful spirits doubt the mid-day prospect of so garish a dawn. They cannot see in the whole system and temper of the times that law of self-restraint under the rule of moral obligation, and of self-sacrifice for the maintenance of great principles which they believe to be essential to the real well-doing of individuals or society. Above all, they look at the growing tendency to treat all religious truth as matter of opinion with many fears for the incoming generation. At such a time it is all important that the national clergy should be not only religious men, but also men of thought and education. After the want of a hearty belief in what they teach, no sign could possibly be worse for our commonwealth than that the priests of the Established faith should be behind their age in the cultivation of their intellects or in the true breadth of their view, especially as to all moral and spiritual subjects. If the clergy appeared to the laity—instead of being men of more divine knowledge than themselves, of a deeper philosophy which combines boldness with sobriety and thought with reverence—to be ignorant or superstitious, too weak or too indolent to grapple with real difficulties, averse to progress and fearful of the light, it is not difficult to see what the end would be. Happily the very opposite is the fact: never were the clergy more earnest, and never, as a class, more enlightened than now. The very troubles of the age attest it. The questions which are vexing the Church, on the one hand as to what appears to us the trivialities of external ceremonialism, and as to the all-important verities of doctrine on the other, alike bear witness to the intense earnestness both of the clergy and of the laity whom they influence. The old sluggard slumberers of the last generation, with their strong port, large pluralities, closed volumes, and neglected parishes, are nowhere. For good or for evil, all are awake; all are hard at work; all are labouring for progress. New churches, new parishes, new schools, new institutions, cover the land. The press, if it labours with the utterances of the doubters and the unbelievers, groans under the issue of sermons, pamphlets, and volumes which speak of the spiritual zeal and mental activity of the clergy; whilst in every department of literature they occupy at this time a leading place. Nor is even this the greatest part of the strength of our clergy for the discharge of their great work. They pervade the land with a leavening presence of immeasurable power. From how many a parsonage-house, whose inmates assert for themselves no high literary claims, is there perpetually flowing forth a stream of civilising elevating influence, which blesses all within its reach, and the widespread existence of which constitutes in a very high degree the strongest might of the national clergy! In the glowing words of Dr. Chalmers as to the parochial clergyman:—

> 'All his spontaneous services bear upon them the unequivocal aspect of pure and disinterested zeal. And this in the midst of a people to whom he is every day more endeared by the kind notices and cordialities of his growing acquaintanceship, gives to all the forthgoings of an earnest parish minister a power over the hearts and habits of families which cannot be realised by any other individual in the commonwealth.'

What may be before us, God knows; but if the Church of England as an establishment be about, as some forebode, to enter on a fierce struggle for her very being, she will at least enter on it at a moment when her labours are greater, more varied, and more successful than they have ever been, and with a body of clergy serving in her parishes, such as for hearty zeal, for firm faith, for varied erudition, and for self-denying toil, probably no Church before her could at any one time have marshalled for her duties in the day of service, or for her safeguard in the hour of peril—

> 'Si Pergama dextrâ
> Defendi possent: etiam hâc defensa fuissent.'

ROYAL AUTHORSHIP.*

(*October*, 1867, *and January*, 1868.)

It is scarcely possible to conceive a work less likely to entice any one to the cares of royal authorship than the 'Catalogue' of Horace Walpole, with its scanty praise and its abundance of carping criticism.

'Frederick, Prince of Wales,' he tells us, 'wrote French songs in imitation of the Regent,† and did not miscarry solely by writing in a language not his own.' ‡ Three letters of James II., which were published at his command by W. Fuller, gentleman, led the unhappy agent into being voted by the House of Commons a notorious cheat; into his being prosecuted by the Attorney-General, and whipped and pilloried. § Charles I. wrote 'most uncouth and inharmonious poetry.' The merit of James I.'s compositions is expressed in the caustic assertion that 'Bishop Montagu translated all his Majesty's works into Latin. A man of so much patience was well worthy of favour.' ‖ Henry VIII. himself comes off very little better, with the suggestion as to the great work which earned for the wearer of the English crown the title of Defender of the Faith (of which Walpole most characteristically says, 'it seemed peculiarly adapted to the weak head of the high church, Anne,') ¶ that 'a little scepticism on his talents for such a performance, *mean as it is*, might make us question whether he did not write the defence of the Sacraments against Luther, as one of his successors ** is sup-

---

* 'The Early Years of His Royal Highness the Prince Consort. Compiled under the Direction of Her Majesty the Queen.' By Lieut.-General the Hon. Charles Grey. London, 1867.
† Philip Duke of Orleans. ‡ Page 278. 4to. of 1798.
§ Ibid. ‖ P. 266, 275. ¶ P. 246. ** Charles I.

posed to have written the Εἰκὼν Βασιλική, that is, with the pen of some Court prelate.' * With the same suggestion of assisted authorship he sweeps away the claim of Edward II. to the composition of the poem attributed to him, believing that 'this melody of a dying monarch is about as authentic as that of the old poetic warbler the swan.' †

The only royal pen to which he allows any real merit is that of Queen Elizabeth, who, 'in the days when,' as Camden says, 'King Edward was wont to call her *his sweet sister Temperance,* applied much to literature.' ‡

Such galling criticisms may be sufficient to repress all ordinary royal authorship, but they could not touch the high motives or sacred feeling which have led to the newest example of such a production. For, we say it advisedly, the work, the title of which is prefixed to this article, is, in truth, the produce of another royal hand, and that, like Elizabeth's, the hand of a female sovereign.

It is true that, in exact contradiction to what Walpole suggested to have been the course of Henry and of Charles in giving a royal sponsorship to works wrought for them by others, here another name is given to what is essentially a royal work. For the volume professes to be 'the early years of the Prince Consort, compiled under the direction of her Majesty the Queen, by Lieut.-General the Hon. C. Grey,' and in many places the mask of authorship is not ungracefully assumed by the gallant General. But every reader of the volume will feel that its real interest is derived from the writing of another; whose presence is never more perceived than when it seems most to be withholden. General Grey's share in the work is indeed very creditably performed.§ He

---

* P. 256. Saunders and Bellarmine ascribed the defence of the Sacraments against Luther to Bishop Fisher, others to Sir Thomas More.
† P. 255. ‡ P. 266.
§ In a second edition the date of the death of the Princess Charlotte should be corrected. It was Nov. 1817, not 1818.

has threaded well together the pearls intrusted to him; but though the threading is his, the pearls are the gift to us of a higher hand.

This is essential to notice, because it is this which gives its real interest to the work. No affected pedantry, no frigid love of conceits, no desire of display, no longing to be enrolled in the catalogue of authors, have led to the writing of this volume. It is a genuine and unmistakable offering of love. It is the fruit of that desire of sympathy which is ever strongest in the tenderest and most human hearts. It is one of those pleas, which when, as here, they are put forth simply and naturally, are absolutely irresistible. It is the Sovereign casting herself in her speechless grief upon the sympathy of her people.

The volume which this represents was first printed only for private circulation in the family and amongst the closest friends of the Queen. But, once in print, when it might possibly be pirated, and when, far more, the certain effect of a wider circulation could be better calculated from what had been the effect of the smaller, then a loving zeal for the Prince's honour, and a noble claim on a nation's truth, overcame all difficulties, and gave it to the world.

The mere fact of such an appeal is a declaration of what he was whose memory lives so fresh in the widow's heart, an appeal the truth and eloquence of which can scarcely be exceeded by any articulate utterance. But, if anything could be added, it is surely to be found in these pages, through which we must hastily carry our readers.

Besides the history of the early days and first married year of Prince Albert's life, the volume contains in the Appendix a most remarkable paper, entitled 'Reminiscences of the King of the Belgians.' It is full of all that long-sighted clearness of vision, which, to an extent rarely equalled, was the faculty of King Leopold. It throws no little light upon much of our contemporary history, and supplies some remarkable facts as to the secret course of matters in the highest quarters.

The troubled waters of the Regency and early reign of George IV., after this lapse of years, show strangely when they are contrasted with the calm and high tone to which the Court of Queen Victoria has made Great Britain accustomed. We can scarcely believe that of a time so near our own, and of our own Royal Family, we can read such an entry as this:—

'The Regent was not kind to his brother. At every instant something or other of an unpleasant nature arose.'

'1820.—Prince Leopold was at Lord Cravens, when the news arrived that a cold which the Duke' [of Kent] 'got at Salisbury, visiting the Cathedral, had become alarming. Soon after the Prince's arrival the Duke breathed his last.

'The Duchess, who lost a most amiable and devoted husband, was in a state of the greatest distress. It was fortunate Prince Leopold had not been out of the country, as the poor Duke had left his family deprived of all means of existence.'

It is strange to read such extracts, and then, whilst their memory is fresh with us, to look at the history of the same Royal Family for the last twenty-seven years. In one thing only was the history of that time and this sadly alike; though now it is the wife, and then it was the husband, upon whom the blow has fallen. But sovereigns have no exemption, God knows, from the sorrows of their subjects. Changing the persons, the griefs of 1861 may be read in the records of 1817:—

'Nov.—Saw the ruin of this happy home, and the destruction at one blow of every hope and happiness of Prince Leopold. He has never recovered the feeling of happiness which had blessed his short married life.'

But to return from the Appendix to the text.

Prince Albert of Saxe-Coburg was born at the Grand Ducal Castle of Rosenau, on the 26th of August, 1819, three months after the birth of the Princess Victoria, to whom (the Duchess of Kent being sister of the Grand Duke of Coburg) he was first cousin.

There is depicted in this volume an intertwining of the early threads of these two lives, which more resembles the beautiful fables of the 'Arabian Nights' Entertainments' than the hard realities of modern life. Some of these passages sound like the records of the sport of one of the Genii (for, *pace* Mr. Lane, we cannot give up for his Jins those genial companions of our boyhood, the Genii), who carries the beautiful young princess off and sets her beside the young prince, whose after-life is restless and homeless, till he can recover the bright vision which once flashed so strangely upon his youth. Mademoiselle Siebold is the first link in the Genii chain, officiating at both these auspicious births. She is called at Rosenau, where the murmuring waters inspire rest and sleep, 'at three, and at six the little one gives his first cry in this world, and looks about like a little squirrel, with a pair of large black eyes'—though from a Royal correction we know that they were really 'blue'— and at the very same time 'she cannot sufficiently describe what a dear little love is the *May Flower*' (the Princess Victoria, born May 24). Again, the good grandmother, who comes in throughout all these pages as the beneficent fairy godmother, in the midst of wise words concerning the early training of the young Prince and his brother, breaks off, as if some golden thread already linked them to each other, into council concerning the young Princess, and prays the anxious mother 'not yet to tease her little puss with learning—she is so young still.' And again she says, ' Bold Albertchen drags Leopold constantly about by the hand. The little fellow is the pendant to the pretty cousin, very handsome, but too slight for a boy; lively, very funny, all good nature and full of mischief.' Visions indeed of what the distant future was to fulfil visited the foreboding thoughts of this lady, of whom we read:—

'The Queen remembers her dear grandmother perfectly well. She was a most remarkable woman, with a most powerful, energetic, almost masculine mind, accompanied with great tenderness of heart and extreme love for nature.' . . . 'A most distinguished person, the King of the Belgians calls her in his Reminiscences.' . . . 'She told the Queen that she had wished earnestly that he should marry the Queen.'

We must add here, for their intrinsic beauty, a few words more, written in a similar strain by the good Duchess, the year before her death, to her daughter, the again widowed mother of a daughter of so great a future, May, 1830:—

'My blessings and good wishes for the day which gave you the sweet Blossom of May! May God preserve and protect the valuable life of that lovely flower from all the dangers which will beset her mind and heart. The rays of the sun are scorching at the height to which she may one day attain. It is only by the blessing of God that all the fine qualities He has put into that young soul can be kept pure and untarnished.'

And so passes away from our pages the figure of this good and remarkable woman. There is an exquisite plaintiveness in the tone in which the last adieu is uttered in these pages by her Royal granddaughter:—

'She had already, at a very early period, formed the ardent wish that a marriage should one day take place between her beloved grandchild Albert and the "Flower of May," as she loved to call the little Princess Victoria. How would her kind, loving heart have rejoiced, could she have lived to see the perfect consummation of her wishes in the happiness, too soon, alas! to be cut short! that followed this auspicious union.'

The early years of the Prince were marked with many indications of unusual truthfulness, affection, and intelligence; whilst his childlike ways and looks (a beautiful record of which adorns the title-page of this volume) attracted to him early notice and favour. We read such records as these: 'Little Albertchen, with his large blue eyes and dimpled cheeks, is bewitching, forward, and quick as a weazel.' 'He is much smaller than his brother and lovely as a little angel, with his fair curls.' As early as when not yet four he was transferred from the tutelage of women to that of Herr Florschütz, of Coburg, a tutor who knew how to deal with the precious charge committed to him. 'I entered,' he says, 'upon the discharge of my important charge with enthusiasm. Every grace had been showered by nature on this charming boy—every eye rested on him with delight, and his look won the hearts of all.' Herr Florschütz had, and deserved to have, the sole direction of the education of the two young Princes until, fifteen years later, they left the University of Bonn. For his faithful and kindly services the Prince ever entertained the warmest gratitude.

The boyish years of the young men were distinguished by no remarkable events, but of none was it more eminently true than of Prince Albert, that 'the boy was father of the man.' The winning childhood passed by natural gradation into a youth not less attractive after its kind. 'He was always,' says his tutor, 'singularly easy to instruct.' 'To do something was with him a necessity.' 'He was rather delicate than robust, though already remarkable for his powers of perseverance and endurance. The same ardent and energetic spirit, which manifested itself in his studies, was shown in the sports of his boyhood; and in these his was the directing mind.' .... 'He was always,' says King Leopold, 'an intelligent child, and held a certain sway over his elder brother, who rather kindly submitted to it.'

The 'submission,' however, was not always yielded without a struggle, and (to maintain his pre-eminence) the native vigour of his character had sometimes to show itself in something more than the assertion of mere moral power; for though he was the younger, the smaller, and the more delicate boy, we read such entries as these from a journal remarkable for its simple truthfulness of delineation, when he was not yet six years old: 'April 9. I got up well and happy; afterwards I had a fight with my brother.' ... 'April 10. I had another fight with my brother; that was not right.'

This early moral handling of his tendency to assert too absolutely his own will seems to have lasted through his youth. 'With his brother,' says the good Florschütz, 'the Prince showed rather too strong a will of his own; and this disposition came out at times even in later years. Surpassing his brother in thoughtful earnestness, in calm reflection, and self-command, and evincing at the same time more prudence in action, it was only natural that his will should prevail, and when compliance with it was not voluntarily yielded, he was sometimes disposed to have recourse to compulsion. But,' he adds, 'the distinguishing characteristics of the Prince's disposition were his winning cheerfulness and his endearing amiability.' How successful he was in enforcing on himself this difficult rule of self-constraint in conscious superiority, is abundantly proved by the intense affection of the brothers to each other. Their lives were spent absolutely together, until the elder brother was twenty, the younger nineteen years of age. Then first they were parted—Prince Ernest joining the Saxon army at Dresden, and Prince Albert commencing a tour through Italy. The relations of their lives may be read in the touching words of the younger brother. 'Ernest,' he writes to Prince William of Löwenstein, ' is now going to Dresden. I shall shortly begin my Italian travels. I shall not set out till Ernest also launches his vessel, so that he may not be left behind alone. The separation will be frightfully painful to us. Up to this moment we have never, as long as we can recollect, been a single day away from each other. I cannot bear to think of that moment.' And, after the separation, he writes again: ' Now I am quite alone. Ernest is gone off, and I am left behind. . . . . Now Ernest has slept through his first night at Dresden. This day will also bring to him the feeling that something is wanting.' Soon after he adds, what would sound strangely philosophic from the pen of any ordinary young man of nineteen, but which, from its depth of thought and simple practicalness, seems to us eminently characteristic of the writer: 'I must now give up the custom of saying *we*, and use the I, which sounds so egotistic and cold. In WE everything sounded much softer, for the WE expresses the harmony between different souls, the I rather the resistance of the individual against outward forces, though also confidence in its own strength.'

But we must return to those earlier days from which this single feature of character has led us away. 'Albert,' is the recollection of Count Mensdorff, who had been his intimate companion from his earliest youth, 'never was noisy or wild. He was always very fond of Natural History and more serious studies, and many a happy hour we spent in the Ehrenburg (the palace at Coburg) arranging and dusting the collections our cousins had themselves made and kept there. From his earliest infancy he was distinguished for perfect moral purity both in word and deed, and to this he owed the sweetness of disposition so much admired by every one.' From his fourth to his nineteenth year his education under Mr. Florschütz, was conducted during the winter months at Coburg or Gotha, and during the rest of the year for the most part at the pleasant country palaces of Rosenau and Reinhardsbrunn, with occasional excursions in Germany or to his uncle's capital, Brussels, or, in 1836, when he was seventeen years old, to England. It was in the course of this visit that he first met his Royal cousin, the Princess Victoria; and there are unquestionable indications that from this time his thoughts turned often to 'the Flower of May,' for whom, as we have seen, the good old Duchess had so long since destined him. Throughout these years the character he was gradually and firmly forming exhibits everywhere the same features. A genuine love of nature, a keen relish for natural history, an ever increasing earnestness in study, a growing acquaintance with and value for art, entire moral purity and deep conscientiousness, appear at every turn. The 'recollections' of his tutor preserve some interesting features of his life :—

'In his early youth Prince Albert was very shy, and he had long to struggle against this feeling. He disliked visits from strangers.'

'He was always fond of natural history, and lost no opportunity of collecting specimens.'

'The active life which he led in the open air strengthened alike the mind and the body. His thirst for knowledge was kept alive and indulged; while under the influence of his bodily exercises he grew up into an active and healthy boy.'

Still,

'He was subject to alarming attacks of croup. At such times the characteristic qualities of his mind displayed themselves very remarkably. I shall never forget the gentle goodness, the affectionate patience, he showed. His heart seemed then to open to the whole world. He would form the most noble projects for execution after his recovery, and, though apparently not satisfied with himself, he displayed a temper and disposition which I may characterise as being in thought and in deed perfectly angelic. I cannot recal these recollections even now without the deepest emotions.'

'Two virtues were conspicuous even in his boyhood, winning for him the love and respect of all. Growing with his growth, these virtues gained strength with years: one was his eager desire to do good and to assist others; the other, the grateful feeling which never allowed him to forget all acts of kindness, however trifling, to himself.'

These high moral qualities were grounded, Mr. Florschütz tells us, on the only firm basis of religion. The youth of Protestant Germany are not commonly admitted to the rite of confirmation until they have reached their seventeenth year; but, in consequence of 'the singularly earnest and thoughtful nature' of the Prince, it was determined not to separate him in that declaration of his faith from the brother whose close companionship he shared; on the elder, therefore, attaining the due age, the younger was suffered to accompany him; and 'on Palm Sunday, 1835, the young Princes were accordingly confirmed. Mr. Florschütz speaks warmly of the earnestness with which Prince Albert prepared himself for the solemn ceremony, and of the deep feelings of religion with which he engaged in it.'

In April, 1837, the scene of the Prince's life changes, for the next year and a half, to the University of Bonn. 'Here,' says Mr. Florschütz, who continued with his Princes throughout this residence, 'he maintained the early promise of his youth by the eagerness with which he applied himself to his work, and by the rapid progress which he made, especially in the natural sciences, in political economy, and in philosophy. Music, also, of which he was passionately fond, was not neglected; and he had already shown considerable talent as a composer.' The Prince describes 'the chief subjects of his studies' in a letter to his father in November, 1837, as 'Roman law, State right, and political economy, and the principles of finance. We also attended two courses of historical lectures by Löbell and A. W. von Schlegel, and a philosophical lecture (anthropology and philosophy) by Fichte. At the same time we shall not fail to give attention to the study of modern languages.'

The enlargement of mind, which was the result of conscientious labour under the quickening influence of men of such various intellectual power as the Bonn professors, could be traced throughout his after life. But the picture of this course at Bonn would be very incomplete, without the lights thrown into it by the friend of his youth, Prince William of Löwenstein. With his equals in age, indeed, as with his elders, there was a continual desire to learn all that was to be learned. 'He liked, above all things, to discuss questions of public law and metaphysics, and constantly, amongst our evening walks, juridical principles and philosophical doctrines were thoroughly discussed.' But with these more serious tastes mingled freely 'a lively sense of the ridiculous—a great talent for mimicking, and drawing caricatures, in which he perpetuated the scenes of his University life. He excelled most of his contemporaries in the use of intellectual weapons, in the art of convincing, in strictly logical argument; so he was distinguished also in all kinds of bodily exercise; in fencing and the practice of the broadsword he was very skilful. Attempts were made at dramatic improvising. Prince Albert was always the life and soul of them, and acted the principal parts; he entered with the greatest eagerness into every study, whether belonging to science or art. He spared no exertion of mind or body; on the contrary, he rather sought difficulties, in order to overcome them.'

There was one other power which his letters reveal as acting on his young life—a power hidden, it seems, altogether from the most intimate of his contemporaries; hardly, perhaps, avowed fully to himself—which may yet have aided in the highest measure that beautiful development of character, to which he was by such first steps gradually attaining. For no power, which is of this world, is so strong in all its influences for good upon such a youthful spirit as his, as the power of an early attachment. Nothing more purifies the blood of youth, nothing spurs it on more certainly to seek in all things to excel, than the presence of such an elevating, inspiriting, and refining influence. And that this was acting on the Prince, his letters very plainly suggest. He had not looked unmoved, in his visit to England, on the fair 'Flower of May.' There is just that refined half-expressed allusion to such a passion, which would be its natural expression from such a man. He communicates to his father, in June, 1838, as he is bidden, a letter from 'our cousin,' and mentions 'a second and still kinder letter from "my" cousin' (the *our* to which he was accustomed drops unintentionally into the *my*) : adding, 'you may easily imagine that both these letters gave me the greatest pleasure.' Under the reserve of the following letter of congratulation on the Queen's accession, a letter eminently characteristic of the writer, with its simple unflattering truthfulness and its calm deep estimate of life by its responsibilities and duties—so rare in youth—we can trace the same secret impulses of affection :—

'MY DEAREST COUSIN,—I must write you a few lines to present you my sincerest felicitations on that great change which has taken place in your life.

' Now you are Queen of the mightiest land of Europe; in your hand lies the happiness of millions. May Heaven assist you and strengthen you with its strength in that high but difficult task !

' I hope that your reign may be long, happy, and glorious, and that your efforts may be rewarded by the thankfulness and love of your subjects.

' May I pray you to think likewise sometimes of your cousins in Bonn, and to continue to them that kindness you favoured them with till now ?'

Just at this time he makes a tour in Switzerland; and, with his passionate love of scenery, is 'quite intoxicated by all' he 'has seen.' Under these electric currents the vision of his life, true to the laws of every high affection, is lighted up with fresh hues, and he sends ' to my cousin ' a small book containing views of the places he had visited :—

' From one of these, the top of the Righi, he sent her a dried "rose des Alpes," and from the other, Voltaire's house at Ferney, which he visited from Geneva, a scrap of Voltaire's handwriting, which he obtained from his old servant. "The whole of these," the Queen adds, " were placed in a small album, with the dates at which each place was visited, in the Prince's handwriting," and this album the Queen now considers one of her greatest treasures, and never goes anywhere without it. Nothing had at this time passed between the Queen and the Prince; but this gift shows that the latter in the midst of his travels often thought of his young cousin.'

Doubtless he did; and who can estimate, in the pure and high character which was so early maturing, what may not have been the value of those 'often thoughts of his young cousin'?

At the close of the summer term of 1838, the Prince quitted Bonn, and, after a short stay at Coburg, proceeded to visit Italy, where he remained till the following May. With his residence at Bonn had terminated the charge of the now Councillor Florschütz, though his affection to such a pupil never varied. Such words as he wrote after the Prince's death are at once a lively exhibition of his own faithful heart, and a grand tribute to the pupil of his love—'I stand daily before the valued picture which but a short time before his death he sent me, to weep for my beloved pupil and friend.'

It is one of the rewards of such a character as we have been examining, that it does secure such affection from such men. So it was to an eminent degree with the Prince; and, though he now lost the company of his old friend, another was found willing to accompany him in his Italian tour, even more fitted from his wide acquaintance with life for such an office, and worthy in every respect to be the companion and the friend of such a Prince. Baron Stockmar had known him from infancy, and had watched, with the delight which only such fidelity as his could feel, the gradual unfolding of that noble character, which, in his secret thoughts, he had for many years hoped to see supporting in her arduous duties the future Queen of England.

We shall only follow the leading of 'the Queen's volume,' if we pause for a moment upon the beautiful episode which embalms the memory of Baron Stockmar. A native of Coburg—he was early attached to the person of Prince Leopold; accompanied him to England, on his marriage; lived with him at Claremont, and was actually present at the death of the Princess Charlotte. To him it was given to prolong for the next generation, and to receive back from it, the affection which had first clung to his own. Indeed he loved the Prince Albert as with a father's love, and watched him with a closeness of observation which gave him, from the Prince's boyhood onward, an almost prophetic insight into his future.

Thus, in 1844, speaking to one with whom he conversed most familiarly of the value of the Prince's life to this country, he said, in words which throughout those days of anxious watching which preceded the Prince's death were ringing in the ears of him who had heard them almost as a knell, 'If ever he falls sick of a low fever, you will lose him!' After the marriage of Prince Albert, the English Court was the Baron's chief residence, until the advancing infirmities of age led him reluctantly, and amidst the loving regrets of all, to return to spend at Coburg the 'aliquid intervalli' between his life-long service and the grave. All who knew revered him. We must quote without omission the golden words, which record the feelings of his royal 'friend:'—

'The Queen, looking back with gratitude and affection to the friend of their early married life, can never forget the assistance given by the Baron to the young couple in regulating their movements and general mode of life, and in directing the education of their children. Lord Melbourne had the greatest regard and affection for, and most unbounded confidence in him. At the commencement of the Queen's reign, the Baron was of invaluable assistance to Lord Melbourne. Lord Aberdeen also, speaking of him to the Queen, said,—" I have known men as clever, as discreet, as good, and with as much judgment: but I never knew any one who united all these qualities as he did. He is a most remarkable man." The Baron had the greatest regard in return for "My good Aberdeen," as he called him.'

Golden words from such a pen! but words altogether deserved. Baron Stockmar was the very pattern of fidelity; for which in its perfectness what various qualities, and those the highest both of heart and mind, are essential! There must be the hearty affection, which is as jealous of any defect as a lover of the honour of his mistress, and yet which cannot take, and so can hardly give, offence; there must be courage, to speak the least welcome truths, and to reprove unsparingly any attempt in others, be they who they may, to flatter or deceive; there must be calm, cool, far-sighted judgment to advise; there must, above all, be absolute disinterestedness, the perfect freedom from one aim of personal ambition, not only in its ordinary vulgar grossness, but in its more refined acting of loving to advise, and to feel the possession of influence. Rare indeed, as his wide experience of men had taught Lord Aberdeen, is such a combination. In the Baron it was so grandly exhibited, that no deficiency on any side made itself visible to the closest gaze of the keenest eye. Twice after his retirement to Coburg from the Court of Victoria and Albert their long-united pathways again crossed each other: once in 1860, when the Queen and Prince visited Coburg in great part to see again their old and long-tried friend; and once again in 1862, when alas! the form of 'the crushed and broken-hearted widow' alone trod the lately rejoicing path. When she was speaking to him of their beloved Prince, and showing him the pictures and photographs of him which covered the table, the Baron exclaimed, 'My dear, good Prince, how happy I shall be to see him again! and it will not be long.' It was not long. On the 9th of July, 1863, the faithful friend closed his eyes to this earth and all its cares.

But we must return to the Prince. His tour took him first to Florence, where he rejoiced in the vast stores of art which were there gathered, as well as in the beauty of the surrounding scenery. 'I am often,' he says, 'quite intoxicated with delight when I come out of one of the galleries.' Here, on principle, and much against his natural inclination, he abandoned himself to the necessary impertinences of ordinary social life :—

'I have,' he tells his friend Prince Löwenstein, 'lately thrown myself entirely into the whirl of society. I have danced, dined, supped, and paid compliments; have been introduced to people, and had people introduced to me; have spoken French and English, exhausted all remarks about the weather; have played the amiable, and, in short, have made "bonne mine à mauvais jeu." You know my *passion* for such things, and must therefore admire my strength of character that I have never excused myself, never returned home till five in the morning, that I have emptied the carnival cup to the dregs.'

How much he would have preferred other pursuits may be gathered from a remark of the Grand Duke Leopold at this very time, who, seeing him kept from the gaieties of the ball-room by an animated discussion with the blind Marquis Apponi, one of the most eminent members of the Tuscan aristocracy, said to Lady Augusta Fox, ' Voilà un prince dont nous pouvons être fiers. La belle danseuse l'attend, le savant l'occupe.'

From Florence he went on to Rome, and thence to Naples, returning homewards by Pisa, Genoa, Milan, and Como. At Rome he found the only ceremony which did not disappoint him, 'the Pope's blessing the people, assembled before the Vatican, from the balcony, amidst the ringing of bells, firing of cannon, and military music.' ' It was really a most imposing scene, though what followed was tedious, and savoured strongly of idolatry.' He had, too, the 'honour of an interview with his Holiness,' whom he found ' kind and civil.' ' I remained with him nearly half an hour. Shut up in a small room, we conversed, in Italian, on the influence the Egyptians had on Greek art, and that again on Roman art. The Pope asserted that the Greeks had taken their models from the Etruscans. In spite of his infallibility, I ventured to assert that they had derived their lessons in art from the Egyptians.'

He himself reviews, in a letter to Prince Löwenstein, in June, 1839, when he had returned to Coburg, the effect of this Italian tour upon him. 'It was,' he says, 'of great advantage to me. It has made an impression on me, not so much by its peculiar incidents as by its general character. My sphere of observation has been doubled, and my power of forming a right judgment will be much increased by my having seen for myself. On the whole, my life was very pleasant. The society of such a man as Baron Stockmar was most precious and valuable to me.'

The great crisis of his life was now approaching. 'When he was a child of three years old, his nurse always told him that he should marry the Queen, and when he first thought of marrying at all, he always thought of her.' After the first visit to Kensington in 1836, these floating images of a possible future gathered themselves up, we believe, in his mind, under the influence of early affection, into a more definite shape; and though 'nothing had passed between him and the Queen,' the future to which his heart now pointed was very different from the shadowy dreamland of his early life.

But now difficulties seemed to intervene. King William IV., with that kindly but bustling interference with everything he could touch, which was one of his most marked characteristics, had set himself against the Coburg alliance, and contemplated one of five other marriages for the Princess. He had, therefore, opposed the Duke of Coburg's visit to England in 1836. Who can say how all that has since passed might have been marred had that visit not have taken place in spite of his opposition? This difficulty was now removed, and the sagacious mind of the King of the Belgians, apprehending all the advantages of such an alliance, used his great influence to promote it. In the early part of 1838 he obtained the Queen's sanction to his opening the matter as one of possible arrangement with the Prince. 'He looks,' the King writes to Baron Stockmar, 'at the question from its most elevated and honourable point of view. . . . . . I have told him that his great youth would make it necessary to postpone the marriage for a few years. . . . . .' 'I am ready,' he said, 'to submit to this delay, if I have only some certain assurance to go upon. But if after waiting, perhaps for three years, I should find that the Queen no longer desired the marriage, it would place me in a very ridiculous position . . . . .' This was now the only remaining difficulty.

The visit of 1836 had favourably impressed the mind of the young Princess. 'The Prince was at that time much shorter than his brother, already very handsome, but very stout, which he entirely grew out of afterwards. He was most amiable, natural, unaffected, and merry, full of interest in everything,—playing on the piano with the Princess his cousin, drawing, in short, constantly occupied. He always paid the greatest attention to all he saw; and the Queen remembers well how intently he listened to the sermon preached in St. Paul's.' This notice of the former visit, the effect of which on the Prince we have already traced, shows that the impression made by it on the other side also was real—strong enough, probably, to make the idea of an alliance at some future time not unacceptable, but not strong enough to lead to the desire of an immediate marriage. On the other hand, the Prince's father objected to any uncertain delay, and the wise Leopold acknowledged the truth of the objection, 'If Albert waits till he is in his twenty-first, twenty-second, or twenty-third year, it will be impossible for him to begin any new career, and his whole life would be marred if the Queen should change her mind.'

In October, 1839, the two brothers came to England on a visit to the Queen; Prince Albert intending to tell her 'that he could not now wait for a decision, as he had done at a former period when this marriage was first talked about.' The natural progress of events soon made any such declaration wholly superfluous. King Leopold remarks to Baron Stockmar on the great improvement in Albert: 'He looks so much more manly, and from his *tournure* one might easily take him to be twenty-two or twenty-three.' Those who remember him at that time well know how well this praise was merited. Rarely have the rich gifts of mind and soul with which he was endowed been enshrined in an outer casket of more beseeming comeliness. His countenance bespoke the rare union of strength, sweetness, and intelligence, which existed within. He was, too, as that keen observer, the King of the Belgians, writes, 'a very agreeable companion. His manners are so gentle and harmonious, that one likes to have him near one's self. I have always found him so when I had him with me, and I think his travels have still improved him. He is full of talent and fun.' All this, too, was accompanied by that secret power over other hearts which accompanied the unbroken inward reign of spotless purity and stainless truth. It was most natural that the affection of such a Prince should be speedily returned; and, whatever were before the obstacles which produced a disinclination to an immediate marriage, five days of familiar intercourse sufficed to break them down. Every heart, we think, must thrill under the power of these words, which record the retrospect cast in later years on this inclination to delay:—

'The Queen cannot think without indignation against herself of her wish to keep the Prince waiting for probably three or four years, at the risk of ruining all his prospects for life, until she might feel inclined to marry. . . . The only excuse the Queen can make for herself is in the fact that the sudden change from the secluded life at Kensington to the independence of her position as Queen Regnant at the age of eighteen, put all ideas of marriage out of her mind, which she now most bitterly repents.

'A worse school for a young girl, or one more detrimental to all natural feelings and affections, cannot well be imagined than the position of a Queen at eighteen without experience, and without a husband to guide and support her. This the Queen can state from painful experience, and she thanks God that none of her dear daughters are exposed to such dangers.'

There was, however, not one day's needless trifling with the Prince's feelings. On the 15th of October the Queen sent for him, and made the communication which (as he writes the same day to the faithful Stockmar, sending him 'the most welcome news possible') made it 'one of the happiest days in his life.' The letter is all that any one would wish to find it; it proceeds: 'Victoria is so good and kind to me, that I am often at a loss to believe that such affection should be shown to me. I know the great interest you take in my happiness, and therefore pour out my heart to you. . . . More, or more seriously, I cannot write to you, for at this moment I am too bewildered.

'Das Auge sieht den Himmel offen,
Es schwimmt das Herz in Seligkeit.' *

'Heaven open wide the glad eye sees,
The heart is bathed in perfect peace.'

The entry in the Queen's journal of the day, which we are permitted to see, is not a little remarkable, 'How I will strive to make him feel as little as possible the great sacrifice he has made! I told him it *was* a great sacrifice on his part, but he would not allow it. . . . I then told him to fetch Ernest. . . . He told me how perfect his brother was.'

All now marched with steps of joy. The announcement was received with universal satisfaction both at home and abroad. 'Nothing,' wrote the King of the Belgians to the Queen, 'could have given me greater pleasure than your dear letter. I had, when I learnt your decision, almost the feeling of old Simeon, "Now lettest thou thy servant depart

* Schiller's 'Lied von der Glocke,' always a special favourite with the Prince.

in peace." Your choice has been for these last years my conviction of what might and would be best for your happiness.'

Throughout the English nation there was the same full approval of the step the Queen was taking. On the 23rd of November the intended marriage was announced by the Queen with admirable self-possession to eighty-three members of the Privy Council, and the preliminary arrangements immediately succeeded. Parliament was opened on the 16th of January, 1840, and the Queen was never cheered more loudly than as she drove down to the Palace of Westminster to announce to the descendants of the ancient Barons of England, and the assembled representatives of her people, her intended marriage. In Parliament itself, though there was the same consentient approval of her marriage, yet matters did not proceed altogether smoothly. On the Prince's Annuity Bill, and on the Naturalisation Bill, the two great parties of the State were brought into active opposition. In the first, the sum proposed by the Government, 50,000*l.* a year, was opposed as excessive, and an amendment of 30,000*l.* a year was carried. In the second, it was proposed to enable the Queen to affix to the future Consort any precedence she chose. This was objected to, on family grounds, by certain members of the Royal family, and as unconstitutional by the Duke of Wellington; and the proposition was dropped. It would scarcely be worth while reviving now the memory of these long-past discussions, were it not to point out the singular fairness with which they are recorded in the Prince's memoir, and the nobleness of character in him which they accidentally elicited. 'The mortification which the refused vote was calculated to occasion to the Queen might,' it is justly admitted, 'have been avoided by proper communications beforehand between Lord Melbourne and the leaders of the Opposition.' 'If, on the one side, the opposition to the proposed vote may be traced, in part at least, to disappointed hope of office, the unconciliatory course pursued on the other may have been influenced by the hope not acknowledged, perhaps, to themselves, of indisposing the young Prince on his first arrival to their opponents, and of seeing the breach widened which already existed between them and the Queen.'

The admission here made is one which marks the singular fairness of the mind which looks back with so mild and equal a judgment upon what at the time was a great annoyance, and was studiously represented as an intended insult. If such a plan was devised, it certainly failed altogether with regard to the Prince. The refusal, of course, pained him at the time; but with that impartial judgment of others, which his own consciousness of perfect fairness taught him, and with his quick and intelligent perception of the bearing of political questions in our land, he at once saw that no disloyalty to the Queen or disaffection to himself had dictated the opposition; and he never showed in his treatment of the Conservative party any grudging or ill will for what he doubted not was on their part a course dictated by nothing else than a conscientious sense of duty.

No other difficulty of any sort was interposed; and when the Prince, after a visit of leave-taking to his native land, which drew forth the strongest expressions of the love for him with which he had inspired his own countrymen, returned again to England, the marriage was at once celebrated. The Prince landed at Dover on Thursday, the 6th of February, and on Monday, the 10th, he was married at the Chapel Royal, St. James's Palace.

Here, by the ordinary rules of romance—and it is a true romance which is pictured in the earlier portion of the volume—the narrative should have closed. But it is, indeed, well that it did not. To do any justice to the great character portrayed, it was necessary to join his manhood visibly to his youth, to show in the first years of his new life what was the fruit of the diligent self-training which had preceded it, and how completely the developed manhood was the bright flower into which the conscientious boyhood had all along promised to burst forth.

The forecasting mind of King Leopold had long perceived the difficulties through which the Queen's husband must pass before he could occupy his true place in the Court and nation. 'His position,' he wrote, October, 1839, to the Queen, 'will be a difficult one; but much, I may say *all*, will depend on your affection for him.' How completely he had that support, and how wisely he used it, these pages show. Lord Melbourne has been often blamed for not having taken more trouble in making a position for the Consort of the Queen. That he did not attempt to do so is certain. But the reason of his conduct was not what his characteristic way of meeting the reproach would seem at first sight to imply. For, instead of being the careless man he liked to appear, he was, in truth, most painstaking and laborious. His unfeigned attachment also to the Queen would have made him exert all his power to secure her this comfort if he had deemed it possible. But his answer, 'What would be the good of making him a position? if he is a fool he will lose it, and if he is a wise man he will make it for himself,' expressed in his own phraseology the conviction that the position must be made by the Prince himself. No one rejoiced more at witnessing the perfect success with which the Prince's high qualities enabled him to make it. When the Regency Bill passed, in August, 1840, through both Houses of Parliament without one voice of opposition, Lord Melbourne said to the Queen, 'Three months ago they would not have done it for him;' adding with tears in his eyes, 'It is entirely his own character.'

And well did he make for himself the fitting position; and yet not without opposition. The first difficulty was in the Royal Household itself. This is touched on in a very few but very telling words in a letter of May, 1840, to Prince Löwenstein, in which the Prince says, 'I am very happy and contented; but the difficulty in filling my place with the proper dignity is, that I am only the husband, not the master in the house.' Fortunately, however, for the country, and still more fortunately for the happiness of the Royal couple themselves, things did not long remain in this condition. Thanks to the firmness, but at the same time gentleness, with which the Prince insisted on filling his proper position as head of the family—thanks also to the clear judgment and right feeling of the Queen, as well as to her singularly honest and straightforward nature—but thanks, more than all, to the mutual love and perfect confidence which bound the Queen and Prince to each other, it was impossible to keep up any separation or difference of interests or duties between them. To those who would urge upon the Queen that, as Sovereign, she must be the head of the house and the family, as well as of the State, and that her husband was, after all, but one of her subjects, Her Majesty would reply, that she had solemnly engaged at the altar to 'obey' as well as to 'love and honour;' and this sacred obligation she could consent neither to limit nor refine away.

A calm unruffled temper, the greatest quickness of perception, a strong will, and a head of singular sagacity, with the unbounded affection of the Royal Mistress of the Palace, soon scattered these difficulties, and enabled the Prince to effect what he had set before himself as one of his special functions—the raising to the highest level the character of the Court. He rested this endeavour on the only true foundation. At the first Easter after the marriage the

Queen and Prince received the Holy Communion together in in St. George's Chapel, Windsor. 'The Prince,' says the Queen's 'Memorandum,' 'had a very strong feeling about the solemnity of this act, and did not like to appear in company either the evening before or the day on which he took it, and he and the Queen almost always dined alone on these occasions.' Having thus begun with consecrating his life by the highest acts of religion, he 'laid down' for himself, we are told, 'from the first, strict, not to say severe, rules for his own guidance. He imposed a degree of restraint and self-denial upon his own movements which could not but have been irksome.'

How true such conduct,—which forbad one painful feeling ever troubling the Royal lady whom he had married,—was to his own feelings of manly affection for his wife the nation may now read in the 'Memorandum' by the Queen. 'During the time the Queen was laid up (after the birth of the Princess Royal) his care and devotion were quite beyond expression.' He refused to go to the play, or anywhere else, generally dining alone with the Duchess of Kent, till the Queen was able to join them, and was always at hand to do anything in his power for her comfort. He was content to sit by her in a darkened room, and to read to her or write for her. 'No one but himself ever lifted her from her bed to her sofa. . . . As years went on, and he became overwhelmed with work, this was often done at much inconvenience to himself; but he ever came with a sweet smile on his face. In short,' the Queen adds, 'his care of me was like that of a mother, nor could there be a kinder, wiser, or more judicious nurse.' How successful his conduct was, is proved by the fact that Scandal never dared in her most malignant mood to associate his name with the lightest hint of any possible suspicion. He might, indeed, have been far more popular during the first years of his married life if he had not imposed upon himself this rule—not only of avoiding evil, but of raising a tone of higher purity in the society in which he moved by a stern rejection and rebuke of every possible approach to levity of conduct.

It was less difficult for such a man to assume his true place in the political world. In spite of the ridiculous jealousy of some feeble minds, who would even have excluded him from 'driving with the Queen in the state carriage, or sitting next to her in the House of Lords,' Lord Melbourne, and his successors in the Premiership, were from the first anxious 'that the Queen should tell him and show him everything connected with public affairs.' The noble spirit in which he entered on this delicate relation to a responsible Ministry prevented the rise of those difficulties which would have sprung up as thistles before a vain, or selfish, or intriguing man. From the time of his first contemplation of his future duties, this breathes everywhere in all his communications. He was resolved, not to be useful or powerful, but to be of such a character that such usefulness should flow naturally forth from what he was in his own inner being. 'I have laid to heart,' he tells Baron Stockmar in November, 1838, 'the friendly advice of your good will as to the true foundation on which my future happiness must rest, and it agrees entirely with the principles of action which I had already in my own reflections framed for myself: an individuality (*Persönlichkeit*), a character, which shall win the respect, the love, and the confidence of the Queen and of the nation, must be the ground-work of my position. This individuality gives security for the disposition which prompts the actions; and even should mistakes (*Missgriffe*) occur, they will be more easily pardoned on account of that personal character: while even the most noble and beautiful undertakings fail in procuring support to a man who is not capable of inspiring that confidence.

'If, therefore, I prove a "noble" Prince (*ein edler Fürst*), in the true sense of the word, as you call upon me to be, wise and prudent conduct will become easier to me, and its results more rich in blessings. I will not let my courage fail. With firm resolution and true zeal on my part I cannot fail to continue noble, manly, and princely in all things.' Remarkable words surely for a young man of twenty, in the contemplation of such a life as lay before him; words which, in fact, reveal the secret of the marvellous success which he achieved. For what he thus nobly designed he grandly executed. When, eleven years afterwards, that great man the Duke of Wellington proposed a scheme which was to issue in the Prince Consort succeeding himself as the Commander-in-Chief of the British Army, the Prince could look undazzled on the glittering offer, and subject it, without one thought of personal distinction, to the calm decision of the most searching judgment, as if he had been dealing with a question which affected another, because he was the inwardly noble man he aspired to be.

'Whilst a female sovereign,' he writes in reply to the Duke of Wellington, 'has a great many disadvantages in comparison with a King, yet, if she is married, and her husband understands and does his duty, her position on the other hand has many compensating advantages, and, in the long run, will be found to be even stronger than that of a male sovereign. But this requires that the husband should entirely sink his *own individual* existence in that of his wife, that he should aim at no power by himself or for himself, should shun all ostentation, assume no separate responsibility before the public; but make his position entirely a part of hers, fill up every gap which, as a woman, she would naturally leave in the exercise of her regal functions, continually and anxiously watch every part of the public business, in order to be able to advise and assist her at any moment in any of the multifarious and difficult questions or duties brought before her, sometimes international, sometimes political, or social, or personal.

'As the natural head of her family, superintendent of her household, manager of her private affairs, sole *confidential* adviser in politics, and only assistant in her communications with the officers of the government, he is, besides the husband of the Queen, the tutor of the Royal children, the private secretary of the sovereign and her permanent minister.'*

And so he discarded the tempting idea of being placed in command of the British Army.

It was this magnanimous resolve ' entirely to sink his own individual existence in that of his wife '—thus aiming at no power by himself or for himself, thus shunning all ostentation—which by degrees allayed the suspicions which the English jealousy of foreigners, the anomalous nature of his position, and even the perception of his great powers of mind, had excited, and gave him, without his seeking it, such an authority in the realm, as a wise, good, and powerful monarch might have rejoiced to possess.

The entire, and if such a word may be used in such a connection, the dutiful love of the Lady of the Land, which every year increased, was the basis on which all this influence ultimately rested. One main interest of this remarkable volume is the ever-recurring proof of the greatness of the wedded love—that rare inheritance, alas! of crowned heads —which for once invested with its sacred brightness the throne of England. It is easy for inferior minds and vulgar natures to question the propriety of such a revelation of the Sovereign's inner life. We believe the deeper and truer view of the effects it will produce is that which has led the illustrious Lady it concerns to sanction its being made. True, deep, earnest love is a great and not a little thing. It elevates every character which it does truly possess. Its real greatness may easily be put out of sight by the pettinesses of a too demonstrative fondness. Such feeble adjuncts of the noble passion should of course be treated as human weaknesses over which the veil of utter secrecy cannot be too closely drawn. But the sight of the majesty of deep affection

* Letter to Duke of Wellington, April 8th, 1850. Windsor Castle. 'Speeches and Addresses of the Prince Consort,' pp. 76-78.

is always ennobling. And there are many circumstances connected with the preceding occupants of the British throne, as well as with these times themselves, which make it wise, because profitable for the nation, to let the veil be somewhat lifted, and the throne be seen to have been the central point of that true, pure, loving, family life which has ever been so dear to the heart of England.

All this is to be seen in these pages not so much in direct expressions of happy love—though these are not few—as in the delight with which the Prince's influence for good on her who loved him best is acknowledged with a simple absence of all self-consciousness which would be charming from any pen in any rank of life, and which is more memorable still from the pen which traced such lines as these:—

'The time spent at Claremont was always a very happy one; the Prince and Queen, being able to take charming walks in the pretty grounds, and neighbourhood. . . . . I told Albert that formerly I was too happy to go to London and wretched to leave it, and how since the blessed hour of my marriage, and still more since the summer, I dislike and am unhappy to leave the country, and could be content and happy never to go to town. This pleased him. The solid pleasures of peaceful, quiet, yet merry life in the country, with my inestimable husband and friend, my all-in-all, are far more desirable than the amusements of London, though we don't despise or dislike these sometimes.'

'The Prince constantly said on arriving at Osborne and Balmoral, and on leaving London,—"How sweet it smells! How delicious the air is! One begins to breathe again!" And how he delighted in the song of birds, and especially of nightingales! listening for them in the happy, peaceful woods at Osborne, and whistling to them in their own peculiar long note, which they invariably answer! The Queen cannot hear this note without fancying she hears him, and without the deepest, saddest emotion. At night he would stand on the balcony at Osborne in May listening to the nightingales.'

How strong these tastes were, and how they mingled themselves with the happiness of that family life which was the admiration of all who really witnessed it, may be read in yet one more extract given us from the 'Queen's Journal' of

Balmoral of October 13, 1856:—'Every year my heart becomes more fixed in this dear paradise, and so much more so now that *all* has become my dearest Albert's *own* creation, own work, own building, own laying out, as at Osborne, that his great taste and the impress of his dear hand have been stamped everywhere.'

Yet with this complete appreciation of nature and the country, the same wise and wholesome influence was employed to prevent the delights of retirement and family life interfering with the duties imposed by her position upon the wearer of the crown. 'The Prince,' we are told, 'though never losing the smallest particle of that intense enjoyment of the country which used to burst forth in such expressions as "Now I am free; now I can breathe;" yet was always anxious that the Queen should spend as much of her time as she could in London.'

The same influence was most usefully exerted in yet higher departments of the duties of the Crown. The Queen has allowed it to be recorded, that 'up to the period of her marriage she had indulged strong feelings of political partisanship.' There were not wanting events in the early days of the marriage which might easily have stamped a like political bias on any one of less robust mental and moral habits than the Prince. 'At Aix-la-Chapelle, on his journey to England, for the marriage, the Prince heard the news of the rejection of the proposed grant of 50,000*l.*, which made a disagreeable impression on him.' The difficulties raised in Parliament to granting him the desired precedence shortly followed. It can cause no matter of surprise that 'the Queen was, as she herself says, most indignant at what had occurred, or that the first impression made on the young Prince's mind by the proceedings in both Houses should have been a painful one.' But his mind had been early made up that to discharge his duties to the nation and the Queen he must stand entirely apart from mere political party. There is an admirable statement of this principle in one of his early letters to the Queen (Dec. 10, 1839), concerning the choice of his future household:—'I should wish,' he says, 'particularly that the selection should be made without regard to politics; for if I am really to keep myself free from all parties, my people must not belong exclusively to one side. Above all, these appointments should not be made mere party rewards. . . . . It is very necessary that they should be chosen from both sides.' To this principle he faithfully adhered. He understood almost intuitively the relations of our political parties; and he cast aside, as their natural result, and springing from no want of loyalty to the Queen or regard to himself, the early vexations which might have eaten deep into the heart of a feebler man. His relation from the first with the leaders of both the great parties in the State was that of amicable fidelity; and all the leading men of the nation soon trusted him implicitly. The chief peril of a female reign was thus happily averted, and the party 'feelings by which the Queen so candidly admits that she was herself biassed at the time of her marriage soon ceased to show themselves under the influence of his judicious counsels.' Thus was prevented what might else have grown into no slight danger to the realm. For, as Lord Bacon has recorded—'When princes that ought to be common parents make themselves as a party, and lean to a side, it is as a boat that is overthrown by uneven weight on the one side.'*

Such was the Prince whom we have had, and whom in the inscrutable providence of God, except in the good which he has done, and the example he has left, we have lost. In these pages it has been our endeavour to make his own acts, words, and letters as much as possible record his character. And after such a record few sentences of mere formal

* Lord Bacon's Works, vol. ii. p. 284.

description can, we think, be needful. Of a noble and distinguished lineage amongst our German kinsmen, he was trained in all the highest excellencies of their best education. In person he was remarkable for a manly beauty in which the presence of intellect made itself felt like strongly-marked features of scenery through the more ordinary graces of a finished landscape. His intellectual gifts were of the highest order. With a keen relish for knowledge of every kind, and great exactness in acquiring and retaining it,—of history, of art, of philosophy, of science, and of nature, he had the master power of casting all acquired facts into such a philosophical order that he was never oppressed by the multitude of his attainments. The higher accomplishments of a liberal education were also his; he was a painter and a musician of no ordinary merit. He possessed the power of reasoning to an eminent degree. In argument on any topic, no man was readier in the use of every lawful weapon of fence. Humour, illustration, repartee, and the strong grasp of vigorous contradiction, all lay hid under that mild and calm exterior. His affections, too, though their outward demonstrations were repressed on principle into a settled sobriety of expression, were quick and strong. How did he return the almost worship of the aged Duchess of Gotha! how did he love his Queen, his brother, and his friends! Here is one instance of the latter too striking not to be inserted, and one which illustrates also the great fairness of his character. When Mr. G. E. Anson was first appointed to be his private secretary, the arrangement was reluctantly acquiesced in by him, because he feared that Mr. Anson's former connection with Lord Melbourne, as private secretary, would give a political colour to the appointment. The objection was, however overruled; and the Prince soon found that he had a thoroughly honest, fearless, and attached servant in Mr. Anson. These were qualities which his truthful and noble nature thoroughly appreciated; and he soon gave to Mr. Anson, not only confidence, but an affection which ripened early, to be early broken in upon by the sudden death of his confidential servant. 'The Prince was deeply affected when the news of Mr. Anson's sudden death arrived, and said to the Queen, "He was my only intimate friend. We went through everything together since I came here. He was almost like a brother to me."'

But the pre-eminent feature, after all, in the character of the Prince was his noble estimate of duty. This was not in him the dull and formal performance, however precise, of a set of external acts; it was the outcoming of his life, and so, like other true comings forth of life, was at once real, vigorous, genial, and perpetual. This was his aim,—not merely to do with any amount of exactness external duties, but to be such that the external performance would be the natural expression of the inward man. 'If I prove,' they are his own grand words, 'a "noble" prince in the true sense of the word, wise and prudent conduct will become easier to me.' And all this was founded on a true principle of religion which had kept his youth spotlessly pure. We believe that the words in which she who knew him best gives utterance to her estimate of his goodness are no exaggeration, when she says, 'God knows vice itself would ever have recoiled from the look alone of one who wore "the lily of a blameless life."' It is not easy to over-estimate the influence for good on our Court and people of such a life as this, placed beside the throne of a young female sovereign. The Queen's words, which we have before quoted, express her estimate of what the gain was in the highest quarter. But it did not stop there; through the Court, and by a thousand channels through the nation, that life daily distilled its purifying, elevating influences. What England might now have been if that young Court had been led astray by the union of such abilities as those possessed by the Prince to such a character as Charles II.'s; what it might have been if the Lady of the land had wedded a mere dull, clownish lout like the husband of Queen Anne, who amongst us can say? Where do we not meet now with the marks of what he did, who has been taken from us in presence, but who is still with us in the virtues of the Court, in the growth of art, in the elevation of science, and in many beneficent institutions for raising the character and increasing the comforts of servants and of poor children, and for securing to the labourer's family a home in which the practice of virtue is rendered possible because its life can be led with decency?

'How this early promise of distinction was fulfilled,' the Queen says in the Memorandum from which this extract is taken, 'how immeasurably all the most sanguine expectations were surpassed, how King Leopold's fondest hopes were realised ten thousand fold, and how the fearful blow which took him from us put an end to all this happiness, and cut short his brilliant and useful career, we all know!'

It was one consequence of the line which he marked out for himself, of 'sinking his own individual existence in that of his wife,' that all this should at the time be unperceived. During the earlier years, accordingly, of his married life he was comparatively speaking unknown. English jealousy of foreign interferences in some quarters, resentment in others at the high tone of virtue which he was felt to enforce, ignorance of what he was in almost all, created and kept alive respecting him misjudgment, with its consequent disaffection. By little and little the truth, as it always will, oozed out. The speeches which from time to time he delivered excited first attention and then astonishment. They were so full of genius, and they were so evidently his own, whilst they announced such high principles in such clear language; they so plainly met some great practical need in so straightforward a manner, and they were so quickly followed by corresponding acts, that his real character and greatness began to be universally appreciated. Men felt in his growing influence, and saw in his perpetual labours, the truth of the words of the great philosophic statesman: 'Princes are like to heavenly bodies which cause good or evil times; and which have much veneration but no rest.'* And then, almost before his sun had risen to its mid-day height, it sunk suddenly, and men found out what they had possessed by the sad process of losing it.

What he would yet more and more, as years passed on, have become to England and to Europe, and so to the whole civilised world, if that large intellect, that calm unerring judgment, and that truthfulness, purity, and justice of character which already had done so much, had been left to expand itself to its full proportions and assert in the sight of all men its real greatness, it *is* impossible to speculate. But that future was not allowed him; he had already done his work and he has entered on his rest.

To such an one we may apply the words in which the great philosophical historian of Rome comments upon the death of Julius Agricola, with an appropriateness which no heathen writer could reach—' Si quis piorum Manibus locus, si, ut sapientibus placet, non cum corpore exstinguuntur magnæ animæ, placidè quiescas; nosque, domum tuam, ab infirmo desiderio . . . ad contemplationem virtutum tuarum voces, quas neque lugeri neque plangi fas est . . . Is verus honos, ea conjunctissimi cujusque pietas. Id filiæ quoque uxorique præceperim, sic patris, sic mariti memoriam venerari, ut omnia facta dictaque ejus secum revolvant.'†

Such was Prince Albert to the land of his adoption. What he was within the closer precincts of family life these pages may make any careful reader know. The subject is still too sacred for any more detailed handling than we have ventured

---

* Bacon's Essays, 'Of Empire.'   † 'C. Cornelii Taciti Jul. Agricol.,' c. 46.

to use. But if there ever was a call upon all that is good and true in this nation for a lifelong sympathy, it is the voice of the Wife, the Mother, and the Queen, as it sounds from this volume. 'I am very glad of it,' was Lord Melbourne's reply to the announcement of the first engagement, adding, with his wonted shrewdness, in quite a paternal tone, 'you will be much more comfortable, for a woman cannot stand alone for any time in whatever position she may be.' Let Her children, let Her people never forget that God's wise though mysterious providence has so ordered Her life, that 'The Queen cannot forbear from adding, "Alas! alas! the poor Queen now stands in that painful position."'

ROYAL AUTHORSHIP.

THE work of which we give the title below* must be considered as the supplement of that volume of royal authorship which we recently brought before our readers. It is a record of that daily life to which the former book so touchingly alluded; and whatever of direct biography future volumes may yet give us, and however skilfully Mr. Theodore Martin may execute his task, nothing from another hand can have the interest which this possesses, nor can any retrospect be animated with the living power which belongs to notes such as these of the days which are passed—jotted down at the time with no thought of publication, but only as the outpouring of a happy heart, fixing in an enduring record the thoughts, feelings, and impressions with which, in a sunshine life spent in high moral and intellectual companionship, it was being daily ennobled. The volume consists of journals written by the Queen during excursions in England, Scot-

---

* 'Leaves from the Journal of Our Life in the Highlands, from 1848 to 1861.' Edited by Arthur Helps. London, 1868.

land, and Ireland. They have the charm which perfect naturalness combined with exquisite gracefulness might give to another writer; but from their actual writer they have a far higher interest. They serve, as nothing which was written for the purpose of doing it could serve, to set before her people the real tone of the life which their Queen has been for so many years continually leading; its simplicity, its truthfulness, its high family affectionateness, its thorough sympathy with all around the royal persons who form the centre of the group, and who, even in hours of unusual rest from public business, are still engaged in discharging family duties with a care and kindness which few households could equal, and perhaps none surpass.

But though this insight into the Royal Family is the main interest of this volume, to which we must return, and of which we must give some exhibition in the way of extracts from these pages, there is about such a volume as this another interest besides this which is so directly personal.

The elements of future history are stored in such a narrative. What would we not give to have such a diary of Henry VII., when, after having won his throne, he was endeavouring to conciliate the subjects amongst whom he made his carefully-planned progresses? or such journals from the pen of Elizabeth, the sovereign who, of all who have sat upon our ancient throne, was the most given to excursions through all her dominions? The short fragmentary notices which we do possess of such royal tours of old, only make us feel the more acutely how precious such relics would be. We have one such record of the first progress made by Henry VII., when the storms through which his succession to the Crown was effected had been sufficiently calmed to allow of his coronation, and he set out in 1486 to show himself as King throughout his wide dominion. We shall preserve the irregular and capricious spelling of the old Cotton MSS.,

ROYAL AUTHORSHIP. 153

and give it exactly as it may yet be read in the British Museum, from what terms itself ' A short and brief Memory by license and correcyon of the first Progress of our Soveraigne Lorde King Henry the VII. After his noble Coronation, Cristemas, and Parlement, holden at his Paleys at Westm̃r. towards the north parties :'—

' In the. . . daye of March he rode his Hors well and nobly accompanyed, at Segnt Johns of London, and rode to Waltham, and from thens the highway to Cambrige where his Grace was honourably receyvede both of the Universite and of the Towne. And from thence he rode by Huntingdon, Stamforde, and to Lincolne, and then his Grace kepte right devoutly the Holy Fest of Ester; and full like a Christen Prynce harde his dyvine servyce in the Cathedral Churche and in no pryve Chapell: and on Shere* thursday he had in the Bysshoppes Halle XXIX pore men to whom he humbly and cristenly for Crysten love with his noble handes did washe ther fete, and gave as grete almes like as other hys noble Progenitors Kynges of England have been accustomed aforetyme: and also on Good Friday after all his offering and observances of halowing of Ryngest† after dyner gave marvelous grete sumes of money in grotes to poore people, besides grete alms to poor Frears, Prysoners, and Layars house of that countrey: and on Sheer Thursday, Good Fryday, Ester Even and Ester day the Bysshop of that See dyd the Dyvyne Servyce, and the Kynge hemself kept every day thus . . . and that same weke he removed unto Nottingham.' ‡

How charming would it be to have Henry's own record of this 'riding forth on his Hors,' well and nobly accompanied; to know what he really felt towards the University of Cambridge; how its high authorities received him; what he ate and drank; and how he fared in the High Halls at Stamford and in the grand old Palace, which at Lincoln looked out over the wide-spread champaign of Lincolnshire.

But of all our sovereigns perhaps Elizabeth, as we have said, took the greatest pleasure in royal progresses, and certainly none could have yielded incidents which it would be

---

* *Shere* or *Sheer* Thursday, so called from the preparation made by shaving and cutting the hair for Easter.

† For medical use against epilepsy, &c.

‡ Ex lib. Cotton, Julius XII., fol. 504.

more delightful to follow closely from the hand of the royal pen than those which must have befallen her. We do not believe in the deep State motives which have been suggested for these frequent pilgrimages, as having been undertaken in order to reduce the power of some whom she suspected, by the expense which they inflicted on her hosts. She seems to have wished to see things with her own eyes; moreover, she evidently enjoyed not a little the incense so freely burned before her in the great provincial houses where she halted. There was, too, apparently about her a certain restlessness of temper, which was perhaps bred partly from the unsettledness of her early years and partly from the strange and unhappy circumstances of her unmarried condition after she became Queen. From her accession, accordingly, almost to the end of her days, she was a great traveller through England, visiting in succession most parts of Surrey, Hampshire, Berkshire, Kent, Sussex, Hertfordshire, Warwickshire, Worcestershire, Essex, Suffolk, Wiltshire. These migrations were continued till 1602, within a few weeks of her death.

In the days of her early troubles, Elizabeth had known other progresses than these to which after her coming to the throne she was so much devoted. After Sir Thomas Wyatt's rebellion (1554), which she lay under some suspicion of favouring, when, at the end of May, she was delivered from close imprisonment in the Tower, she was sent under the command of Sir Henry Bedingfield and Lord Williams of Thame,* to the Royal manor of Woodstock. The first night of her journey she lay at Richmond, where—being watched all night by the soldiers, and all access of her own private attendants utterly prohibited—she began to be convinced that orders had been given to put her privately to death. The next day she reached Windsor, where she was lodged in the Dean's house. She then passed to Lord Williams' seat at

* Nichols' 'Progresses of Elizabeth,' i. 7.

Ricot, in Oxfordshire, where, to Bedingfield's great disgust, she 'was verie princelie entertained.' Arriving at Woodstock she was kept in the Gate House of the Palace, and her expectations and feelings may be gathered from three lines which Holinshed records her to have written with a diamond on her chamber window:—

> 'Much suspected, by* me
> Nothing proved can be,
> Quoth Elizabeth prisoner.'

Having after many months obtained her release, she set out on her first day's journey from Woodstock to Ricot in such tempestuous weather that 'her hood and the attire of her head were twice or thrice blown off'—disarrangements of her dress which she was compelled to remedy under a hedge near the road, as Bedingfield would not suffer her to make use of a neighbouring gentleman's house for the purpose. Perhaps the remembrance of these early trials made her love to haunt the same places when at the noonday of her power she could visit them in the pride of her sovereignty; for Woodstock and 'Rycort' are amongst the most frequent of her progresses, and are the scenes of some of her grandest receptions. Thus, in 1592, having been 'entertained magnifically' by the Lady Russell at Bissam, and the Lord Chandos at Sudley, where she was welcomed as the 'Queene of this island, the wonder of the world and Nature's glory,' she passed on to Ricorte, where on Sunday, being received in the garden with 'sweete musicke of sundry sorts, she is presented with gifts which purport to come from all quarters: an "Irish lacque," bringing her a Darte of gold set with diamonds, with this motto in Irish, I fly onely for my sovereign; a shipper from Flanders delivered a key of golde set with diamonds, with this motto in Dutch, I onlie open to you; a French page brings a sword of golde set with

---

* *By*, in the old sense of *against*.

diamonds and rubyies, with this motto in French, Drawen only in your defence; and a truncheon set with diamonds, with the motto in Spanish, I do not commande but under you.'*

In these progresses she sometimes threw off her state, as when after visiting Kenilworth Castle in 1572, she returned very late at night to Warwick, and 'because she woold see what chere my Lady of Warwick made, she sodenly went into Mr. Thomas Fisher's house, and there fynding them at supper, satt downe awhile, and after a little repast rose agayne, leaving the rest at supper, and went to visite the good man of the house, Thomas Fisher, who at that tyme was grevously vexed with the gowt.' †

Very different then was an excursion, even through these home counties, for anything we know: we may form some idea of the change by comparing our own experience of a journey from London to Edinburgh with that accomplished at the death of Elizabeth by a 'hasty Hudson' of that day. Instead of being whirled along by the easy speed of an express train, when Sir Robert Carey reached Edinburgh to bring to James I. the news of his succession to the throne he was 'admitted to the King bebloodied with great falles and bruises' as the consequences and witnesses of his speed.'‡ The Queen's temporary absence from the capital, even in one of the midland counties, in those days difficult of travel, led to such provisions being made as would not a little astonish the magnates of the city of London if they were thought needful upon the starting of the royal train for distant Balmoral. Thus when she set forth on her progress of 1572 she wrote first to the Lord Mayor that she had appointed for his assistance 'during this time of our progress

---

* 'Progresses,' &c., 1592. Quoted by Nichols, vol. ii. p. 592.

† From a MS. called the 'Black Book,' belonging to the Corporation of Warwick, fol. 65—70. Quoted by Nichols.

‡ 'Millington's True Narration,' given in Nichols' 3rd volume.

and absence in remote parts from thence, the Archbishop of Canterbury, the Bishop of London, and others . . . . that they shall join with you to devise . . . . for quiet order to be continued in our said city.'

Future generations will turn to the 'Leaves from the Journal of our Life,' of Queen Victoria, with the same historical interest with which we gaze into the comparatively unpersonal records of the progresses of Elizabeth. But with this difference: that instead of seeing a brocaded figure receiving the incense of an antique and almost barbarous flattery, or toying with Leicester, or simulating a romantic passion for the Duke of Anjou at the very moment when she is frigidly rejecting his proposals—whilst the whole mystery of her remarkable life, her real relations with Leicester and Essex, with Burleigh and Cecil, are almost hidden from us—our descendants will have the great figures of the historical portrait set before them with a minuteness of description, a completeness of detail, and a delicacy of touch, which will, after any lapse of time, reproduce before them the real life of the present century in its best proportions.

This is in truth the master interest of this volume. Mr. Arthur Helps, who at the Queen's command has edited it, gives a clear and concise account both of the original composition of the volume and of the circumstances which led to its publication:

'During one of the Editor's official visits to Balmoral, Her Majesty very kindly allowed him to see several extracts from her journal relating to excursions in the Highlands of Scotland, and afterward to progresses in England, Ireland, and the Channel Islands. He was much interested by them; and expressed the interest which he felt. It then occurred to Her Majesty that these extracts, referring, as they did, to some of the happiest hours of her life, might be made into a book, to be printed privately, for presentation to members of the Royal Family and Her Majesty's intimate friends; especially to those who had accompanied and attended her in these tours.

'It was then suggested to Her Majesty by some persons, among them a near and dear relative of the Queen, and afterwards by the Editor, that this work, if made known to others, would be very interesting to them as well as to the Royal Family and to Her Majesty's intimate friends. The Queen, however, said that she had no skill whatever in authorship; that these were, for the most part, mere homely accounts of excursions near home; and that she felt extremely reluctant to publish anything written by herself.

'To this the Editor respectfully replied, that, if printed at all, however limited the impression, and however careful the selection of persons to whom copies might be given, some portions of the volume, or quite as probably incorrect representations of its contents, might find their way into the public journals. It would, therefore, he thought, be better at once to place the volume within the reach of Her Majesty's subjects, who would, no doubt, derive from it pleasure similar to that which it had afforded to the Editor himself. Moreover, it would be very gratifying to her subjects —who had always shown a sincere and ready sympathy with the personal joys and sorrows of their Sovereign—to be allowed to know how her rare moments of leisure were passed in her Highland home, when every joy was heightened, and every care and sorrow diminished, by the loving companionship of the Prince Consort. With his memory the scenes to which this volume refers would always be associated.

'Upon these considerations Her Majesty eventually consented to its publication.'

The editor proceeds to describe the volume as containing—

'A record of the impressions received by the Royal Author in the course of these journeys, as might hereafter serve to recall to her own mind the scenes and circumstances which had been the source of so much pleasure. All references to political questions, or to the affairs of Government, have, for obvious reasons, been studiously omitted. The book is mainly confined to the natural expressions of a mind rejoicing in the beauties of nature, and throwing itself, with a delight rendered keener by the rarity of its opportunities, into the enjoyment of a life removed, for the moment, from the pressure of public cares.'

The practised hand of Mr. Helps supplies us further with some of the literary characteristics of the volume: he notices—

'The picturesque descriptions of scenery in which the work abounds; the simplicity of diction throughout it; and the perfect faithfulness of narration which is one of its chief characteristics; for in every page the writer describes what she thinks and feels, rather than what she might be expected to think and feel.

Every one who reads the book, and no book will be more widely read, must feel the truth of these descriptions of its style and composition. The excursions in England and the Channel Islands which are recorded in this volume, were made in the summer and autumn of 1846, and consisted of a yacht visit to Devonshire, Cornwall, and Guernsey and Jersey. One or two extracts will do more than any description to bring the passing scenes of such record before the reader's eye :—

' *On board the Victoria and Albert, Dartmouth, Thursday, August* 20, 1846.—We steamed past the various places on the beautiful coast of Devonshire which we had passed three years ago till we came to Babbicombe, a small bay, where we remained an hour. It is a beautiful spot, which before we had only passed at a distance. Red cliffs and rocks with wooded hills, like Italy, and reminding one of a ballet or play where nymphs are to appear—such rocks and grottoes, with the deepest sea, on which there was not a ripple. We intended to disembark and walk up the hill ; but it came on to rain very much, and we could not do so. We tried to sketch the part looking towards Torbay. I never saw our good children looking better, or in higher spirits. I contrived to give Vicky* a little lesson by making her read in her English history.'

Two days later the Journal, dated Plymouth, Saturday, August 22, says :—

' Albert was up at six o'clock, as he was to go to Dartmoor Forest. At ten I went in the barge with the two children, the ladies, Baron Stockmar, and Lord Alfred Paget, and landed at Mount Edgcumbe . . . . There were crowds where we landed, and I feel so shy and put out without Albert . . . . A little after twelve we returned to the yacht, which had been beset with boats ever since six in the morning. Albert returned safely to me at one o'clock, much pleased with his trip, and said that Dartmoor Forest was like Scotland . . . . Poor Lord Mount Edgcumbe is in such a sad, helpless state ; but so patient and cheerful.'

' *In Guernsey Bay, off St. Pierre, Guernsey, Sunday, August* 23.—On waking, the morning was so lovely that we could not help regretting that

---

* The Princess Royal.

we could not delay our trip a little, by one day at least, as the Council which was to have been on the 25th is now on the 29th. Albert thought we might perhaps manage to see one of the Channel Islands, and accordingly it was settled that we should go to Guernsey, which delighted me, as I had so long wished to see it. The day splendid .... The sea the whole way was as calm as it was in '43 .... As we approached we were struck by the beauty of the Guernsey coast, in which there are several rocky bays, and the town of St. Pierre is very picturesquely built, down to the water's edge .... We anchored at seven, immediately opposite St. Pierre, and with the two islands on the other side of us.'

'*August* 24.—This island with its bold point, and the little one of Cornet with a sort of castle on it (close to which we were anchored), and the three islands of Herm, Jethou, and Sark, with innumerable rocks, are really very fine and peculiar, especially as they then were in bright sunlight. We both sketched, and at a quarter to nine got into our barge with our ladies. The pier and shore were lined with crowds of people, and with ladies dressed in white, singing "God save the Queen," and strewing the ground with flowers. We walked to our carriage, preceded by General Napier, brother to Sir Charles (in Scinde), a very singular-looking old man, tall and thin, with an aquiline nose, piercing eyes, and white moustaches and hair. The people were extremely well-behaved and friendly, and received us very warmly as we drove through the narrow streets, which were decorated with flowers and flags, and lined with the Guernsey militia, 2000 strong, with their several bands. Some of the militia were mounted.

'The vegetation beyond the town is exceedingly fine ; and the evergreens and flowers most abundant. The streets and hills steep, and the view from the fort, which is very high (and where General Napier presented me with the keys), is extremely beautiful. You look over the bay of Guernsey, and see opposite to you the islands of Herm, Jethou, and Sark ; with Alderney, and the coast of France, Cape de la Hague, to the left in the distance, and to the right in the distance, Jersey .... They belonged to the Duchy of Normandy, and have been in our possession ever since William the Conqueror's time. King John was the last of their sovereigns who visited them. We drove along the pier, and then embarked amidst great cheering. It was all admirably managed ; the people are extremely loyal.'

After the interruption of the Council the excursion was resumed, and the Journal thus records its course:—

'*On board the Victoria and Albert, off St. Heliers, Jersey, Wednesday, September* 2, 1846.—At a quarter past seven o'clock we set off with Vicky, Bertie,* Lady Jocelyn, Miss Kerr, Mdlle. Gruner, Lord Spencer, Lord

---

* The Prince of Wales.

Palmerston, and Sir James Clark, and embarked at Osborne pier. There was a good deal of swell. It was fine, but very cold at first. At twelve we saw Alderney, and between two and three got into the Alderney Race, where there was a great deal of rolling, but not for long. We passed between Alderney and the French Coast—Cape de la Hague—and saw the other side of Alderney; and then, later, Sark, Guernsey, and the other islands. After passing the Alderney Race it became quite smooth; and then Bertie put on his sailor's dress, which was beautifully made by the man on board who makes for our sailors. When he appeared, the officers and sailors, who were all assembled on deck to see him, cheered, and seemed delighted with him.

'The coast of Jersey is very beautiful, and we had to go nearly all round in order to get to St. Heliers . . . . The red cliffs and rocks, with the setting sun gilding and lighting them all up, were beautiful. At last, at a quarter to seven, we arrived in this fine large bay of St. Aubin, in which lies St Heliers; and after dinner we went on deck to see the illumination and the bonfires.'

'*Off St. Heliers, Thursday, September* 3.—A splendid day. I never saw a more beautiful deep blue sea, quite like Naples; and Albert said that this fine bay of St. Aubin, in which we lie, really is like Naples. Noirmont Point terminates in a low tower to our left, with St. Aubin and a tower on a rock in front of it; farther in, and to our right, Elizabeth Castle, a picturesque fort on a rock, with the town of St. Heliers behind it.

'The colouring and the effect of light were indescribably beautiful. . . . We landed at the stairs of the Victoria Harbour, amid the cheers of the numberless crowds, guns firing, and bands playing; were received, as at Guernsey, by all the ladies of the town, very gaily dressed, who, strewing flowers on our way, conducted us to a canopy, where I received the address of the States and of the militia.

'We then got into our carriage and drove along the pier; Colonel Le Couteur, my militia aide-de-camp, riding by my side, with other officers, and by Albert's side Colonel Le Breton, commanding the militia, who, 5000 strong, lined the streets, and were stationed along the pier. The States walking in front. The crowds were immense, but everything in excellent order, and the people most enthusiastic; the decorations and arches of flowers were really beautifully done, and there were numberless kind inscriptions.

'We then proceeded . . . . through the interior of the island, which is extremely pretty and very green—orchards without end, as at Mayence. We passed the curious old tower of La Hougue Bie, of very ancient date, and went to the castle of Mont Orgeuil, in Grouville Bay, very beautifully situated, completely overhanging the sea, and where Robert, Duke of Normandy, son of William the Conqueror, is said to have lived.'

The home voyage was propitious. The evening at Falmouth

'beautiful, and the sea as smooth as glass, and without even a ripple. The calmest night possible, with a beautiful moon, when we went on deck; every now and then the splashing of oars and the hum of voices were heard; but they were the only sounds, unlike the constant dashing of the sea against the vessel, which we heard all the time we were at Jersey.'

The next day they anchor off Penzance amidst a 'crowd of boats.'

'*Mount's Bay, Cornwall, Saturday, September 5.*—Numbers of Cornish pilcher fishermen, in their curious large boats, kept going round and round, and then anchored, besides many other boats full of people. They are a very noisy, talkative race, and speak a kind of English hardly to be understood.

'During our voyage I was able to give Vicky her lessons.'

Soon after the Corporation of Penryn come on board—

'Very anxious to see "the Duke of Cornwall," so I stepped out of the pavilion on deck with Bertie, and Lord Palmerston told them that that was "the Duke of Cornwall;" and the old mayor of Penryn said that "he hoped he would grow up a blessing to his parents and to his country."'

There were other manifestations of Cornish interest in the Duke:—

'Just below Truro the whole population poured out on foot and in carts, &c., along the banks, and cheered, and were enchanted when Bertie was held up for them to see. It was a very pretty, gratifying sight.

'We went straight on to Swan Pool, outside Pendennis Castle, where we got into the barge, and rowed near to the shore to see a net drawn.'

On the 9th of September the excursion ended at Osborne.

There are journals of two visits to Ireland, the first in 1844 and the second in 1861. The first commences with Cork, which is pronounced to be—

'Not at all like an English town, and looking rather foreign. The crowd is a noisy, excitable, but very good-humoured one, running and pushing about, and laughing, talking, and shrieking. The beauty of the women is very remarkable, and struck us much; such beautiful dark eyes and hair, and such fine teeth; almost every third woman was pretty, and some remarkably so. They wear no bonnets, and generally long blue cloaks; the men are very poorly, often raggedly dressed; and many wear blue coats and short breeches with blue stockings.'

The Royal party, after visiting Dublin, come in for some characteristic rejoicings at Castors, the seat of the Duke of Leinster,

'One of the kindest and best of men. After luncheon we walked out and saw some of the country people dance jigs, which was very amusing. It is quite different from the Scotch reel; not so animated, and the steps different, but very droll. The people were very poorly dressed in thick coats, and the women in shawls. There was one man who was a regular specimen of an Irishman, with his hat on one ear. Others in blue coats, with short breeches and blue stockings. There were three old and tattered pipers playing. The Irish pipe is very different to the Scotch; it is very weak, and they don't blow into it, but merely have small bellows which they move with the arm.'

The tour takes them on to Belfast, and thence by a stormy passage to Scotland.

The main part of the volume, as the title intimates, consists of journals which record the daily life of the Royal party in their Highland home. This is preceded by notes of three visits which preceded their settlement at Balmoral in 1848. The first visit was in 1842, which took them in succession to Dalkeith, Dalmeny, Dupplin, Scone, Dunkeld, Taymouth, Drummond Castle, and gave them a good introduction to the northern kingdom. During this visit the Prince had his first experience of deer-stalking, which the need of exertion of every sort, both of mind and body, at once recommended strongly to him. He gives his first impression of it in a letter to the late Prince of Leiningen:—

'Without doubt deer-stalking is one of the most fatiguing, but it is also one of the most interesting of pursuits. There is not a tree or a bush behind which you can hide yourself. . . . One has, therefore, to be constantly on the alert in order to circumvent them, and to keep under the hill out of their wind, crawling on hands and knees, and dressed entirely in grey.'

The journal marks in the entry of September 14th the affection to her northern dominion already created in the Queen's mind by a first visit to it:

'This is our last day in Scotland; it is really a delightful country, and I am very sorry to leave it.'

In 1844 a visit follows to Blair Athole, and in 1847 a tour succeeds round the West coast. Throughout these Journals there are many of those natural touches which constitute one especial charm of the whole volume. Here are one or two examples:—

'About three miles beyond Dundee we stopped at the gate of Lord Camperdown's place: here a triumphal arch had been erected, and Lady Camperdown and Lady Duncan and her little boy, with others, were all waiting to welcome us, and were very civil and kind. The little boy, beautifully dressed in the Highland dress, was carried to Vicky, and gave her a basket with fruit and flowers. I said to Albert I could hardly believe that our child was travelling with us—it put me so in mind of myself when I was the "little Princess." Albert observed that it was always said that parents lived their lives over again in their children, which is a very pleasant feeling.

'Nothing could be quieter than our journey, and the scenery is so beautiful! It is very different from England: all the houses built of stone; the people so different—sandy hair, high cheek-bones; children with long shaggy hair and bare legs and feet; little boys in kilts. Near Dunkeld, and also as you get more into the Highlands, there are prettier faces. Those jackets which the girls wear are so pretty; all the men and women, as well as the children, look very healthy. We saw Birnam Wood and Sir W. Stewart's place in that fine valley on the opposite side of the river. All along such splendid scenery, and Albert enjoyed it so much—rejoicing in the beauties of nature, the sight of mountains, and the pure air.

'We got out at an inn (which was small, but very clean) at Dunkeld. Such a charming view from the window! Vicky stood and bowed to the people out of the window. There never was such a good traveller as she is, sleeping in the carriage at her usual times, not put out, not frightened at noise or crowds, but pleased and amused.'

'*Blair Castle, Blair Athole, Thursday, September* 12.—We took a delightful walk of two hours. We went through the wood, along a steep winding path over-hanging the rapid stream. These Scotch streams, full of stones, and clear as glass, are most beautiful; the peeps between the trees, the depth of the shadows, the mossy stones, mixed with slate, &c.,

which cover the banks, are lovely; at every turn you have a picture. We were up high, but could not get to the top; Albert in such delight; it is a happiness to see him, he is in such spirits.

'He said that the chief beauty of mountain scenery consisted in its frequent changes.

'As we left the wood we came upon such a lovely view—Ben-y-Ghlo straight before us—and under these high hills the river Tilt gushing and winding over stones and slates, and the hills and mountains skirted at the bottom with beautiful trees; the whole lit up by the sun, and the air so pure and fine; but no description can at all do it justice, or give an idea of what this drive was.

'Oh! what can equal the beauties of nature! What enjoyment there is in them! Albert enjoys it so much; he is in ecstasies here. He has inherited this love for nature from his dear father.'

Here is the first account of one of those half-accompanied deer-stalks which allow of ladies sharing in the wild pleasures of the Highlands:—

'We stopped at the top of the Chrianan, whence you look down an immense height. Here the eagles sometimes sit. Albert looked about in great admiration. We then went nearly to the top of Cairn Chlamain, and here we separated, Albert going off with Peter, Lawley, and two other keepers, to get a "quiet shot," as they call it; and Lady Canning, Lord Glenlyon, and I went up quite to the top, which is deep in moss. Here we sat down and stayed some time sketching the ponies below—Lord Glenlyon and Sandy remaining near us. The view was quite beautiful, nothing but mountains all around us, and the solitude, the complete solitude, very impressive. We descended this highest pinnacle, and proceeded on a level to meet Albert. We met him shortly after; he had had bad luck, I am sorry to say. We then sat down on the grass and had some luncheon; then I walked a little with Albert and we got on our ponies. As we went on towards home some deer were seen in Glen Chroime, which is called the "Sanctum;" where it is supposed that there are a great many. Albert went off soon after this, and we remained on Sron a Chro for an hour, I am sure, as Lord Glenlyon said by so doing we should turn the deer to Albert, whereas if we went on we should disturb and spoil the whole thing. So we submitted. Albert looked like a little speck creeping about on an opposite hill. We saw four herds of deer, two of them close to us. It was a beautiful sight.

'As the sun went down the scenery became more and more beautiful, the sky crimson, golden-red and blue, and the hills looking purple and lilac, most exquisite, till at length it set, and the hues grew softer in the sky and the outlines of the hills sharper. I never saw anything so fine. It soon, however, grew very dark.

'At length Albert met us. He had been very unlucky, and had lost his sport, for the rifle would not go off just when he could have shot some fine harts; yet he was as merry and cheerful as if nothing had happened to disappoint him.

'We saw a flight of ptarmigan, with their white wings, on the top of Sron a Chro; also plovers, grouse, and pheasants.'

This was the last day of the visit to Blair Athole :—

'I rode back on "Arghait Bhean"* for the last time, and took a sad leave of him and of faithful Sandy McAra.'

'Lord Aberdeen was quite touched when I told him I was so attached to the dear, dear Highlands, and missed the fine hills so much. There is a great peculiarity about the Highlands and Highlanders; and they are such a chivalrous, fine, active people. Our stay among them was so delightful. Independently of the beautiful scenery, there was a quiet, a retirement, a wildness, a liberty, and a solitude that had such a charm for us.'

This affection for the

'Land of brown heath and shaggy wood,
Land of the mountain and the flood,'

was not a little increased by the succeeding visit to the West of Scotland, and led before long to the purchase of Balmoral as what it is so desirable that the Queen of Great Britain should possess—a really Highland home. Here is the record of its 'first impressions :'—

'*Balmoral, Friday, September* 8, 1848.—We arrived at Balmoral at a quarter to three. It is a pretty little castle in the old Scottish style. There is a picturesque tower and garden in front, with a high wooded hill: at the back there is wood down to the Dee; and the hills rise all around. At half-past four we walked out, and went up to the top of the wooded hill opposite our windows, where there is a cairn, and up which there is a pretty winding path. The view from here, looking down upon the house, is charming. To the left you look towards the beautiful hills surrounding Loch-na-Gar, and to the right, towards Ballater, to the glen (or valley) along which the Dee winds, with beautiful wooded hills, which reminded us very much of the Thüringerwald. It was so calm, and so solitary, it

---

* 'This pony was given to me by the Duke of Athole in 1847, and is now alive at Osborne.'

did one good as one gazed around; and the pure mountain air was most refreshing. All seemed to breathe freedom and peace, and to make one forget the world and its sad turmoils.

'The scenery is wild, and yet not desolate. Then the soil is delightfully dry. We walked beside the Dee, a beautiful, rapid stream, which is close behind the house. The view of the hills towards Invercauld is exceedingly fine.'

Excursions, drives, deer-stalking, incognito journeys, with some of the incidents which in Eastern garb delighted the great Haroun Alraschid, soon followed. To a few of these we shall treat our readers. Here is the first ascent of Loch-na-Gar:—

'*Saturday, September*, 16, 1848.—At half-past nine o'clock Albert and I set off in a postchaise, and drove to the bridge in the wood of Balloch Buie, about five miles from Balmoral, where our ponies and people were. Here we mounted, and were attended by a keeper of Mr. Farquharson's as guide, Macdonald*—who, with his shooting jacket, and in his kilt, looked a picture— Grant† on a pony, with our luncheon in two baskets, and Batterbury‡ on another pony. We went through that beautiful wood for about a mile, and then turned and began to ascend gradually, the view getting finer and finer; no road, but not bad ground—moss, heather, and stones. Albert saw some deer when we had been out about three-quarters of an hour, and ran off to stalk them, while I rested; but he arrived just

---

* 'A Jäger of the Prince's, who came from Fort Augustus in the west; he was remarkably tall and handsome. The poor man died of consumption at Windsor, in May, 1860. His eldest son was attaché to the British Legation in Japan. He died in 1866. The third son, Archie, is Jäger to the Prince of Wales, and was for a year with the beloved Prince.'

† 'Head-keeper. He had been nearly twenty years with Sir Robert Gordon, nine as keeper; he was born in Braemar in the year 1810. He is an excellent man, most trustworthy, of singular shrewdness and discretion, and most devotedly attached to the Prince and myself. He has a fine intelligent countenance. The Prince was very fond of him. He has six sons—the second, Alick, is wardrobe-man to our son Leopold: all are good, well-disposed lads, and getting on well in their different occupations. His mother, a fine, hale, old woman of eighty years, 'stops' in a small cottage which the Prince built for her in our village. He, himself, lives in a pretty Lodge called Croft, a mile from Balmoral, which the Prince built for him.'

‡ 'A groom (now dead some years) who followed me in his ordinary dress, with thin boots and gaiters, and seemed anything but happy. He was replaced by a gillie.'

a minute too late. He waited for me on the other side of a stony little burn, which I crossed on my pony, after our faithful Highlanders had moved some stones and made it easier. We then went on a little way, and I got off and walked a bit, and afterwards remounted, Macdonald leading my pony. The view of Ben-na-Bhourd, and indeed of all around, was very beautiful; but as we rose higher we saw mist over Loch-na-Gar. Albert left me to go after ptarmigan, and went on with Grant, while the others remained with me, taking the greatest care of me. Macdonald is a good honest man, and was indefatigable, and poor Batterbury was very anxious also.'

This last extract introduces us to what is one of the most noticeable features of this life in the Highland home—the relations between the Queen and Prince and their Scotch servants. These were of the most friendly nature; and evidently one great charm of days spent so much in the open air and in absolute dependence on the care, skill, and conduct of their attendants, was that the peculiarities of the Highland character made such intimacy possible without any loss of that perfect respect which prevented its ever tending towards familiarity or rudeness. The establishment of such relations fell in exactly with the character both of the Queen and of the Prince. Not the least remarkable amongst those 'Speeches' which first acquainted the people of England generally with the nobleness of the Prince's nature, was that which he delivered in May, 1849, on the foundation of the Servants' Provident Society. How beautiful is the language in which he sketches out what ought in a Christian household to be the relation between the masters and the servants:—

'Who would not feel the deepest interest in the welfare of their domestic servants? Whose heart would fail to sympathise with those who minister to us in all the wants of daily life, attend us in sickness, receive us upon our first appearance in this world, and even extend their cares to our mortal remains; who live under one roof, form one household, and are part of one family?' *

---

* 'Speeches and Addresses of the Prince Consort,' p. 96.

What a noble utterance it is! and how specially needful for these times, when all such bonds as these seem to be too generally relaxing under the influence of a subtle selfishness which conceals its hateful acting under the garb of non-interference on the one side, and independence on the other! How is service elevated from servitude when it is thus baptised with the spirit of mutual regard, of offices rendered with love and received with gratitude, when the personality neither of the master nor the servant is destroyed by their official relations.

No less accordant with the Sovereign's own character is this loftier view of these family relations. Mr. Helps has well remarked on this feature in his introduction, when he notices

'The Patriarchal feeling (if one may apply such a word as "patriarchal" to a lady) which is so strong in the present occupant of the throne. Perhaps there is no person in these realms who takes a more deep and abiding interest in the welfare of the household committed to his charge than our Gracious Queen does in hers, or who feels more keenly what are the reciprocal duties of masters and servants.

'Nor does any one wish more ardently than Her Majesty does, that there should be no abrupt severance of class from class, but rather a gradual blending together of all classes—caused by a full community of interests, a constant interchange of good offices, and a kindly respect felt and expressed by each class to all its brethren in the great brotherhood that forms a nation.

'Those whose duty it has been to attend upon the Queen in matters of business must have noticed that her Majesty, as a person well versed in the conduct of affairs, is wont to keep closely to the point at issue, and to speak of nothing but what is directly connected with the matter before her. But whenever there is an exception to this rule, it arises from Her Majesty's anxious desire to make some inquiry about the welfare of her subjects—to express her sympathy with this man's sorrow, or on that man's bereavement—to ask what is the latest intelligence about this disaster, or that suffering, and what can be done to remedy or assuage it—thus showing, unconsciously, that she is, indeed, the Mother of her People, taking the deepest interest in all that concerns them, without respect of persons, from the highest to the lowest.'

With personal attendants, as we commonly find them in

England, such intimacy is scarcely possible; and to minds longing to substitute for the wretched hollowness of mere paid services this acceptance, with honour on the one side and love on the other, of the conditions of domestic life, the power of resuming 'patriarchal' relations was evidently most grateful. Instances of it, and of the degree in which every particular of the life and family of such attendants became matter of kindly interest to their royal masters, are perpetually reappearing in this volume. They are such as these:—

'We then came to a place which is always wet, but which was particularly bad after the late rain and snow. There was no pony for me to get on; and as I wished not to get my feet wet by walking through the long grass, Albert proposed I should be carried over in a plaid; and Lenchen* was first carried over; but it was held too low, and her feet dangled; so Albert suggested the plaid should be put round the men's shoulders, and that I should sit upon it. Brown and Duncan, the two strongest and handiest, were the two who undertook it, and I sat safely enough with an arm on each man's shoulder, and was carried successfully over. All the Highlanders are so amusing, and really pleasant and instructive to talk to —women as well as men—and the latter so gentlemanlike. As we went along I talked frequently with good Grant.'

'We saw where the Dee rises between the mountains, and such magnificent wild rocks, precipices, and corries. It had a sublime and solemn effect; so wild, so solitary—no one but ourselves and our little party there.

'Albert went on further with the children, but I returned with Grant to my seat on the cairn, as I could not scramble about well. I and Alice rode part of the way, walking wherever it was very steep. Albert and Bertie walked the whole time, Albert, talking so gaily with Grant. Upon which Brown observed to me in simple Highland phrase, "It's very pleasant to walk with a person who is always 'content.'" Yesterday, in speaking of dearest Albert's sport, when I observed he never was cross after bad luck, Brown said, "Every one on the estate says there never was so kind a master; I am sure our only wish is to give satisfaction." I said they certainly did.'†

How well founded was this belief in the Prince's thought-

* Princess Helena.

† 'We were always in the habit of conversing with the Highlanders—with whom one comes so much in contact in the Highlands. The Prince highly appreciated the good-breeding, simplicity, and intelligence, which make it so pleasant, and even instructive to talk to them.'

ful kindness towards his attendants comes well out in such a notice as this:—

'At the bridge at Mar Lodge, Brown lit the lanterns. We gave him and Grant our plaids to put on, as we always do when they have walked a long way with us and drive afterwards.'

'Old John Gordon amused Albert by saying, in speaking of the bad road we had gone, "It's something steep and something rough," and " this is the only best," meaning that it was *very* bad—which was a characteristic reply.'

Here is another instance of the personal interest of the Queen and Prince in all that belonged to their attendants:—

'*September* 16, 1850.—We reached the hut on Loch Muich at three o'clock. At half-past four we walked down to the loch, and got into the boat with our people; Duncan Brown,* P. Cotes, and Leys rowing. They rowed mostly towards the opposite side, which is very fine indeed, and deeply furrowed by the torrents, which form glens and corries where birch and alder trees grow close to the water's edge.

'The moon rose, and was beautifully reflected on the lake, which, with its steep green hills, looked lovely. To add to the beauty, poetry, and wildness of the scene, Cotes † played in the boat; the men, who row very quickly and well now, giving an occasional shout when he played a reel. It reminded me of Sir Walter Scott's lines in the 'Lady of the Lake':

---

* 'The same who, in 1858, became my regular attendant out of doors everywhere in the Highlands; who commenced as gillie in 1849, and was selected by Albert and me to go with my carriage. In 1851 he entered our service permanently, and began in that year leading my pony, and advanced step by step by his good conduct and intelligence. His attention, care, and faithfulness cannot be exceeded; and the state of my health, which of late years has been sorely tried and weakened, renders such qualifications most valuable, and indeed most needful, in a constant attendant upon all occasions. He has since most deservedly been promoted to be an upper servant, and my permanent personal attendant. (December, 1865.) He has all the independence and elevated feelings peculiar to the Highland race, and is singularly straightforward, simple-minded, kind-hearted, and disinterested; always ready to oblige; and of a discretion rarely to be met with. He is now in his fortieth year. His father was a small farmer, who lived at the Bush on the opposite side to Balmoral. He is the second of nine brothers—three of whom have died—two are in Australia and New Zealand, two are living in the neighbourhood of Balmoral; and the youngest, Archie (Archiebald) is valet to our son Leopold, and is an excellent, trustworthy young man.'

† 'Now, since some years, piper to Farquharson of Invercauld.'

> "Ever, as on they bore, more loud
> And louder rung the pibroch proud.
> At first the sound, by distance tame,
> Mellow'd along the waters came,
> And, lingering long by cape and bay,
> Wail'd every harsher note away."

We were home at a little past seven; and it was so still and pretty as we entered the wood, and saw the light flickering from our humble little abode.'

'*September* 12, 1850.—We went with the children and all our party to the Gathering at the Castle of Bracmar, as we did last year. There were the usual games of "putting the stone," "throwing the hammer," and "caber," and racing up the hill of Craig Cheunnich, which was accomplished in less than six minutes and a half; and we were all much pleased to see our gillie Duncan,* who is an active, good-looking young man, win. He was far before the others the whole way. It is a fearful exertion. Mr. Farquharson brought him up to me afterwards.'

'Duncan, in spite of all his exertions yesterday, and having besides walked to and from the Gathering, was the whole time in the water.'

Here is an incident of the same temper with the Duke of Athole:

'Where the road for carriages ends, and the glen widens, were our ponies. There we saw old Peter Frazer, the former head-keeper there, now walking with the aid of two sticks!

'We started on our ponies, the Duke and his men (twelve altogether) on foot—Sandy McAra, now head-keeper, grown old and grey, and two pipers, preceded us; the two latter playing alternately the whole time, which had a most cheerful effect. The wild strains sounded so softly amid those noble hills; and our caravan winding along—our people and the Duke's, all in kilts, and the ponies made altogether a most picturesque scene.

'One of the Duke's keepers, Donald Macbeath, is a guardsman, and was in the Crimea. He is a celebrated marksman, and a fine-looking man, as all the Duke's men are. For some little time it was easy riding, but soon we came to a rougher path, more on the "brae" of the hill, where the pony

---

* 'One of our keepers since 1851: an excellent, intelligent man, much liked by the Prince. He, like many others, spit blood after running the race up that steep hill in this short space of time, and he has never been so strong since. The running up hill has in consequence been discontinued. He lives in a cottage at the back of Craig Gowan (commanding a beautiful view) called Robrech, which the Prince built for him.

required to be led, which I always have done, either when it is at all rough or bad, or when the pony has to be got on faster.

'The Duke walked near me the greater part of the time; amusingly saying, in reference to former times, that he did not offer to lead me, as he knew I had no confidence in him. I replied, laughingly, "Oh, no, only I like best being led by the person I am accustomed to."

'.... Lunched at a place called Dalcronachie, looking up a glen towards Loch Loch—on a high bank overhanging the Tilt. A few minutes brought us to the celebrated ford of the Tarff (Poll Tarff it is called), which is very deep, and after heavy rain almost impassable. The Duke offered to lead the pony on one side, and talked of Sandy for the other side, but I asked for Brown (whom I have far the most confidence in) to lead the pony, the Duke taking hold of it (as he did frequently) on the other side. Sandy McAra, the guide, and the two pipers went first, playing all the time. To all appearance the ford of the Tarff was not deeper than the other fords, but once in it the men were above their knees —and suddenly in the middle, where the current, from the fine, high, full falls, is very strong, it was nearly up to the men's waists. Here Sandy returned, and I said to the Duke (which he afterwards joked with Sandy about) that I thought he (Sandy) had better take the Duke's place; he did so, and we came very well through, all the others following, the men chiefly wading—Albert (close behind me) and the others riding through.'

Nor was this interest in their attendants confined to, though it was so eminently drawn forth by, the Highlanders. Here is a note of the first stay at Alt-na-Giuthasach:—

'Margaret French, my maid Caroline's maid, Löhlein,* Albert's valet, a cook, Shackle,† and Macdonald, are the only persons with us in the house, old John Gordon and his wife excepted.'

'The scenery is beautiful here, so wild and grand—real severe Highland scenery, with trees in the hollow. We had various scrambles in and out of the boat and along the shore, and saw three hawks and caught seventy trout. I wish an artist could have been there to sketch the scene; it was so picturesque—the boat, the net, and the people in their kilts in the water and on the shore. In going back Albert rowed and Macdonald steered: and the lights were beautiful.

---

* 'This faithful and trusty valet nursed his dear master most devotedly through his sad illness in December, 1861, and is now always with me as my personal groom of the chambers or valet. I gave him a house near Windsor Castle, where he resides when the Court are there. He is a native of Coburg. His father has been for fifty years Förster at Fülbach, close to Coburg.'

† 'Who was very active and efficient. He is now a Page.'

'After dinner we walked round the little garden. The silence and solitude, only interrupted by the waving of the fir-trees, were very solemn and striking.'

Such natural kindness must indeed have won the hearts of a people so constitutionally loyal as the Highlanders, and throw back a stream of sunshine on the daily life of those whose height of station too commonly robs them of the richer colouring which belongs to the lower valleys; neither was it confined to the immediate members of the Royal household. Here is to us a delightful entry:—

'*Saturday, September* 26, 1857.—Albert went out with Alfred for the day, and I walked out with the two girls and Lady Churchill, stopped at the shop and made some purchases for poor people and others; drove a little way, got out and walked up the hill to Balnacroft, Mrs. P. Farquharson's, and she walked round with us to some of the cottages to show me where the poor people lived and to tell them who I was. Before we went into any we met an old woman, who, Mrs. Farquharson said, was very poor, eighty-eight years old, and mother to the former distiller. I gave her a warm petticoat, and the tears rolled down her old cheeks, and she shook my hands and prayed God to bless me: it was very touching.

'I went into a small cabin of old Kitty Kear's, who is eighty-six years old—quite erect, and who welcomed us with a great air of dignity. She sat down and spun. I gave her also a warm petticoat. She said, "May the Lord ever attend ye and yours, here and hereafter; and may the Lord be a guide to ye, and keep ye from all harm." She was quite surprised at Vicky's height; great interest is taken in her. We went on to a cottage (formerly Jean Gordon's), to visit old widow Symons, who is "past fourscore," with a nice rosy face, but was bent quite double; she was most friendly, shaking hands with us all, asking which was I, and repeating many kind blessings: "May the Lord attend ye with mirth and with joy; may He ever be with ye in this world, and when ye leave it." To Vicky, when told she was going to be married, she said, "May the Lord be a guide to ye in your future, and may every happiness attend ye." She was very talkative; and when I said I hoped to see her again, she expressed an expectation that "she should be called any day," and so did Kitty Kear.[*]

'We went into three other cottages: to Mrs. Symons's (daughter-in-law to the old widow living next door), who had an "unwell boy;" then across a little burn to another old woman's; and afterwards peeped into

---

[*] 'She died in Jan. 1865.'

Blair, the fiddler's. We drove back and got out again to visit old Mrs. Grant (Grant's mother), who is so tidy and clean, and to whom I gave a dress and handkerchief, and she said, " You're too kind to me, you're over kind to me, ye give me more every year, and I get older every year." After talking some time with her, she said, " I am happy to see ye looking so nice." She had tears in her eyes, and speaking of Vicky's going, said, " I am very sorry, and I think she is sorry hersel';" and, having said she feared she would not see her (the Princess) again, said : " I am very sorry I said that, but I meant no harm ; I always say just what I think, not what is fut" (fit). Dear old lady; she is such a pleasant person.

'Really the affection of these good people, who are so hearty and so happy to see you, taking interest in everything, is very touching and gratifying.'

Here, to vary the scene, comes in what cannot fail to interest all our lady readers : the very form and words of that utterance at all times, even to Royal lips, most difficult to frame—a proposal :—

'*September* 29, 1855.—Our dear Victoria was this day engaged to Prince Frederick William of Prussia, who had been on a visit to us since the 14th. He had already spoken to us, on the 20th, of his wishes ; but we were uncertain, on account of her extreme youth, whether he should speak to her himself, or wait till he came back again. However, we felt it was better he should do so ; and during our ride up Craig-na-Ban this afternoon, he picked a piece of white heather (the emblem of " good luck "), which he gave to her ; and this enabled him to make an allusion to his hopes and wishes, as they rode down Glen Girnoch, which led to this happy conclusion.'

Here are some of their healthy amusements, some of them requiring spirit enough to enter into them. Many a fine lady, we suspect, would shrink from taking the Queen's share in a ' drive ' in the Balloch Buie :—

'*September* 18, 1848.—We mounted our ponies, Bertie riding Grant's pony on the deer-saddle, and being led by a gillie, Grant walking by his side. Macdonald and several gillies were with us, and we were preceded by Bowman and old Arthur Farquharson, a deerstalker of Invercauld's. They took us up a beautiful path winding through the trees and heather in the Balloch Buie ; but when we had got about a mile or more they discovered deer. A " council of war " was held in a whisper, and we turned back and went the whole way down again, and rode along to the keeper's lodge, where we turned up the glen immediately below Craig Daign, through a beautiful part of the wood, and went on along the track till we came to the foot of the craig, where we all dismounted.

'We scrambled up an almost perpendicular place to where there was a little *box*, made of hurdles and interwoven with branches of fir and heather, about five feet in height. There we seated ourselves with Bertie, Macdonald lying in the heather near us, watching and quite concealed; some had gone round to beat, and others again were at a little distance. We sat quite still, and sketched a little; I doing the landscape and some trees, Albert drawing Macdonald as he lay there. This lasted for nearly an hour, when Albert fancied he heard a distant sound, and, in a few minutes, Macdonald whispered that he saw stags, and that Albert should wait and take a steady aim. We then heard them coming past. Albert did not look over the box, but through it, and fired through the branches, and then again over the box. The deer retreated; but Albert felt certain he had hit a stag. He ran up to the keepers, and at that moment they called from below that they "had got him," and Albert ran on to see. I waited for a bit; but soon scrambled on with Bertie and Macdonald's help; and Albert joined me directly, and we all went down and saw a magnificent stag, "a royal," which had dropped, soon after Albert had hit him, at one of the men's feet. The sport was successful, and every one was delighted—Macdonald and the keepers in particular;—the former saying, "that it was her Majesty's coming out that had brought the good luck." I was supposed to have "a lucky foot," of which the Highlanders "think a great deal." We walked down to the place we last came up, got into the carriage, and were home by half-past two o'clock.'

Some of the most enjoyable days recorded in the Journal were those on which, all state having been thrown aside, excursions were made under a strict incognito. Here are one or two extracts, put together from different trips of this character:—

'A few seconds brought us over to the road, where there were two shabby vehicles, one a kind of barouche, into which Albert and I got, Lady Churchill and General Grey into the other—a break; each with a pair of small and rather miserable horses, driven by a man from the box. Grant was on our carriage, and Brown on the other. We had gone so far forty miles, at least twenty on horseback. We had decided to call ourselves *Lord and Lady Churchill and party,* Lady Churchill passing as *Miss Spencer,* and General Grey as *Dr. Grey!* Brown once forgot this, and called me "Your Majesty" as I was getting into the carriage; and Grant on the box once called Albert "Your Royal Highness;" which set us off laughing, but no one observed it.

'We had a long three hours' drive.

'Most striking was the utter, and to me very refreshing, solitude. Hardly a habitation! and hardly meeting a soul! It gradually grew dark. We stopped at a small half-way house for the horses to take some water; and the few people about stared vacantly at the two simple vehicles.

'The mountains gradually disappeared—the evening was mild, with a few drops of rain. On and on we went, till at length we saw lights, and drove through a long and straggling "toun," and turned down a small court to the door of the inn. Here we got out quickly—Lady Churchill and General Grey not waiting for us. We went up a small staircase, and were shown to our bed-room at the top of it—very small, but clean—with a large four-post bed which nearly filled the whole room. Opposite was the drawing and dining-room in one—very tidy and well-sized. Then came the room where Albert dressed, which was very small. The two maids (Jane Shackle* was with me) had driven over by another road in the waggonette, Stewart driving them. Made ourselves "clean and tidy," and then sat down to our dinner. Grant and Brown were to have waited on us, but were "bashful" and did not. A ringletted woman did everything; and, when dinner was over, removed the cloth and placed the bottle of wine (our own which we had brought) on the table with the glasses, which was the old English fashion. The dinner was very fair, and all very clean.'

'*Wednesday, September* 5.—A misty, rainy morning. Had not slept very soundly. We got up rather early, and sat working and reading in the drawing-room till the breakfast was ready, for which we had to wait some little time. Good tea and bread and butter, and some excellent porridge. Jane Shackle (who was very useful and attentive) said that they had all supped together, namely, the two maids, and Grant, Brown, Stewart, and Walker (who was still there), and were very merry in the "commercial room." The people were very amusing about us. The woman came in while they were at dinner, and said to Grant, "Dr. Grey wants you," which nearly upset the gravity of all the others: then they told Jane, "Your lady gives no trouble;" and Grant in the morning called up to Jane, "Does his lordship want me?" One could look on the street, which is a very long wide one, with detached houses, from our window. It was perfectly quiet, no one stirring, except here and there a man driving a cart, or a boy going along on his errand. General Grey bought himself a watch in a shop for 2*l*.!

---

* 'One of my wardrobe-maids, and daughter to the Page mentioned earlier.'

'At length, at about ten minutes to ten o'clock, we started in the same carriages and the same way as yesterday, and drove . . . . . to Tomantoul . . . . . the most tumble-down, poor-looking place I ever saw. . . . . .

'We mounted our ponies a short way out of the town. We came upon a beautiful view, looking down upon the Avon and up a fine glen. There we rested and took luncheon. While Brown was unpacking and arranging our things, I spoke to him and to Grant, who was helping, about not having waited on us, as they ought to have done, at dinner last night and at breakfast, as we had wished; and Brown answered, he was afraid he should not do it rightly; I replied we did not wish to have a stranger in the room, and they must do so another time.

' . . . . . In order to get on, as it was late, and we had eight miles to ride, our men—at least Brown and two of the others—walked before us at a fearful pace, so that we had to trot to keep up at all. Grant rode frequently on the deer pony; the others seemed, however, a good deal tired with the two long days' journey, and were glad to get on Albert's or the General's pony to give themselves a lift; but their willingness, readiness, cheerfulness, indefatigableness, are very admirable, and make them most delightful servants. As for Grant and Brown they are perfect—discreet, careful, intelligent, attentive, ever ready to do what is wanted; and the latter, particularly, is handy and willing to do everything and anything, and to overcome every difficulty, which makes him one of my best servants anywhere.

'What a delightful, successful expedition ! . . . . To my dear Albert do we owe it, for he always thought it would be delightful, having gone on many similar expeditions in former days himself. He enjoyed it very much.'

Here is a second excursion :—

'At a quarter past seven o'clock we reached the small quiet town, or rather village, of Fettercairn, for it was very small—not a creature stirring, and we got out at the quiet little inn "Ramsey Arms," quite unobserved, and went at once upstairs. There was a very nice drawing-room, and next to it a dining-room, both very clean and tidy—then to the left our bed-room, which was excessively small, but also very clean and neat, and much better furnished than at Grantown. Alice had a nice room, the same size as ours; then came a mere morsel of one (with a "press bed"), in which Albert dressed; and then came Lady Churchill's bed-room just beyond. Louis and General Grey had rooms in an hotel, called "The Temperance Hotel," opposite. We dined at eight, a very nice, clean, good dinner. Grant and Brown waited. They were rather nervous, but General Grey and Lady Churchill carved, and they had only to change the plates, which Brown soon got into the way of doing. A little girl of the house came in to help—but Grant turned her round to prevent her looking at us! The landlord and landlady knew who we were, but *no one else* except the coachman, and they kept the secret admirably.

'The evening being bright and moonlight and very still, we all went out, and walked through the whole village, where not a creature moved, ... hearing nothing whatever—not a leaf moving—but the distant barking of a dog! Suddenly we heard a drum and fifes! We were greatly alarmed, fearing we had been recognised; but Louis and General Grey, who went back, saw nothing whatever. Still, as we walked slowly back, we heard the noise from time to time—and when we reached the inn door we stopped, and saw six men march up with fifes and a drum (not a creature taking any notice of them), go down the street, and back again. Grant and Brown were out, but had no idea what it could be. Albert asked the little maid, and the answer was, " It's just a band," and that it walked about in this way twice a week. How odd! It went on playing some time after we got home. We sat till half-past ten working, and Albert reading—and then retired to rest.'

'*Saturday, September* 21.—Got to sleep after two or three o'clock. The morning was dull and close, and misty, with a little rain; hardly any one stirring; but a few people at their work. A traveller had arrived at night, and wanted to come up into the dining-room, which is the "commercial travellers' room;" and they had difficulty in telling him he could *not* stop there. He joined Grant and Brown at their tea, and on his asking "What's the matter here?" Grant answered, "It's a wedding party from Aberdeen." At "The Temperance Hotel" they were very anxious to know whom they had got. All, except General Grey, breakfasted a little before nine. Brown acted as my servant, brushing my skirt and boots, and taking any message, and Grant as Albert's valet.

'At a quarter to ten we started the same way as before.' . . . . .

'At Kingussie there was a small, curious, chattering crowd of people—who, however, did not really make us out, but evidently suspected who we were. Grant and Brown kept them off the carriages, and gave them evasive answers, directing them to the wrong carriage, which was most amusing. One old gentleman, with a high wide-awake, was especially inquisitive.

'We started again, and went on and on, passing through the village of Newton of Benchar, where the footman McDonald * comes from.'

In the midst of these scenes of family affection, amusement, and repose, the distant sounds of the great world, of

---

* 'He died at Abergeldie, last year, of consumption; and his widow, an excellent person, daughter of Mitchell, the blacksmith, at Balmoral, is now my wardrobe maid.'

which those withdrawn persons were yet the living heart, come upon our ears with a solemnity and strangeness of intrusion. Here is one of rejoicing:—

'*September* 10, 1855.—All were in constant expectation of more telegraphic despatches. At half-past ten o'clock two arrived—one for me, and one for Lord Granville. I began reading mine, which was from Lord Clarendon, with details from Marshal Pélissier, of the further destruction of the Russian ships; and Lord Granville said, "I have still better news;" on which he read, "From General Simpson—*Sevastopol is in the hands of the Allies.*" God be praised for it!'

Here is a second instance, in another tone; one which will be read with interest wherever the English tongue or any translation of it can be read:—

'*Alt-na-Giuthasach, Thursday, September* 16, 1852.—We were startled this morning at seven o'clock, by a letter from Colonel Phipps, enclosing a telegraphic despatch with the report from the sixth edition of the "Sun," of the Duke of Wellington's death the day before yesterday, which report, however, we did not at all believe. Would to God that we had been right; and that this day had not been cruelly saddened in the afternoon.

'We walked a long way on the top of the very steep hills overhanging the loch . . . . . Here I suddenly missed my watch, which the dear old Duke had given me; and, not being certain whether I had put it on or not, I asked Mackenzie* to go back and inquire. We walked on until we reached the higher part of the Glassalt. . . .

'Then we began the descent of the Glassalt.

'We got off our ponies, and I had just sat down to sketch, when Mackenzie returned, saying my watch was safe at home, and bringing letters: amongst them there was one from Lord Derby, which I tore open, and alas! it contained the confirmation of the fatal news, that England's, or rather Britain's pride, her glory, her hero, the greatest man she ever had produced, was no more. Sad day! Great and irreparable national loss!

'Lord Derby enclosed a few lines from Lord Charles Wellesley, saying that his dear great father had died on Tuesday at three o'clock, after a few hours' illness and no suffering. God's will be done! The day must have come; the Duke was eighty-three. It is well for him that he has been taken when still in the possession of his great mind, and without a long illness,—but what a *loss!* One cannot think of this country without "the Duke,"—our immortal hero!

---

* 'One of our keepers, and a very good man; he lives at Alt-na-Giuthasach.'

'In him centred almost every earthly honour a subject could possess. His position was the highest a subject ever had,—above party,—looked up to by all,—revered by the whole nation,—the friend of the Sovereign. And *how* simply he carried these honours! With what singleness of purpose, what straightforwardness, what courage, were all the motives of his actions guided. The Crown never possessed—and I fear never *will*—so *devoted*, loyal, and faithful a subject, so staunch a supporter! To *us* (who, alas! have lost now so many of our valued and experienced friends), his loss is *irreparable*, for his readiness to aid and advise, if it could be of use to us, and to overcome any and every difficulty, was unequalled. To Albert he showed the greatest kindness and the utmost confidence. His experience and his knowledge of the past were so great too; he was a link which connected us with bygone times, with the last century. Not an eye will be dry in the whole country.

'We hastened down on foot to the head of Loch Muich; and then rode home, in a heavy shower, to Alt-na-Giuthasach. Our whole enjoyment was spoilt; a gloom overhung all of us.

'We wrote to Lord Derby and Lord Charles Wellesley.'

Amidst all the utterances of politicians, historians, and poets, there is to our mind a grandeur of its own in the simplicity of these words of sorrow from the throne of England.

It is easy, even without knowing the weight of those golden chains of reserve and ceremony with which kings are fettered, to imagine the enjoyments which such an interlude in Royal life as Balmoral afforded when its halls were lighted with that brightness of family affection which played so continually there. For, amidst all the keen relish for nature and for freedom which these pages betray, still the one ever prevailing sentiment of every page of the Journal is the love of the appreciating wife for the grand husband whom Providence had given her. Always this is re-appearing. The 'love for Balmoral' itself based itself on this far deeper affection:—

'*October* 13, 1856.—Every year my heart becomes more fixed in this dear Paradise, and so much more so now, that *all* has become my dearest Albert's *own* creation, own work, own building, own laying out, as at Osborne; and his great taste, and the impress of his dear hand, have been stamped everywhere. He was very busy to-day, settling and arranging many things for next year.'

There is a continual perception of his love of learning everything which was to be learned:—

'We rode the whole way, and Albert only walked the last two miles. He took a Gaelic lesson during our ride, asking Macdonald, who speaks it with great purity, many words, and making him talk to Jemmie Coutts. Albert has already picked up many words.'

His shortest absence clouded all the scene:—

'*September* 14, 1859.—I felt very low-spirited at my dearest Albert having to leave at one o'clock for Aberdeen, to preside at the meeting of the British Association.'

'So sad not to find my darling husband at home.'

We can conceive some critics finding fault with such revelations as these. But we believe them to be entirely wrong in their estimate of man's nature, and we are confident that the general assent of all deeper minds will reverse their sentence.

To numbers amongst her subjects these unintentional delineations of the character and mode of life of the highest persons in the realm—thorough sun-pictures as they are, catching the passing emotions of the hour, and writing them down with a passionless exactness—will be not a little welcome. Their effect must be to quicken the emotions of that loyalty which at this moment, more than almost any other, is of such value to this nation. For they substitute for the lifeless names of king and queen the living queenly Person to whom the abstract theory of loyalty must, unless it is a very cold abstraction indeed, be able to attach itself. They show her as the mistress of her household, entering with a most unusual affectionateness of care into the individual welfare of every attendant on her person; as, even in the disturbances of a tour, herself teaching her Royal children; as mingling, by a most natural transition, with these domestic duties the cares of the Head of the larger family of the State; above all, they show her as a loving wife, delighting in her husband's companionship; proud, as a wife should be, of his grace and intellect; admiring his noble person; entering with intense zest into all his successes, from the triumph of the successful deer-stalk to his winning the applauses of the gathered scientific sages:—

'*September* 15, 1859.—I heard by telegram last night that Albert's reception was admirable, and that all was going off as well as possible. Thank God.'

'All the gentlemen spoke in very high terms of my beloved Albert's admirable speech, the good it had done, and the general satisfaction it had caused.'

And alas!—we must say it—for this land, and alas! for that true mother, wife, and queen, they shew her—when the blow had fallen and the pall was drawn over that life of love,—suffering as none can suffer but one in that height of station which for the most part is barren of such happiness as she knew, and which by its very exaltation leaves her now with a consciousness of loneliness which not even such a bereavement would bring upon the humblest of her subjects. How touching is such an entry as this!—

'Grant told me in May, 1862, that, when the Prince stopped behind with him, looking at the Choils which he intended as a deer-forest for the Prince of Wales, and giving his directions as to the planting in Glen Muich, he said to Grant, "You and I may be dead and gone before that." In less than three months, alas! his words were verified as regards himself! He was ever cheerful, but ever ready and prepared.'

The heart of any man must be judicially hardened who can read without emotion the last entry of the last Highland excursion:—

'We went back on our side of the river; and if we had been a little earlier Albert might have got a stag, but it was too late. The moon rose and shone most beautifully, and we returned at twenty minutes to seven o'clock, much pleased and interested with this delightful expedition. Alas! I fear our *last* great one! (*It was our last one!*—1867.')

The only words which can follow this entry are those in which the royal writer pours forth in the dedication of the volume the whole of her heart :—

'To the dear memory of him who made the life of the writer bright and happy, these simple records are lovingly and gratefully inscribed.'

THE ARCHBISHOPS OF CANTERBURY OF THE REFORMATION.

(*October*, 1868.)

THE two last volumes of the Dean of Chichester's 'Lives of the Archbishops,' beginning with the archiepiscopate of Warham, and ending with the death of Cranmer, contain the records of the great crisis of the English Reformation. The work has from the first steadily increased in interest. Not only has the Dean's hand become readier in the performance of its task, but the subjects of his pen have been connected with greater national events, and far richer original matter has been open to his examination. The battles of the Kites and Crows have passed on through the demigod period, and become the contentions of men in circumstances somewhat like our own, and with objects at least analogous to those for which we are striving.

This new interest rises to its height in these last two volumes. The Reformation period must always rivet the attention of Englishmen. For then, whatever evils were inseparable from it, was the birth-time of their liberties both in Church and State. Its long sufferings were but travail pangs, and though many of the attendant operations were rudely managed, with no little loss of vital energy and threatenings of still greater evils, yet was the birth at last gracious, and on those who were the instruments of its accomplishment must always rest with the deepest interest the enquiring gaze of after generations.

* 'Lives of the Archbishops of Canterbury.' By Walter Farquhar Hook, D.D., F.R.S., Dean of Chichester. Vols. VI. and VII. New Series. Reformation Period. 2 vols. London, 1868.

Never, perhaps, was this more the case than at the present time, when we are passing again through many struggles both of religious thought and of national policy not unlike those with which our fathers grappled. For the great questions which stirred so deeply the souls of our Reformers, that they were ready to burn and to be burnt at a thousand stakes to procure their settlement, seem, after a torpor of three hundred years, to have suddenly reawoke amongst us, and we have almost each one of us again to examine the Pope's claim to supremacy and infallibility with all the train of teaching which is involved in such an admission:—the necessity of auricular confession; the celibacy of the clergy; the maiming, for the laity, of the great Sacrament of the Eucharist; the cultus of the blessed Virgin Mary; the offering of masses for the quick and dead; and purgatory with its pains, its indulgences, and its corresponding pecuniary advantages. Questions of public policy, too, which were then in course of settlement, and the settlement of which has been thenceforward interwoven with the very warp of our national life, are all suddenly re-opened. The existence of a Church really national—the only bulwark as our fathers believed, and as our children may find to their cost, against the arrogance and the usurpations of Rome—is suddenly threatened. For if England and Ireland be one united kingdom, with one Established Church, and not two separate monarchies loosely allied by the overshadowing of two Crowns Imperial resting for the time upon one brow, the destruction of the Church's nationality in one island must logically imply its destruction as a national Church in both, although it may still survive as an anomaly in one. To build this up, which it is now so lightly proposed to pull down, was, in fact, the master aim of the great Reformation statesmen. Thus, in the grand old English of the Statute of Appeals, it was declared that:—

'By divers sundry old authentic histories and chronicles it is manifestly declared and exposited that this realm of England is an empire and hath so been accepted in the world; governed by one supreme head and king, having the dignity and royal estate of the imperial crown of the same; unto whom a body politic compact of all sorts and degrees of people, divided in terms by names of spiritualty and temporalty, be bound, and ought to bear next to God a natural and humble obedience. . . . the body spiritual whereof having power when any cause of the law divine happened to come in question, or of spiritual, having declared, interpret, and shewed by that part of the body politic called the spiritualty, now usually called the English Church, which also hath been reported and also found of that sort, that both for knowledge, integrity and sufficiency of numbers it hath been always thought to be, and is also at this hour, sufficient and meet of itself without the interfering of any exterior person or persons, to declare and determine all such doubts, and to administer all such offices and duties as to their room spiritual doth appertain.'

It was on this foundation of the unquestioned existence of a national Church of the empire, as a body spiritual, that the usurped claim of the Bishop of Rome to interfere with this kingdom was by enactment fully and for ever excluded, and all attempts to re-introduce his jurisdiction was branded with the guilt of treason against the high reserved nationality of the realm which centered in the Crown of England. How well that bulwark was conceived, how straight its lines were devised and drawn across the main stream and flow of Papal aggression, how deeply laid were its foundations, how well compacted were its stones, has been shown beyond the possibility of question by all succeeding events: by its standing, under Henry VIII. and Edward VI., the first buffet of those proud waves, by its speedy restoration from the demolition attempted under Philip and Mary, and by its continuance from Elizabeth to Victoria as the very breakwater of our nationality against whatever storms have burst from time to time upon us from the dark and turbulent depths of that spiritual Black Sea, which has never ceased to rage against our borders. This it is now proposed to raze, because its existence proclaiming of necessity the incorporation of Ireland with Great Britain is a standing insult to those who are thus reminded that they are no longer what their fathers were, an independent kingdom, entitled to an independent spiritualty. When such proposals are made, there must, for all thoughtful men, be a peculiar interest in studying anew the history of that time when these defences were erected. Then, too, it must be the course of wisdom to see why our forefathers toiled so hard to raise them, and what may be our condition when we have agreed to their demolition.

It may be presumed that it would be by alleging the exceeding importance of the era described in these two volumes that the publisher (for it is not credible that their respected author had anything to do with it) has called them a 'new series.' But the idea of a 'new series' is really at variance with the whole aim and purpose of these volumes and of every line in them from their first beginning. For one leading object of the Dean has evidently been to show the unbrokenness of this Church of England from the beginning until now; to exhibit it one and the same body from the mission of Augustine to the present hour; to show it protesting against the rising aggressions of Rome under the Plantagenets, and completing and enforcing the protest with the brave hearts and strong hands of the Tudor kings.

'When we speak,' he says, 'of the continuity and perpetuity of the English Church, we only affirm an historical fact. By both Church and State measures had been adopted to annihilate the Papal authority in England, long before any notion was entertained of dealing with any points of doctrine. In the twenty-eighth year of Henry's reign, when King and Parliament and Church were vehement in their opposition to Protestantism, some of the chief Acts against the Pope and his pretensions were passed in Parliament. . . . . The Church of England was anti-papal before it was reformed; at the commencement of the dispute between the Church of England and the Court of Rome, in the sixteenth century, the State accepted as a fact what the Church affirmed, that the work to be done by the co-operation of the civil and ecclesiastical authorities in England was not the displacing of the old Church and the supplanting of it by some new sect, but the gradual reformation of that old Catholic Church, which had been established here in the first instance by the joint labour and devotion of Augustine the first Archbishop of Canterbury, and Ethelbert King of Kent, the Bretwalda.'

One chief merit of these volumes may be traced to the distinctness with which their author has throughout realised this unbroken continuity of the Church of England. For it has saved him from the necessity of considering Cranmer as in any real sense the founder of a new Communion, and so has made it easy for him to draw his character with absolute impartiality. The Romanist who charges him with the crime of founding, instead of the old Catholic Church of England, the new schismatic body which has replaced it, and the ultra-Protestant who believes that he and his fellows founded a new Church at the Reformation, are alike incapable of such impartiality: to the one he is from first to last an apostate and a traitor; to the other he is, with the like universal applause, a saint and a martyr. In these pages he is one in a long line of Archbishops of Canterbury. He is distinguishable from others especially by the circumstances of his episcopate. His days are cast when a mighty change was passing over the minds of his countrymen; in that change he himself largely participated, and few were themselves borne along by the current more palpably and completely. Something he contributed towards the change; he is to be tried, like other men, by what he was, by what he affected, by what he let slip. There is here no temptation to exaggerate either his excellences or his defects. He was neither a demigod whose personality is lost on the rise of a new empire, nor a convicted villain who treasonably overturned a well-balanced kingdom. Viewed as he was, and not through these distorting media, he appears to be rather an ordinary man: affectionate, forgiving, gentle, caring for and making good provision for his family, very fond of field sports, physically brave, but morally not over courageous, sincerely religious, a great master of English, a diligent student of his Bible, and, though not eager for intellectual or spiritual discoveries, with a mind slowly but surely receptive of increased measures of truth as they were presented to him.

But this is by no means the only advantage which the clear mastery of this truth has given to the writer of these volumes. It has aided him as an historian as well as a biographer. It has kept him clear from the strange confusion which represents the Church of England before the Reformation as having been a spiritual body almost independent of the State, and since the Reformation as an Act of Parliament establishment which has consciously renounced its claims to an independent spiritual personality. In truth, before the Reformation, as well as since the Reformation, the Church of England was, on one side, an Act of Parliament Church. It was a branch of the one Holy Apostolical Church, settled within this realm, welcomed by the realm, honoured, endowed, established; and so exercising upon certain honourable conditions its spiritual functions in the land. What the Crown, the Parliament, and the people claimed was not to have created the spiritual body, with its creeds, doctrines, ministry and sacramental life; but to have created, and so to have the right to enforce, and if need were to modify, the conditions under which that life and ministry were exercised. All the struggles of the Acts of Provisors and the like were the exercise of this power of the realm over the external conditions through which the spiritual power acted. At the time of the Reformation this struggle reached its most critical point. The State, and to a great degree the national clergy also, felt that the original conditions of acknowledged nationality under which the spiritual body ought to act had been infringed. The nation rose in all ranks and orders to rectify these broken conditions. The strife at its beginning was limited to this. But, as soon as it broke out, it became evident that the violation of these more outward conditions was itself an effect of yet higher obligations, and that the great deposit of religious truth itself had been corrupted by its guardians. The second wave broke upon the crest of the first, and the religious reformation rolled in upon the ecclesiastical. The Church, which had been the subject of old Acts of Parliaments, became the subject of new Acts, which aimed at restoring the old compact between the spirituality and the temporalty to their original conditions, and guarding for the future against the evils of the past. But whilst as an establishment the Church was brought, as the consequence and punishment of former Popish insolence, under straiter bonds, there was no leaven of real Erastianism in the change. From first to last the spiritual power, and the ecclesiastical conditions under which it was to be exercised in England, are kept wholly distinct in the Acts of Henry VIII. 'The Institution of a Christian Man' laid clearly down this principle. 'Christ and his Apostles did institute and ordain in the New Testament, besides the civil powers and governance of kings and princes, that there should also be continually in the Church militant certain other ministers and officers, who should have special power, authority, and commission under Christ to preach and teach the word of God to His people, to dispense and administer the sacraments of God unto them, and by the same to confer and give the graces of the Holy Ghost.' 'This office, this power, this authority was committed and given by Christ and his apostles to certain persons only: that is to say, to priests or bishops, whom they did elect, call, and admit thereunto by their prayers and imposition of hands.' * The English language is scarcely capable of being made to express a declaration more at variance than

---

* 'Formularies of Faith,' 101-104, quoted in 'Lives of Archbishops,' vol. ii. pp. 164, 165.

this with what we read in the Erastian press of the day as the result of the change intended and wrought by the Reformation on the old English Church and its pretensions.

The Dean's treatment of his subject has risen with its requirements; and these two volumes, though marked throughout with the strongest family resemblance to those before them, are in every respect far the best of the series. There is more study of original documents, more grasp of character, a bolder announcement of principles, and a broader and more philosophic estimate of the flow of the events which he describes, both in their causes and in their consequences. The story, moreover, turns itself more naturally round the two Archbishops, and there is more power shown of seizing upon and delineating character.

This, indeed, is one of the Dean's strongest points. There is a vein of humour peeping out through the whole narrative, giving to it a deep human interest for the reader. Without such a vein of humour in the depictor, all delineations of character must be utterly tame and lifeless. A man must have lived amongst his fellows, must have read their characters, must have seen their weaknesses, sympathised with them in their struggles, and admired their great qualities, before the history of the past will give up to him living men and women, instead of mere names or stiff brocaded figures. There is, of course, a danger attending such a power. From more than one popular writer of history it is not difficult to extract the secret of his success in painting the broad panorama of history. He selects a picturesque period, in which many actors appear naturally on the scene. It may be a rebellion, a conspiracy, or a council. He analyses their characters, settles in his own mind from the hints dropped concerning them their resemblance to still living men, whom he can study in their actual words and deeds; and he then proceeds to paint, under the old dress and label, with the old name, one or other of the men who move and act around him according to what he has assumed to be their similitude to the dead. This produces, no doubt, a life-like and interesting narrative ; but it is a work of fancy, not of history. Such historical portraits may be speaking likenesses of the living men actually drawn, but they are no more real historical characters than was the hero of the sermon of the young dissenting preacher who moved his audience to tears by the touching portrait which he drew from the text, 'Tekel, thou art weighed in the balances and art found wanting.' The Tekel of the moving discourse was quite as real a man as are the heroes of some of our recent popular historians. Strong conscientiousness and sterling good sense keep the Dean from such slips ; and where he sees these parallels, instead of substituting the living analogue for the dead man, or playing, with a sort of literary ventriloquism, the trick which is attributed to St. Dunstan, and speaking himself through silent lips, he points out—dangerously sometimes to gravity—with his humorous pen, the reproduction of the present in the past.

We have already said that these volumes rise above the level of the earlier narrative. They are thoroughly readable, and will amply repay careful reading, not only from the great events they so faithfully chronicle, but also from the mode in which the narrative is put together. That same quaint humour of which we have spoken knits into a pleasant unity the present and the past. Thus, 'in most monasteries,' he tells us, ' there arose two sets ; what would now be called " the fast set" would bring against the " strict set" the accusation so easy to make, and so difficult to disprove—of hypocrisy.' So with a sly glance at certain modern practices of Lenten obligations, he records of Warham's day, that, ' although men ate and drank to repletion, and some of the feasters were obliged in retirement to rehabilitate their constitutions by submitting to a course of physic and blood-letting, still the dietary consisted exclusively of fish. The taste of the piscivorous multitude may not have been discriminating when regaling on well-concocted conger, and ling, and halibut, disguised under various condiments and sauces, . . . on which the genius of the artist who presided over the culinary department must have been called into full play, . . . they may have thought the difference slight between fish and flesh.' He finds, too, when noting the applause which followed a singularly dull speech of the good Archbishop, with a glance all our readers will appreciate, the opportunity of suggesting that its enthusiastic reception only proved 'that Warham was endued with sweetness of voice and a natural eloquence, such as we ourselves occasionally witness in preachers who, inferior in point of ability, are surrounded by attentive, applauding, and enthusiastic auditors.' Does the living experience of a Dean of Chichester force itself to light under the statement concerning Collet, that the Dean found it more difficult to contend with the Cretan bellies of the underlings of his Church than to struggle against the Bœotian intellects of his opponents at Oxford? Nor are the laity altogether spared. It would not require Mr. Croker's ingenuity in suggestion to piece a living name to the remark apropos to some overbearing men in the day of Warham, that 'many a lordly persecutor assumes to be, and has the character of being, a philanthropist.' It is difficult not to believe that the paper of the day had just been thrown down upon the study-table of the Deanery at Chichester, when the sentence concerning the Parliament of 1529 was penned, and the then 'Lords Spiritual were' pronounced 'guilty of the unpardonable fault of despairing of the fortunes of the Spiritual republic.'

One danger must beset such a writer; he is in danger of forgetting that he is a Church historian, as well as a biographer, and so of indulging in colloquial expressions, which the grave muse of history can scarcely endure : we allude to such expressions, to give but a single instance, as 'the old Duchess who appears to have been folly itself.'

One other suggestion we would make for the after volumes and the reprints of them—the insertion of a running date in the margin of each page. This would not only be a great assistance to the reader, but it would force upon the writer a stricter observance of chronological order in his narrative, and prevent the tendency to repetition, of which there is room for occasional complaint.

A valuable introductory chapter opens the first of these volumes. In this are well laid down the broad general principles on which all ecclesiastical history must be written and read, if 'by history we mean anything more than annals or a dry statement of facts—a corpse without a soul.'

In this too are contained discussions (after the manner of dissertations) of subjects which could neither be passed over without manifest incompleteness or introduced into the text of the narrative without a perpetual interruption of its flow. Thus in this chapter, amongst other matter, three important dissertations will be found : one on the identity of the Reformed with the Early Church of England ; one on the supremacy of the Crown ; and one on the character of Crumwell (the spelling which the Dean adopts to keep clear the distinction between the Minister of Henry VIII. and the usurping Protector) and his suppression of the monasteries. Each of these is very ably written, and of great importance to all who would understand the Ecclesiastical history of the time. We have already quoted from the first : in the second it is distinctly shown that the assertion of the supremacy of the Crown was no new pretension, first urged at the æra of the Reformation, but had been from time immemorial the claim of the English Crown, enforced or suffered to sleep according to the strength of the monarch on the throne; but always reasserted and perpetually re-enforced by statutory enactments. Forgotten as this is by numbers, no fact in history is more certain. Sir Edward Coke's reports on the case of Caudrey, to which the Dean refers, prove conclusively that Henry VIII.'s statute on the supremacy of the Crown was but the giving the authority of a declaratory Act to the old common law of the land. Professor Brewer, in his preface to the 'Letters and Papers of Henry VIII.' (vol. ii.), well sums up the whole argument in these words: 'As a right, though not always as fact, the supremacy of the King had continued immemorial; the usurpations upon that right were resisted and modified by the energy and will of the Sovereign.'

There never was a time when it was more important to make this truth universally known and recognised. For, on the one hand, there is a party—ably represented by the ingenious writer of what we must term the Romance of the Reign of Henry VIII., under the title of a 'History of England, from the Fall of Wolsey to the Death of Elizabeth'—who delight to speak of the Reformation changes as being an abandonment on the part of the Church of England of her claim to be an integral part of the Church Catholic—a spiritual body, with spiritual power given by our Lord through His apostles—and an acceptance of a new position as holding from the will of the State alone her authority and position as a religious body; whilst on the other side there are those who groan over the utter loss of spiritual liberty at the Reformation, and who, under the garb of a spurious Catholicism, preach disaffection to their fathers' Church. These last conveniently forget that, antecedently to the Reformation, Convocation could pass no canons without the King's consent; that no bull or ecclesiastical constitution could be published in this kingdom without his sanction;

that the bishoprics of England, being of royal foundation, were filled by the Crown as donatives before it granted to the Chapters the modified rights conferred by the allowance of the Congé d'Elire; and that under the Congé d'Elire the Sovereign still so effectually selected the Bishop to be elected that Warham could write in 1522 to Cardinal Wolsey, 'Whereas I am informed that it hath pleased the King's most noble Grace to name to the bishopric of London Master Cuthbert Tonstall, Master of the Rolls, at your Grace's special recommendation, furtherance, and promotion, I thank your Grace, therefore, as heartily as I can.' Equally oblivious, in their longing for reunion with Rome, are men of this school of the troubles which long before the Reformation embittered the relations of this land with the Papal communion; nor do they seem to have heard that though the Pope continually renewed his efforts to obtain the recognition of his claim to be the fountain-head of ecclesiastical jurisdiction before the Reformation quite as earnestly as after it, these efforts were resisted and put down by the Crown and by the law of England. These great principles were indeed endangered, as the Dean points out, amidst the various struggles of the Reformation and the Laudian period:—

'The distinction between the royal and the sacerdotal powers was totally disregarded by Crumwell and the unprincipled men who formed the Government of Edward VI.; and the royal supremacy was too often permitted to encroach on the sacerdotal powers through the weakness, the servility, and want of fixed principles on the part of Archbishop Cranmer. Much injury was done to the cause of the Church through the mistaken policy of our leading ecclesiastics under the unfortunate dynasty of the Stuarts. To strengthen their position against the Roman non-conformists on the one hand, and the Puritan non-conformists on the other, they exaggerated the royal perogative.'

But, in spite of these accidental perversions, the doctrine of the Church of England was at all times essentially that which the Convocation declared in 1534, and which Parliament subsequently ratified; that 'the Pope of Rome hath no greater jurisdiction conferred upon him by God in Holy Scripture in this kingdom of England than any other foreign Bishop.'* The Dean quotes at length from Mr. Gladstone's remarks on the Royal supremacy, the clear and memorable statements which set so courageously forward the true position of spiritual freedom, secured alike by law and practice to the Church of England. If the truth on this subject were more generally borne in mind, we should be delivered from those Erastian claims on the one hand, and from those disloyal diatribes on the other, with which extreme men create, renew, prolong, and embitter those dissensions and disputes which so grievously injure the Church's power, and at times threaten even to rend her asunder.

The great figures on the canvas of these volumes are the two Archbishops, Henry VIII., Crumwell, and Cardinal Wolsey. They are all carefully and conscientiously drawn, with alleged warrants for the actions from which their characters are inferred, and with many a Hans Holbein feature, with his lifelike reproduction of the past, and his tender, discriminating touch, as they pass before us.

With no specific attempt to give a character of Henry VIII., we know not any pages in which he so continually reveals himself. Without at all subscribing to the truth of that recent portraiture, in which he is drawn as the model of self-sacrifice—divorcing Catherine, putting to death her successor, marrying Jane Seymour before the block was dry on which Anne Boleyn suffered, all against his own instincts, for the sake of his people—we think there is ample evidence that the opposite view, which represents him as a barbarous tyrant, who never spared man in his anger or woman in his lust, is, to say the least, almost as far from the truth. There were many noble traits marked upon his strong masculine

* Wilkes, iii. 767.

character. In an age of almost universal licentiousness, scandal never fixed a charge upon him, save in the case of the intrigue with the daughter of Sir John Blunt, to which the young Duke of Richmond owed his birth. He was loved as well as feared by all who came into close relation to him. He thoroughly appreciated truth and manliness in others. His relations with Cranmer have often a touching tenderness about them. He believed in his people, and estimated thoroughly the sterling worth and strength of nature which belonged to them. England never stood more alone and yet never held a higher tone than under him. The estimation in which in return the English people manifestly held him is alone sufficient to show the injustice of the utterly black character which is commonly attributed to him. It is quite clear that their loyalty to him living, and their deep regret for him when dead, rested not so much on a nice calculation of the evils which a disputed succession might inflict upon the land, as upon their recognising in him the true kingly embodiment of their own national character. They honoured the intense strength of his will, the geniality which ever lit up those burly features and threw a halo even over acts of violence and bloodshed, his strong and capacious intellect, his large attainments, and the general wisdom which was stamped upon his counsels. Cranmer's affection for him, and his regard for Cranmer, both witness to this character in Henry. The Dean more than once attributes to him an inclination for having his views combated, so long as he knew that he could at the last enforce them as he would. This hardly does justice to the real forbearance and geniality of the man. There were times when Cranmer opposed him on matters as to which any opposition must have touched him to the quick. Such were the Archbishop's letter as to the innocence of Anne Boleyn; such his interference when the Earl of Essex fell. And yet on these, as on all other occasions, he treated

Cranmer with unvarying kindness and manifest consideration. These are great qualities for a king—for a Tudor.

In these Lives it is with Henry's connexion with the Church of England that we are most concerned. Any attempt to represent him as what is commonly meant by a Protestant is simply absurd. He began, as every one knows, by being a bigoted Papist; he prided himself on his refutation of the early Reformed doctrines. The imputation that he 'first saw Gospel light in Boleyn's eyes' is in one sense, no doubt, literally true. No doubt it was the almost unrivalled deceitfulness of Clement, the long delays, the inexhaustible treachery of the old man, his incessant trimming between his fear on the one hand of losing England and on the other of provoking the Emperor, which opened Henry's eyes—as nothing could have opened them which did not closely touch himself—to the vast evils of the Pope's usurped supremacy. Thus he was led to take up the old English quarrel of preceding generations. So far as directly regarded the other points in discussion between the Reformers and their opponents, Henry was to the end a maintainer of the old learning. The Act of the Six Articles was specially his own, enacted against the the will of Crumwell, then his First Minister, and in spite of the public opposition of Cranmer. Political necessity made him at one time court the alliance of the German Powers, but he had no real sympathy from first to last with them or with their views. The effect of these peculiarities of Henry's character upon the process of the English Reformation cannot be over-rated. This gave to it, in its first ebullition, its distinctive character of being mainly and pre-eminently a restoration of the independence of the English Church. It steadied and delayed the movement, and it kept the agents close, as no other Reformers were kept, to the old faith, wherever it had not been hopelessly corrupted.

No part of these volumes has been prepared with more

diligence and care, or executed with more success, than that which exhibits the character, principles, and actions of Crumwell. The figure stands life-like on the canvas before us, from his strange wandering and doubtful youth, through his ambitious, busy, unprincipled, merciless successes, down to the sudden and overwhelming ruin which in a few short hours buried all his greatness. The Dean has beyond a doubt truly and successfully sketched the strange career, and estimated the character of this man. Trained, after the wild experiences of his youth, under Wolsey, he had acquired the lore which made him in that troubled time—when Francis of France and Charles V. of Spain and Germany had to be played against each other—a great foreign minister. His connexion with the fallen Cardinal seemed at first to threaten, but did indeed beyond anything else build up, his fortunes. Shakespeare's unequalled drama, and the commonplace repetition of moralists on history, have tended to create an impression that his fidelity to his ruined master indicated some noble unselfishness in his own mind. We see no trace of such a contradiction, for so it assuredly would be, of every after exhibition of his character. It is true that to a certain degree he clung to the fallen Cardinal; but it was only as the ivy clings to the fallen trunk until it has found another stem around which to entwine itself. Crumwell had no other patron to whom at once to turn, and therefore he adhered to Wolsey. He was far too shrewd an observer of men, and too good a judge of character, to fear provoking any anger of the King by such a short-lived fidelity. Probably he had counted carefully all chances, and was convinced that the King, who would need some one to fill the place which Wolsey had occupied, would be won to regard him favourably by some exhibition of his allegiance to his old patron. It is clear that he was at this time intriguing to be taken into the King's service, for he writes to Cavendish :—' I intend, God willing, this afternoon when my Lord hath dined, to ride to London, and so on to the Court, where I will either make or mar ere I come again.' If he did, as we think, reckon upon this display of fidelity to Wolsey as likely to recommend him to the King, the result fully justifies his sagacity, for Henry at once adopted the services he offered, and with a most pliant alacrity he transferred his fidelity from the fallen Minister to his new master. The Dean suggests, with great reason, that Wolsey's real estimate of Crumwell's character was that of a clever selfish man:—

'I have come to the conclusion that Wolsey had no confidence in Crumwell's sincerity, and that Crumwell did not treat his fallen master with consideration and kindness. He was obliged to defend him, for he had no other course to pursue; but he was in a state of the greatest alarm for his own safety. . . The Cardinal in one letter entreats him as one who had neglected to come to him, when he had been expected to repair to him "as soon as Parliament was broken up." He entices him to come, by saying that he has things to say to him concerning his own self—as if he knew the selfishness of the man.'

The same conviction, combined with a high estimate of Crumwell's great powers, and his special aptitude from charms of manners for obtaining influence, led the haughty Cardinal to fawn upon the servant in whose fidelity he could scarcely believe. 'My own entirely-beloved Crumwell,' he writes. 'My own aider in this my intolerable anxiety and heaviness.' 'My own trusted and most assured refuge in this my calamity.' 'My only refuge and aid.' The Dean finds no ground for believing that these were the utterances of a true affection, but bespoke the Cardinal's earnest desire to retain the services of a sagacious man whom he suspected but wished to employ.

As soon as he was transferred to the King's service he showed himself to be a thoroughly reliable tool in Henry's hand. Throughout he acted on the principles he avowed in that conversation with Reginald Pole (for questioning the veracity of which the Dean says forcibly 'no reason can be alleged except the principle of rejecting every historical fact which does not agree with our pre-conceived opinions'), in which he recommended Machiavelli to him as his teacher, and avowed for himself the intention of 'first discovering what are the secret wishes of the King, and then, in carrying them into effect, making them appear by special arguments to be consistent with the dictates and requirements of morality and religion.

All Crumwell's after-life justified this low opinion which his first patron formed of his moral character. His religion was from first to last dictated by the exigencies of political party, or the claims of his own selfish interest. He threw in his lot with the Reformers, and has been lauded as a saint and 'man of God' by the inaccurate and inveracious Foxe; but neither his character nor his conduct exhibit any marks of piety save that of standing by his faction, and providing for himself. He was greedy of gain, and so rapacious in seizing on and amassing it, that, though utterly profuse and prodigal in spending money, he died possessed of immense wealth. No one trusted him, unless, which is far from certain, the rugged, humorous, quaint Hugh Latimer did so. If Latimer really had any faith in him, it may have been the same defects of his own character which made him offensively facetious and flippant in his letter to Crumwell when appointed to preach at the burning of poor Forest, and 'unhandsomely merry' at the condemnation of Sir Thomas More, or possibly, as we would hope of one who died so bravely for his faith, from the greatness of his own sincerity, which made him unable to suspect or detect the duplicity of the wily statesman to whom the support of such a man was as invaluable as in the present day the support of a great religious leader might be to the irreligious and even profligate head of a political party. Certainly Crumwell's course was not calculated to inspire such trust. He was a zealous supporter of the Reformers when advancing their cause enabled him to suppress the religious houses and enrich himself and his dependants out of their spoils; but when the imperious will of Henry required the enactment of the 'Act of Six Articles, or, as the Puritans, who liked to give hard names to hard acts, called it, the whip with six strings,' Crumwell acquiesced (for his name stands on the list of the committee from which in fact it emanated): although it declared the truth of transubstantiation, justified the receiving the Communion in one kind, prohibited the marriage of the clergy, and continued private masses, vows of chastity, and the retention of auricular confession. In like manner, zealous as he was against the chantries, or at least against their endowments, yet, as the Dean points out,—

'At a time when he was at the head of the ultra-Protestant party [June, 1529], he leaves twenty shillings to each of the five orders of Friars within the City of London, to pay for his soul. He directs his executor "to engage a priest to sing for his soul three years next after his death, and to pay him for the same twenty pounds." Five or six years afterwards he had occasion to correct his will, when the bequests for prayers to be made for his soul were retained; and it is proved that this was not an oversight, for, as regarded the priest who was to pray for the dead, he desired him to continue his services for seven years, and he increased his stipend from 20*l.* to 40*l.* 12*s.* 6*d.* What religion he had would appear to be superstition; and the superstition of an irreligious man induces him to seek the advantages whilst he avoids the responsibilities of religion.'

We differ from the Dean's suggestion that the fall of Crumwell was unconnected with the disgust which Henry entertained to Anne of Cleves. It is almost certain that Crumwell had taken a leading part in promoting that marriage. It was a supreme part of his foreign policy to encourage every alliance between Henry and the Protestant Powers of Germany. Crumwell's personal interests were too deeply involved in this, not to make him thoroughly in earnest in securing it. He had offended the Papal party beyond all possibility of forgiveness. He had to bow his head to the heavy storm of the Six Articles, which were designed rather to prevent the Protestant party from wrangling against the six points, than to enforce the six points themselves as matters of necessary dogmatic belief; but if the Roman party regained their power he would too probably have, not merely to bow his head to such an Act of Parliament, but to lose it on the block, a contingency which few men were less ready to court than Thomas Crumwell. Now past experience had shown him how greatly the King's mode of viewing questions was affected by his domestic relations; and Anne of Cleves might be able to effect what the shameful fall of Anne Boleyn had prevented his accomplishing. He was, therefore, bent upon promoting this match. Partly because he wished well to the Reformers, but more especially because he wished for security for himself. The Dean suggests that Anne of Cleves could not have been the occasion of Crumwell's disgrace, because the King 'instead of venting his anger upon Crumwell, confided to him his disappointment, and consulted him as to the means by which he might extricate himself from his contract.'

'Besides,' he adds, 'it was after her arrival that Crumwell received his earldom.' A study of the original documents not only brings us to an opposite conclusion, but reconciles these facts with it. The King's personal disgust with his contracted Queen was intense; he found too that the political object he had in view in the alliance was not likely to be secured; he regarded the whole matter as Crumwell's arrangement; he had suggested it, he had obtained the flattering pictures and reports of the Queen's beauty which her actual appearance so rudely contradicted, he had even endeavoured to lessen the King's disappointment 'by suggesting that she had a queenly manner.' If she had been a subject of the realm, the King would no doubt have taken at once his course in his own high handed manner. But he feared embroiling the nation at the same time with the Emperor, the King of France, and the German Princes; the threads of the whole mesh-work of foreign politics were in Crumwell's hands, and the King called on him to find a remedy, which would at once set him free from the marriage he hated, and prevent the mischief which, if it were abruptly broken off, he apprehended to the realm, and gave him his earldom to strengthen his hands for the necessary negotiation. It was only when he proved resourceless that expectation turned in the King's mind into disgust; and then the destruction of the lately powerful minister was sudden, not, as we think, because 'Henry delighted to raise his favourites to a giddy eminence of greatness, that their fall might be the heavier when in his caprices or his vengeance he thought fit to hurl them to the bottom of the pit,' but because there had been accumulating against the day of his disgrace innumerable causes and instruments of his destruction. 'Crumwell had failed in every promise he had made the King.' As the fruit of his foreign policy the Crown was wholly without allies, the Pope was hostile to the death, the Emperor alienated, Francis was unwon, the German Princes stood suspiciously aloof; at home religious animosities, always peculiarly distasteful to Henry, were embittering the divisions of the lieges; even the dissolution of the monasteries, the only matter in which the great Malleus Monachorum had succeeded thoroughly, had been a disappointment. Their wealth, which was to have enabled Henry to govern without a Parliament, had slipped like water through his fingers; his share had gone in gambling and magnificences; a few of his nobles had been greatly enriched, no one more so than Crumwell himself, but the common people, whom the religious houses had supported, were ready to revolt; the friends of the monasteries were made his enemies; Crumwell's boasted Government had been on all sides a failure, and as the crown of all it had fettered the King with a marriage engagement which he abhorred, and from which Crumwell could not or would not help to free him. The course of the minister, a bad, bold, hypocritical, unscrupulous, venal man in the day of his elation, was crowded with acts of cruelty, licence, violence, lawlessness, venality, which could not bear examination. For such a man there could be no intermediate condition between eminence of power which was above punishment, and an immediate certainty of destruction. He stumbled, and the darkening wings of the vultures crowded round him. He fell; and he fell irretrievably and abjectly: pleading for life, the late haughty, overbearing minister ended his supplication to the King with the cry 'Written at the Tower with the heavy heart and trembling hand of your Highness's most miserable prisoner and poor slave. I cry for mercy—mercy—mercy!'

The universal rejoicing at his fall throughout all classes attests the harshness of his rule; the insolence of his conduct in prosperity, and the want of dignity in his evil day. That its immediate cause should have been the King's disgust at the newly contracted marriage, and at his minister for having arranged it, is a remarkable instance of Nemesis. Crumwell, a secret Romanist, had for lucre and power put himself at the head of the Protestants; and by success in negotiating (as a zealous Reformer) this Protestant alliance, he lost his power, his honour, and his life.

In his judgment on the suppression of the monasteries, the Dean holds the scale with the even hand and entire fairness which is so honourably conspicuous in his pages. He shows that it had at all times belonged to the King of right to visit all collegiate and monastic institutions; that eighty-one alien priories, that is, priories in England affiliated to religious houses abroad, had been sequestered by King John; that thirty more had been sequestered by Edward III., restored in the first year of Henry IV., but again suspended in his sixth year; that Henry V. had by Act of Parliament suppressed the alien priories and vested their estates in the Crown; that throughout the middle ages, and before the Reformation was thought of, the creators of colleges, such as Walter de Merton, and William of Wykeham, had found the means of endowing their great foundations from similar sources; that many of these monasteries were no longer the homes of industry, holy living and devotion, but centres of idleness and moral corruption; that the distinction, moreover, between Church property and monastic property was most marked, and that no notion of peculiar sacredness then attached to the holdings of the monasteries; that they were institutions to be judged of simply by their results; and that they had long ceased to effect in any real degree the useful purposes for which they had at first been founded. They no longer sustained either religion or learning, whilst their inmates had for a long period given no eminent person either to the Church or State. 'The secular clergy maintained their position throughout the reign of Henry VII., and with Wolsey at their head through the early part of his son's reign the Regulars had forfeited the respect and esteem of the public.'

The Dean has therefore no professional censures for the resumption by the State of property of which it might justly regard itself as the trustee, provided only that the mode of resumption was fitting, and the uses to which the resumed property was put were of the nature of a cy-pres redistribution. Under Crumwell's influence he shows that neither of these necessary conditions were observed. Instead of a careful examination of the separate cases of the religious houses, the idlest tales were judged sufficient to justify the dissolution of venerable societies; whilst the rack and other instruments of torture were freely used under the direct persona superintendence of Crumwell, to extort from an unwilling witness or too retentive culprit the secrets they were supposed to hide. Mr. Tytler, as quoted in these pages, does not scruple after examining the original documents to say, that 'they exhibit Crumwell as equally tyrannical and unjust, despising the authority of the law, and unscrupulous in the use of torture.' At the same time he used without scruple every other instrument to obtain his ends, stirring up the populace against all religion by having 'the ordinances of the Church burlesqued, and things most sacred turned into ridicule by divers fresh and quick wits, by whose industry the country was inundated with pictures, jests, songs, and interludes.' The property of the monasteries having by such means got into Crumwell's hands, the purposes for which these estates ought to have been reserved were almost entirely forgotten, and what might have made provision for sound instruction and increased means of public worship was lost in gambling and dissipation, or basely given over to the hangers-on of Crumwell and the Court, to build up private fortunes out of public spoils.

It is well that at the present time the warning which this appropriation of the confiscated estates of the religious houses suggests should be with all distinctness repeated. All experience teaches us that whether or no other curses attend upon such confiscation, the curse of misappropriation has attached itself with unvarying fixedness to all such acts.

The regular series of history in these volumes contains the lives of William Warham and Thomas Cranmer. Warham was Archbishop from 1503 to 1532. He was educated at Winchester and New College, and after leaving Oxford first practised as a lawyer in the Court of Arches: there he attracted the attention of Archbishop Morton, was brought under the keen eye of Henry VII., and according to the custom of that day was sent, then it seems in Holy Orders, as legal adviser to Sir Henry Poynings on his embassy to detach the Duke of Burgundy from the side of Perkin Warbeck. He soon after became precentor of Wells, Master of the Rolls, Archdeacon of Huntingdon, and Principal of a Hall (St. Edward's) at Oxford, whilst he was actively engaged in the foreign affairs of the English Government, and sent frequently abroad to discharge the duties of a diplomatist. In 1501 he was on the King's appointment elected Bishop of London, though not consecrated, in consequence as it seems of being on one of his continental embassies, for more than a year afterwards. Warham was one of those men whom Henry VII. loved to promote. Able, wary, and moderate, untroubled with any genius, and with whom conscientious principle never knotted itself into a crotchet or subsided into impracticable obstinacy. In 1502 he resigned the Mastership of the Rolls; but could not escape from the trammels of his lay dignity, as before the year was out he was appointed Lord Keeper of the Great Seal; and within another six months was translated to the Archiepiscopal See of Canterbury and appointed Lord Chancellor, the pay of which high office when he received it was only 100 marks raised for him afterwards to 200*l.*, and garnished with such moderate perquisites only as a common velvet bag for the Great Seal, value 15*s.*; for winter robes to enable him to sit in Court in December, 26*l.* 13*s.* 4*d.*, with certain tuns of Gascon wine. How must the record of such stinted payments stir the virtuous wrath and kindle the love of such happy times of frugality in the souls of our great Manchester economists. Warham remained Chancellor through the reign of Henry VII., and in spite of many attempts to resign it earlier, it was not until the year 1515 he succeeded in getting free by handing it over to the keeping of Wolsey. Between

Wolsey and himself there existed to his death the relations natural to a wise and wary, though somewhat timid statesman, who held the higher ecclesiastical position, with a minister of master intellect, of uncontrollable ambition, and unwearied administrative vigour.

Warham was a reformer before the Reformation. He was the intimate friend of Erasmus; and from an expression in one of Erasmus's letters which has been supposed to be addressed to Warham, the Dean raises the question, Was Warham a married man? It is rather difficult to gather to which side the balance inclines as one weighs the evidence in the judgment of the impartial Dean. The expression of Erasmus is unequivocal—'Bene vale cum dulcissima conjugali liberisque dulcissimis.' Jortin supposes that there is an error in the heading of the epistle, which should have been addressed to Lord Mountjoy. We have no doubt that this or some such solution is the truth. The Dean is quite right in the estimate which he forms of the moral results of enforced celibacy amongst the clergy. 'Only persons,' he says, 'of very strict religious principles objected to the residence of a concubine in the house of a clergyman.' . . . If the parties were secretly married 'the marriage was voidable, but [not] void, and if the marriage were proved the legitimacy of the children was not disputed.' Still a clergyman by marriage 'violated the canons of the Church or the Statutes of the land, hence the marriage was generally clandestine.' 'Wolsey was himself a concubinary priest.' The Dean seems on the whole to favour the idea of Warham's secret marriage as accounting for Wolsey's 'despotic influence over his mind.' But this is at once accounted for by the accustomed yielding of the gentle and less vigorous, to the more energetic will and mind; and for ourselves we dismiss the suggestion as wholly incompatible with the records of Warham's character and conduct. So far from living, as it has been asserted, merely to support his Order, Warham had himself attempted a reform of the ecclesiastical courts, the great abuse of the day, and had begun a visitation of the monasteries. But he found the sons of Zeruiah too strong for his trembling or aged hand; and acquiesced in the desire of Henry VIII. for Wolsey's cardinalate and legantine powers, mainly as it seems in the hope that the red hat and the weight of a *legatus a latere* might make another powerful enough to enforce the reforms which were beyond his own strength and which yet he saw to be essential to the safety of the Church. Wolsey was not generous in his use of the superior powers which this higher authority conferred upon him, and Warham sometimes meekly resisted but more frequently patiently resigned himself to the assumptions of the power he had by acquiescence invoked. For the same reason he seems to have withdrawn himself from public life. The Dean quotes Sebastian Giustiniani as asserting that Warham the peace-loving minister of Henry VII. could not acquiesce in the ambitious projects of Wolsey's war policy, and so absented himself from the Council when it was resolved to assist the Emperor against the King of France. And this is by no means an improbable solution of his retirement. In domestic politics Warham and Wolsey were at one: save that Warham somewhat inactively desired the reforms which Wolsey vehemently effected. More than fourscore years pressed upon the venerable head of the Primate, and it was but natural that he should to a great degree withdraw himself from political life, and retire into the learned leisure he so dearly loved. This he shared freely with many of the leaders of the 'new learning.' What he was amongst them, some beautiful sentences of Erasmus have recorded.

'Now Erasmus is almost transformed into an Englishman,' he writes to Abbot St. Bertin. 'Of those who are kind to me, I place in the first place

Warham, Archbishop of Canterbury. What genius! What copiousness! What vivacity! What facility in the most complicated discussion! What erudition! What politeness! From Warham, who is truly royal, none ever parted in sorrow! With all these qualities, how great is Warham's humility, how edifying his modesty. He alone is ignorant of his eminence; no one is more faithful or more constant in friendship.'*

So wrote Erasmus of Warham: we, of the present century, might almost fancy that these were Bunsen's words, and that he wrote them concerning Archbishop Howley.

But more than one important matter was yet to trouble Warham's age. First, the question of the King's marriage with Catherine pressed heavily upon him. He took indeed no leading part in helping forward the divorce, yet he leaned strongly to the King's side, and the King would have been well content if the Pope would have committed to him the determination of his matrimonial suit. 'Ther canne,' Henry urged to Clement, 'be no person in Christendome more indifferente, more miet, apt, and convenient than the sayd Archbishop, who hath lernyng, excellent high and long experience, a man ever of a singular zele to justice.' It could not suit the crafty policy of the dissimulating Clement to commit the judgment of the King's cause to such a man. But it is a strong argument in favour of Henry's motives, and of the real justice of his cause, that such a man as Warham adhered to him in it till the end.

The other matter which troubled the close of Warham's life was the Act for the Submission of the Clergy. Wolsey had fallen; and in falling drew down upon the clergy the charge of treason for their admission of his legantine powers. They were proceeded against under the præmunire statute, and had to purchase their forgiveness by a large benevolence. The King required, for the future safeguard of the supremacy of his Crown, that the clergy should bind themselves

* Erasmi Epist. to the Abbot of St. Bertin.

to make no canons in their convocations without the King's sanction. This was no sacrifice of any spiritual power which was really theirs. It was altogether in the spirit of the ancient Church constitution of the land. It conceded no lawful power of the spirituality. In making this concession the spirituality did not profess to receive from the State the power of making canons or constitutions. On the contrary, it assumed that the power of making such rules rested of necessity with the body spiritual, but that it was according to the word of Christ and the teaching of the Apostle that she should not exercise her power within a Christian kingdom, save by a licence from the anointed King. To this Warham counselled the clergy voluntarily to submit; and after a long struggle, the course of which may be read at length in the Dean's biography, the concession was agreed to *in verbo sacerdotii*.

It was almost the last act of Warham. Between the hours of two and three on the 22nd day of August, 1532, William Warham was at rest. There does not appear to be the slightest foundation for the assertion that 'he withdrew himself heartbroken into his palace at Lambeth.'* Such men do not die heartbroken, and there had been nothing, if it had been otherwise, to break his heart. The Dean's conception of his character is the true one. He was a reformer, but a conscientious and a cautious reformer. He saw his primacy drawing to its close, marked, with his entire concurrence, by the re-assertion of the Crown's supremacy and the submission of the clergy to it; he feared that after he was gone these admissions might be so enlarged as to sacrifice what he could not have yielded. Against such a course, which might be 'to the hurt, prejudice, or limitation of the powers of the Church, or to the subverting, enervating, derogating from or diminishing the laws, customs, privileges, prerogatives, pre-

* Froude, i. p. 369.

eminence, or liberties of our metropolitan Church of Canterbury,' he, on his dying bed, signed before the notary his protest, declaring that such in all he had agreed to, he did 'neither will, nor intend, nor with clear conscience was able to consent to the same.'* And so, consenting to a lawful reform, and protesting against what he deemed the licence into which it might be lengthened out, he calmly yielded from his dying hand the crozier he had borne peacefully and with honour through so many a stormy year. Any one who remembers the portrait of him, painted by Hans Holbein, which appeared some two or three years back in the Exhibition at Kensington, will feel how truly the countenance of the man expressed his character. The intellectual, gentle, disciplined face, the refined and well-proportioned features, and the light subdued by quietness which overspread them, well represented the churchman with whom Erasmus loved to converse, and whom Holbein delighted to draw.

Rumour had already fixed on Stephen Gardyner, Bishop of Winchester, as the successor of Warham; but the King had other views, and Cranmer, who had done good service in promoting the divorce from Catherine, was selected for the post, and duly elected and consecrated with the assent of the Papal authorities. The Dean triumphantly vindicates him from the vulgar charge of having sought and accepted the office, whilst he disbelieved in the doctrines which its acceptance implied him to hold. He did not seek, but shrank from the primacy, and delayed as long as he could venture, after the King's nomination, to return and take possession of it He was singularly unambitious; his desires pointed to literary ease amidst family life. As he returned to England he married, as a second wife, a niece of his friend Osiander. He would not have contracted this second marriage if he had in any degree looked to the primacy. It is

* Burnet's 'Collectanea.'

'extreme injustice to represent him as a Protestant in disguise during the reign of Henry.' He 'was not a Protestant before the commencement of the reign of Edward VI.,' even if, 'in the modern acceptance of the term, a Protestant he ever became.' 'The real work of the Reformation was the changing of the mass into a communion, and this involved the dogma of transubstantiation. . . . Henry VIII. was dead before Cranmer renounced transubstantiation, and until he did that it is a mistake to speak of him as a Protestant.' The Dean, in clearing him from this imputation, guards himself from being supposed to have any 'inclination to vindicate the character of Cranmer.' We entirely acquit him of such a charge. Though ready generously to find any possible excuse for many of his faults, he sometimes, we think, judges him too severely. An instance of what we mean occurs in the narrative of one of the earliest and most painful acts of Cranmer's archiepiscopate—the pronouncing sentence of nullity on the supposed marriage between Henry and Catherine, where he is spoken of as 'simulating the character of a just judge, when he had deliberately come to deliver an iniquitous judgment. But he never seems to have been conscience-striken for his conduct on this occasion.' Now why is it to be supposed that the judgment Cranmer delivered was in any sense 'iniquitous'? In the expressed convictions of many of the best and wisest men of the day, the dispensation granted by Julius II. for Henry's marriage was, as dispensing with a law of God, utterly void and of no effect. If this were so, the marriage had never really existed; it was voidable, and it was his bounden duty, on complaint, to declare it void. That this was Cranmer's conscientious and deliberate conviction is well-nigh certain. No man had more deeply studied the whole question. No man had more opportunity of knowing that, even at Rome itself, this was the opinion of the

Canonists. He may probably have known what Paolo Sarpi records, that when the Pope delegated the cause to the Cardinal Campeggio and the Cardinal of York, in order

'to facilitate the resolution that the solemnities of the judgment might not draw the cause in length, a brefe was framed, in which he was declared free from that marriage with the most ample clauses that ever were put into any Pope's Bull, and a Cardinal sent into England with order to present it after some few proofes were passed, which he was sure would easily be made. And this happened in the yeere 1524. But Clement judging it fitter for compassing his designs upon Florence . . . to joyne himself with the Emperour than to continue in the friendship of France and England, in the year 1529, he sent Francis Campana unto Campeggio with order to burne the brefe and proceed slowly in the cause.'*

There seems to us no reason for doubting that with whatever painful sympathy for Catherine, Cranmer must have felt bound as an honest man to give this judgment, and if so to give it clearly and speedily.

The further progress of the reformation of religion is traced in the following pages with a master's hand. The Dean shows that

'Neither Henry nor Cranmer was a theorist. They had no particular schemes of their own to carry. They found the Church of England bowed down by the galling tyranny of Rome, through powers gradually usurped. When they had asserted the freedom of the National Church, and declared the King to be " in all causes and over all persons civil and ecclesiastical within his dominions supreme," they had to legislate not with a view to further their preconceived opinions, but simply to meet the difficulties arising from the circumstances in which they were placed. In an age of inquiry they soon discovered that the Catholic Faith, though always preserved in the three Creeds, had been obscured by superincumbent superstitions; and they sought, as they were discovered one by one, to remove them.'

In this work throughout Henry's reign, he and the Archbishop worked in the main steadily together, though

'Henry was of a conservative temper and would move slowly, whilst Cranmer, though slow to receive a truth, laboured eagerly when he had

---

* 'History of Council of Trent,' lib. i. p. 68. N. Brett's translation, edit. 3.

accepted it for its promulgation. Both were frequently inconsistent: the one urged on by his passions, the other retarded by his weakness.'

It was of God's great mercy to this Church and nation, first, that two men of these opposite temperaments were acting together, one from the throne of England, the other from the marble chair of Canterbury, to guide the coming changes; and next, that the changes themselves were but remedies for immediate practical evils. There was in the nation a widespread dissatisfaction with the whole body of Papal corruptions. If the first attack on these had been conducted by one who had once been what Luther describes himself to have been, a 'most mad Papist,' and who in his first intoxication from newly discovered truth had appealed to that feeling, and had found the strength with which to carry his reforms in the passions of the populace, England's Church might have become what the religious systems of Saxony, of Geneva, and Scotland have been. But the first energy of the English Reformation was spent in demolishing the master evil of the Pope's usurped supremacy, and denying its sister vice of his infallibility. Slowly, cautiously, and like an ebbing tide rather than with the violence of a cataract, with reluctant pauses and seeming returns, the stream of feeling turned against those distinctly doctrinal errors which had affected the great mysteries of the Christian Church; and this branch of the Reformation was in consequence approached calmly and dealt with moderately, so that the evil parasites were removed without shaking the truth round which they had wound themselves, and to which they clung. The final separation by synodical act of the English Church from the Roman obedience, was the consequence of the strong reaction of English feeling, when the Pope reversed the Primate's judgment, and required Henry, under pain of excommunication, to put away his new Queen. Then, on the 7th of April, 1534, it was declared in the English Convocation that ' the

Bishop of Rome hath no greater jurisdiction given him in this realm of England than any other foreign Bishop;'* and so was finally asserted by England's clergy that separation from the Papacy, which the sealing of the Act of the King's Supremacy with the blood of Fisher and Sir Thomas More proclaimed with so terrible an energy for the Laity. Other reformations panted and paused in their course. It was three years later before the joint influence of Cranmer and Crumwell obtained a license from the King permitting the Bible, then called Matthew's Bible, to be freely bought and sold, and a command that a copy of it should be set up in every church. Strype records † that the Archbishop rejoiced on that day more 'than had there been given him a thousand pounds,' with him rejoiced a multitude as at the free opening in the desert of the springs of water. 'With what joy,' says Strype, 'that version of the Bible was received, not only amongst the learneder sort and those that were noted for lovers of the Reformation, but generally all England over, amongst all the vulgar and common people.' This version, revised by Cranmer, was reprinted in the four following years under the title of 'The Great or Cranmer's Bible.' The same year witnessed the publication of the 'Bishop's book,' the 'Institution of a Christian man,' which dealt freely with many points of Roman error. This has been fixed upon by Professor Blunt as the highest point reached by the tide of reform in the reign of Henry.

The following year, 1539, saw the enactment of the Six Articles, supported by the King, and bravely opposed in the House of Lords by Cranmer. The Dean considers these articles as a measure of policy and not of religion. The King perceived the danger which was accruing to the realm from the spread of religious dissension, and this Act was passed not against a wrong belief on the six points, but

* Wilkins's 'Council,' iii. 769.   † Strype's 'Cranmer,' p. 64.

against an open contradiction of the still received opinion. In common with Dr. Maitland the Dean believes that 'it was meant to intimidate rather than to hurt.' It was beyond all question, so far as the immediate prospect of the Reformation was concerned, a distinctly reactionary measure. It had one effect which greatly disturbed the comfort of the Archbishop. For it compelled him to send back his wife to her German relations. The enactment which made it felony for a clergyman to live with his wife was mainly aimed at Cranmer, and may account in some measure for the boldness with which at first he opposed the Bill. The Dean's pages contain some amusing traits of poor Mrs. Cranmer's sufferings during her life of semi-concealed matrimony, especially Sanders' story of her misfortunes when travelling with the Archbishop, but packed away for safety in a chest. His enemies tried hard to wound him from this side. But in this, as in so many other matters, Cranmer had the hearty support of the King. There is nothing which redounds more to Henry's credit than his relations with Cranmer from first to last. Surrounded as Henry was with utterly selfish, unprincipled men, he seems to have delighted in the singleheartedness of the Primate. It was the King who detected the plots formed against the Archbishop, and the King who defeated them. Opposition could not alienate him from Cranmer, and so it was till the unlooked-for end, when having sent for the Archbishop for the last offices of religion, he died wringing hard the Archbishop's hand in token 'that he put his trust in God through Jesus Christ.'

There is no little light thrown back on Cranmer himself, from this unalterable affection of such a man as Henry. From first to last his character appears to us transparently clear. He was thoroughly honest; devoid of any gifts of genius; patient, laborious, and religious; true to his convictions, but liable to have those convictions varied by the force of circumstances or the arguments of others; he was true to his friends and forgiving to his enemies; with some spasmodic exertions of vigour he was deficient in strength of character; he was easily governed by women—Anne Boleyn and Catherine Howard seem equally to have practised on his simplicity; and he became himself the husband of two women, neither of whom leave upon our mind an impress of notable worthiness. 'Black Joan' of the 'Dolphin' may have abused his inexperienced youth; but the second Mrs. Cranmer seems in his life to have manifested little delicacy, and when he was dead to have been voracious of after marriages. But for Henry's constant fidelity and friendly care, Cranmer would hardly have kept his footing in that slippery Court; and after Henry's death it was not long before troubles began to entangle him. Left by Henry's will at the head of the Council of Regency, he soon became almost a cypher in its deliberations. He did, indeed, resist the precipitate haste with which, for purely worldly motives, the Protector sought to carry forward religious changes for which Cranmer was unprepared. For at this time 'he did not hesitate to offer masses for the repose of Henry VIII. and of Francis I.' Accordingly 'the foreign reformers of the Calvinistic School complained of Cranmer that he was lethargic and lukewarm, unworthy to carry out the Reformation to its full extent even when the cards were in his hands.' One of the reasons assigned by the Duke of Northumberland, in 1552, for desiring the preferment of John Knox, or as his Grace writes it, Mr. Knocks, to the Bishopric of Rochester, was that he would be 'a whetstone to quicken and sharpen the Bishop of Canterbury, whereof he hath need.' The Dean shows conclusively the falsehood of this charge. He traces the gradual enlightenment of Cranmer's mind as to the doctrine of transubstantiation with the legislation to which it led; he shows the revisions rendered necessary by these changes in the

Missal, and gives a succinct and valuable review of our Liturgical offices from Augustine to Osmund, from Osmund to Cranmer, and from Cranmer to Juxon.

The Archbishop was far more at home in these pursuits than in the perplexing public affairs in which the sudden decay of young Edward VI. and the Northumberland conspiracy soon involved him. Here all the peculiar traits of his character come out. His honest reluctance to signing Edward's unjust and unconstitutional will—the overbearing of his judgment by the signature of all the Judges except Hales, and of his convictions by his tenderness to the young King in his agony, and the fatal signature—all are in keeping with Cranmer's character from first to last. The scene is well drawn by the Dean in a few vigorous words:—
' Cranmer stood at the side of the couch to receive the last request of one whom he revered as a dying saint. "I hope," said Edward, " I hope that you will not stand out, and not be more repugnant to my will than all the rest of the Council. The Judges have informed me that I may lawfully bequeath my Crown to the Lady Jane, and that my subjects may lawfully receive her as Queen, notwithstanding the oath which they took under my father's will." The King had learned his lesson well. Cranmer still hesitated. He quitted the royal presence, he consulted the Judges who were in attendance, he returned to the sick chamber, he took a last look at his godson, and he signed the fatal document. This, considering the light in which Cranmer had regarded the subject, was an awful fall. He fell; but it was not from fear of death—he fell because he would not hurt the feelings of the dying youth.' Yet to his honour it should be remembered that of the twenty-three names pledged to maintain Edward's device, one name only was withheld from immediate allegiance to Mary when her cause was triumphant, and that was the name of the uncertain but honest Cranmer.

On Mary's accession his long concluding troubles broke at once upon him. He might have fled the kingdom; but deeming it his duty to remain, and over-estimating his strength of purpose, he stood to his post. He was soon imprisoned in the Tower, where he 'found his friends Ridley and Bradford; and five days after in came a venerable octogenarian—as light-hearted, as hard-headed, and as strong-minded as ever—Bishop Latimer. The friends availed themselves of the opportunity to read over the New Testament " with great delectation and peaceful study."' But this was not long to last. His trial and condemnation for treason; his removal to Oxford; his distant view of the glorious martyrdom of Ridley and Latimer; his condemnation; his degradation by the Pope through the triumphant hands of Bonner; followed one another in a rapid succession. Then came the cunning tampering with his weakness of those saddest days of Cranmer's life — the genial dinners, the pleasant games at bowles, the deferential arguments, and all the other crafty wiles of the enemy—and then came their fruit—the first scarcely-extorted and scanty recantation—its aggravated repetition—still, as it seems to us, ever turning in Cranmer's mind on a half-equivocation; on rejecting all heresies and adhering constantly to one holy and Catholic Church; and then, according to the certain course of every man who once allows himself to palter with the simple truth, the utter fall and the shameless degradation. A terrible sadness it was to all true-hearted men—a fearful triumph for the children of lies. We would not by any word of ours lessen all its evil. And yet we cannot but feel an indignation, deep as our sad sympathy for him, with the shallow-hearted critics who — never having known the uttermost bitterness of that storm which was passing over him—the mingled addresses of softness and severity which tried every weak part of his great soul, and who themselves would probably in a less tempest make, if it were possible, a yet completer shipwreck—can find an evil pleasure in insulting and defaming the fallen man.

Better far is it to gather up the lights of his last revival, to remember his bold confession, his patient endurance of every godless violence, his self-revenge upon his traitorous right hand, to see him

> 'Outstretching flame-ward his upbraided hand,
> . . .
> Amid the shudd'ring throng doth Cranmer stand,
> Firm as the stake to which with iron band
> His frame is tied; from the naked feet
> To the head, the victory complete.' *

So Cranmer passes from our view, kindly in character from first to last, persecuting not as Bonner persecuted, from a boisterous cruelty; not as Crumwell persecuted, from the dictates of policy, or for the satisfaction of his greed of gold and selfish lust of power; but reluctantly, on the constraint of principles then universally held to be indisputable, and with perpetual endeavours to save the victims whom he thought himself compelled to sacrifice. He believed as all then believed, that it was as much a duty to condemn to death the convicted murderer of souls as the convicted murderer of bodies. In common with the other Reformers of that day, he was ready to put men and women to death, not for holding, but for teaching, false doctrines; not for being heretics, but for being heresiarchs. He had not the power of mind or spirit which could raise him so far above the age in which he lived, that he could take a broader view of the great question with which circumstances compelled him to grapple.

That the English Reformation was wrought by men of this calibre is perhaps its most notable characteristic. Un-

---

* 'Eccles. Sonnets,' by W. Wordsworth, 27, p. 394.

doubtedly it is to this fact that the Church of England owes its absolutely single and separate character amidst all the reformed communions. It bears the mark and impress of the intellectual or spiritual peculiarities of no single man. Herein at once it is marked off from the Lutheran, the Calvinist, the Zuinglian, and other smaller bodies. On each one of them lay, as the shadow on the sleeping water, the unbroken image of some master mind or imperial soul. The mind of that founder of the new faith, his mode of thought and argument, his religious principles, and his great defects were reproduced in the body which he had formed, and which by a natural instinct appropriated and handed on his name. And so it might have been with us too, had there been amongst the English Reformers such a leader. If Wycliffe —the great forerunner of the Reformation, whose austere figure stands out above the crowd of notables in English history*—if Wycliffe had lived a hundred and thirty years later than he did, his commanding intellect and character might then have stamped upon the religion of England the essential characteristic of a sect. But from this the goodness of God preserved the Church of this land. Like the birth of the beautiful islands of the great Pacific Ocean, the foundations of the new convictions which were so greatly to modify and purify the mediæval faith were laid slowly, unseen, unsuspected, by ten thousand souls, who laboured, they knew not for what, save to accomplish the necessities of their own spiritual belief. The mighty convulsion which suddenly cast up the submarine foundations into peak and mountain, and crevasse, and lake, and plain, came not from man's devising, and obeyed not man's rule. Influences of the heaven above, and of the daily surrounding atmosphere, wrought their will upon the new-born islands. Fresh convulsions changed, modified, and completed their shape, and

* 'Froude,' vol. ii. p. 13.

so the new and the old were blended together into an harmony which no skill of man could have devised. The English Reformers did not attempt to develope a creed or a community out of their own internal consciousness. Their highest aim was only to come back to what had been before. They had not the gifts which created in others the ambition to be the founders of a new system. They did not even set about their task with any fixed plan or organised set of doctrines. Their inconsistencies, their variations, their internal differences, their very retractations witness to the gradualness with which the new light dawned upon them, and dispelled the old darkness. The charges of hypocrisy and time-serving which have been made so wantonly against Cranmer and his brethren, are all honourably interpreted by the real changes which took place in their own opinions. The patient, loving, accurate, study of Holy Scripture was an eminent characteristic of all these men. Thus the opinions they were receiving from others who had advanced far before them in the new faith were continually modified by this continual voice of God's Word sounding in their ears, and by corresponding changes in their own views. Thus they were enabled by God's grace, out of the utter disintegration round them, to restore in its primitive proportions the ancient Church of England.

Surely, in bringing to an end this review of their great enterprise, we may well say with the late Professor Blunt,—

'God grant that a Church which has now for nearly three centuries, amidst every extravagance of doctrine and discipline which has spent itself around her, still carried herself as the mediator, chastening the zealot by words of soberness, and animating the lukewarm by words that burn— that a Church which has been found on experience to have successfully promoted a quiet and unobtrusive and practical piety amongst the people such as comes not of observation, but is seen in the conscientious discharge of all those duties of imperfect obligation . . . . which laws cannot reach —that such a Church may live through these troublous times to train up our children in the fear of God when we are in our graves—and that no strong delusion sent amongst us may prevail to her overthrow to the eventual discomfiture (as they would find, too late, to their cost) of many who have thoughtlessly and ungratefully lifted up their heel against her.'*

* Professor Blunt's 'History of the Reformation,' pp. 233-4.

KEBLE'S BIOGRAPHY.*
(*July*, 1869.)

BIOGRAPHY is often spoken of as if it was a peculiar department of literature, and was to be judged of by rules of its own. To a certain degree, of course, this is true; but it is true only when taken with very marked exceptions and very wide allowances. For biography absolutely changes its character with the varying circumstances of its subject. If the man whose life is recorded is himself in his idiosyncrasy the really interesting matter, then the writing of that life may be a simple biography—a monograph, as the naturalist would call it. But if that which is noteworthy is not so much what the man was, as what the man did, then the biographer becomes in great measure an historian. Whatever was the field in which his subject lived and laboured,—political life, military affairs, science, art, literature, or even opinion,—the history of the times in which he acted, discovered, worked, wrote, or thought, become an essential element in the story of his life; and must be known, understood, and handled, if the biography is to have any high merit. Moreover the men he lived with, those who helped, and those who hindered him; those whom he influenced, and those who influenced him; must all be called up before the reader to make the scene in any degree complete. It is this which makes the task of a biographer, except in the case of the mere writer of a monograph, so difficult; it might almost be said so impossible. If indeed the intention of the 'Life' is merely to reproduce the man whose life is written; and if that life, as is often the case, was one of great sameness, and little else than

---

* 'A Memoir of the Rev. John Keble, M.A.' By the Right Hon. Sir. J. T. Coleridge. Second Edition. London, 1869.

the repetition of a single idea, then there is no great difficulty in writing it, just as it requires no great artistic skill to produce a tame portrait of an inexpressive face; but then the consequence in both works of art is the same—that you have a dull result. You get a sort of sign-post face, very interesting, no doubt, to weary travellers who are looking out for it as connected with their own coming personal comforts, but of no other use whatever to man or beast. A great part of the extant religious biography is of this character. A dull portraying of dull men who had received certain ascertained formularies of thought, and reproduced them in their lives; very much as parish schoolboys, with a great amount of creaking of pencils and rubbing of fingers, reproduce, with an average inaccuracy, poor copies set them on shallow scratched slates. If the man whose character is to be depicted were indeed a typical man, even the monograph writer has his own difficulties; just as from the same cause it requires a consummate artist to paint faces, which have in them that infinite amount of different powers, and those ever-varying expressions of countenance which belong to genius. But if to this difficulty be added those which result from the necessity of painting great events in which the man to be represented took part, and a number of other men with whom he mingled, the demands of the work upon the powers of the artist are almost infinitely increased.

It is not very easy to say what is the proper time after the closing of such a life for reproducing it in a biography. If that time be delayed until prejudice has died away, until the mob of little things has perished, and only the great events or features remain, you may succeed in securing a sort of stern truthfulness for the picture, but it is at the expense of losing all the delicate lights and passing shadows on which the beauty and, to a great degree, the value of the work depends. On the other hand, if the work be that of a contemporary, it is almost impossible but that the figure of the narrator, and not that of his subject, will be the main feature of the picture. You will find the peculiar views and feelings of the writer flavouring everywhere the character of him whom he is seeking to reproduce. Almost the only contemporary writer who has altogether escaped this danger is Boswell; and it is this, above everything, which is the charm of the 'Life of Johnson.' It is Johnson everywhere, Boswell nowhere. He is a mere mirror, without a wave in the glass to distort, without a hue to colour the image of the great, rugged, wise, affectionate, inconsistent sage on whom you are never tired of gazing. But then the biographer must possess Boswell's extraordinary deficiencies as well as his remarkable powers, before he can ever hope to copy such a model. There must be not only the power of appreciating and reverencing his great subject, but there must be the same utter want of self-appreciation and self-respect which possessed the 'jackal who led the lion Johnson forth,' and then painted him in his prowlings, before we can ever have again a 'Boswell's Life of Johnson.'

A biography lately noticed in these pages illustrates all that has been said. The 'Lives of Lord Lyndhurst and Lord Brougham' are really the narrative of the impressions made on a self-conscious, ambitious, remarkably coarse, and not over-scrupulous rival, by the sayings and doings of two great competitors for power and fame, who had, as he thought, overshadowed his own career. The biography he professes to have supplied does not really contain the lives of Copley and Brougham, but the history of how Copley and Brougham surpassed Campbell, and the attempt to prove how mistaken the world was in allowing them to have done so.

Professed autobiography does not escape this difficulty, because as to the writer himself it is commonly not the record of what he was, or even suspected that he was, but of what he wished himself pre-eminently, and his readers in their measure to believe him to have been; whilst as to others, it is too often the history only of the writer's mind in relation to those he lived with, not the real portraiture of the men themselves. So Burnet, in his 'Life and Times,' lightens or darkens the shadows on the figures round him, just as they satisfied or crossed his ever-bristling personal vanity; so that a courtier, who had unluckily disturbed the studied *pose* of the legs on whose proportions he prided himself, appears in his pages as a rogue entirely wanting in all moral principle.

If the 'Life of John Keble' be tested by the application of these principles, it must be pronounced to be one which combined for its writer almost all the difficulties which have been glanced at. It was, as Sir John Coleridge warns his readers in his deprecatory introduction, one which could furnish only 'a most uneventful story.' 'Few persons have lived so long, and achieved so great a name, about whom there is so little of change or incident to record. His life was passed in his father's house, in his college-rooms, in his curacies or in his rectory, in occasional long vacation rambles, in visits to the sea-side, in the alleviation of sickness. He earnestly avoided publicity.'

This might be the outline life of many another English clergyman. The filling in, which makes it Keble's life, is the showing how it came to pass that such a man was the author of a volume of religious poetry, by far the most remarkable and popular in our language; whilst he himself, in spite of his ever shunning publicity, became one mainspring of a great religious movement, which is still more than any other affecting for good, or for evil, or for both, the present and future tone of the Church of England. Now, a biography which is rightly to tell this story, must be full of the man himself whose life is being written; it must especially catch and fix the finer, and therefore the more evanescent features of his genius, his spiritual being, his moral, his family, and his social life. Its writer, if he is to discharge perfectly his work, must ever reproduce Keble, and not himself, and Keble not as he seemed to himself to be, but as he was. This last would be especially needful. For in such a character, the divergence between the true man and the self-contemplated ideal would necessarily be as wide as possible. He would ever view himself through a diminishing, and often through a discolouring medium. Great humility—and Keble was full of the deepest humility—is almost as certain a misrepresenter of a man to himself as vanity or self-assertion. The best, perhaps the only method, by which to succeed in writing such a life as this, would be by letting the man portray himself through his letters and his conversation. This Sir John Coleridge has endeavoured to do, and a large and a most interesting portion of his volume is made up of letters, interwoven into what aims at being a sort of connected narrative. But there is one striking fault in this portion of the work. A mind so sensitive and affections so warm as Keble's, assumed to a great degree with friends whom he highly regarded, the character of him with whom he was conversing. This was probably the cause of what his biographer very happily notices as being the special characteristic of his 'Lyra Innocentium,' which is very rightly described as a book not *for* children, but *about* children.

'It follows them,' says Sir John, 'through their cradle life and infancy, their childhood sports, troubles and encouragements, and warnings; it unfolds the lessons which Nature and the lessons which Grace teaches them; it dwells on their sicknesses, their deaths. No one perhaps but a parent can fully enter into all parts of it, and yet he who wrote it did not marry young, and never was a father. It is matter of wonder how one so circumstanced could ever have known enough of children from infancy to have written such a volume, yet I am persuaded that the more one has seen of them, the more will the life-like truth of the painting strike one. It will naturally be asked where and how did he acquire his knowledge. First, and above all, I think, in his feeling about them, in which the heartiest tenderness was mingled with something amounting almost to reverence.'

This is no doubt the true solution of the question. In writing about children, he set himself beside them, and became one of them. He evidently possessed this almost unconscious dramatic power, which most of those who have high gifts of genius do possess, in an eminent degree. But this solution reaches beyond the particular question of his knowledge of children. It is the key to a great deal more in Keble's mind; it made him somewhat unable to appreciate excellence in those of whom he strongly disapproved, morally or religiously. It made him apt to exaggerate to himself the intellectual qualities of those whose spiritual attainments he venerated. As a mere critic—

'He never could,' says his biographer, 'separate the work from the author; and to a great extent they are inseparable; but there is danger of disparaging good poetry on account of a supposed bad writer of it, and even more, perhaps, of overrating an indifferent work, from a liking and high estimation of the author. I do not think Keble entirely escaped either danger.'

The effect of this seems to have been that, as certain animals unconsciously assume the colours of their food and surroundings, so his mind assimilated itself to the intellectual hue of the friend with whom he was for the time in close and intimate communication. Consequently, a correct estimate of his mind could be formed only from his communication with many different friends. As in matters of mere intellect, he sank to a lower as easily as he rose to a higher note, his communications with a friend whose moral qualities he thoroughly respected, but who was greatly his own intellectual inferior, would quite unconsciously fall to a pitch far below his own, and exhibit also from their unintended artificiality a certain monotony, which would really be foreign to his nature. A selection from his letters to men of many different minds alone could correct this, and was therefore most desirable. But unhappily the letters in this book are almost all written to the author of the 'Life.' He himself regrets this, though not exactly for the reason just stated. But it is the more deeply to be lamented, because the reason alleged for the non-insertion of other letters seems to be so remarkably insufficient:—

'It may be said,' is Sir John Coleridge's statement, 'that I might have added . . . . much to the interest of my memoir if I had made more use of his letters to other friends, and less of those to myself. There is much truth in this remark, and I have done what I could to comply with it. But it is not every possessor of his letters to whom I could properly apply.'

Now if it appeared that all which could be done had been done, though the result would still have been unfortunate, there could have been no ground for complaint. But this does not appear to have been at all universally the case. Efforts, we are told in the first edition, were made, and failed to obtain a series of letters addressed to the late Mr. Hurrell Froude. Since the publication of the first edition a packet of these letters has been found, and some extracts from them appear in the second edition. Whether greater pains might not have earlier obtained these we cannot say, but as to two other sets which would have been, at least, of equal importance, no such attempt, it is avowed, was ever made, and the reason given for not making them is not only entirely insufficient, but may have led to the same result in any other number of instances. It is that, in the writer's opinion, the possessors of letters should have volunteered to supply them unasked :—

'I suppose Dr. Pusey possesses large numbers of important and interesting letters. He had always been so kind to me, that I should be ungrateful if I doubted his readiness to help me—*indeed to volunteer his help*—wherever he felt he could do so properly. . . . . *I have therefore never applied to him*; and for reasons not exactly the same, but of the same kind, I have pursued the same course with Dr. Newman. The work, no doubt, suffers in consequence.'

Most assuredly it does, and to a degree which its writer can scarcely appreciate. He shrank from this repetition of quotations from one series only of letters with characteristic modesty, through fear of 'lying open to the imputation of bringing my own name too forward.' No one who knows the accomplished author could possibly admit the correctness of such an imputation. But the damage to the work reaches far beyond this. It imparts to Mr. Keble throughout these pages a monotony of thought, feeling, expression, and view, which is the inevitable consequence of giving, as the reach and compass of his intellectual life, the expression of that life to one single friend whom he knew thoroughly, and to whose pitch of mind he for very love, when in direct communication with him, always attuned his own. The consequence is, that we have a perpetual repetition of Keble *à la* Coleridge, and a great lack of Keble *au naturel*. A single photograph of Keble would give an utterly different impression of what his countenance really expressed from that which Mr. Richmond's admirable portrait conveys. The features were in themselves poor; from his exceeding gentleness and touching modesty there not unfrequently lay upon them an expression almost of feebleness; but as affection, humour, imagination, earnestness, severity, tenderness, or intellectual excitement stirred them, they varied, and brightened, and glowed until the light of genius darted from them. All this the single photograph would miss—all this the magic pencil of Mr. Richmond, recording in one master sketch the manifoldness of his subject, has most happily preserved. It is so with this biography. It could not but be intensely interesting; for any one complete view of such a man must rivet the attention. But still it is unhappily one view; and the result is, that there is left upon the reader's mind a certain impression of intellectual feebleness in its subject which is altogether incompatible with what the friends of Keble know, and his writings prove that he indeed was. The extracts from the recently-discovered packet of Keble's letters to Hurrell Froude abundantly confirm this view. They are, indeed, very scanty in bulk, only reaching to four that we can discover; yet these four give a view of Keble's character which no part of the correspondence with Sir John Coleridge at all exhibits. They show a readiness and depth of sympathy with a far younger man which is eminently touching; whilst they disclose, besides certain touches of humour, some veins both of difficulty and resource in his own mind, which set him before us in quite a new light. Some of these will be found in our later pages, and without them we think that the character of the writer would have been very inadequately portrayed. What we have occasion to notice as to these makes us only the more earnestly desire that Sir John Coleridge had drawn his general picture from a more diversified collection of details.

Another blemish in the volume may probably be traced to the same cause. There is a continually recurring tone of apology for the introduction of extracts from letters and the like, which most certainly ought not to have been omitted. But as these, from the singleness of the quarry which Sir John Coleridge has worked, have continually, directly or indirectly, some reference to himself, his own modesty leads to their being introduced with such weakening sentences as:—'These are, it may be, little facts; but I do not like to pass them over in silence.' 'It seemed to me right to state the simple truth regarding it.' 'He wrote to me a letter, much of it on the same subject, but I do not like to omit other parts so full of affection.' 'I cannot believe I do wrong in publishing these passages.'

Whilst we are expressing our partial agreement with Sir John Coleridge's most modest depreciation of his work, we must point out two other defects, the amendment of which, if possible, in some future edition, would, we think, add very greatly to the value of the volumes. The first is, that from anxiety to follow out a subject on which he has entered to its conclusion, the biographer has so often rendered intricate the chronology of the 'Life' as effectually to puzzle the reader's enquiries when it was that any particular line of thought predominated in Keble's mind, or when it was that he adopted any special course of action. Now, in his 'Life,' this is a peculiar defect; for, as we are told, very considerable changes even on the most important subjects and on those to which he was wholly devoted did so pass over him; and it is therefore a matter of special interest to know when and under what external influence of circumstances or of persons these changes occurred—a set of enquiries which the mode pursued in this narrative renders it almost impossible to pursue with any hope of reaching a satisfactory conclusion.

Another defect we venture to point out to the distinguished author is a certain carelessness of composition which suggests the sense of a lack of that classical execution which ought to find its place in the biography of so ripe a scholar as Keble. One or two instances—by no means the most striking which might be quoted, though the first which come to hand—will suffice to illustrate the sort of writing referred to. Speaking of the choice of a college for his son by Mr. Keble's father, we read:—

'Mr. Keble had been himself a scholar and Fellow of Corpus Christi College, and it was natural that he should desire to place his sons at the same college; I dare say, too, that the value of *the* scholarship [what scholarship?], *its* certainly leading to a fellowship, and the good preferment which the college offered [to whom?] were not without *their* weight in determining his choice.'

Again, speaking of a volume of sermons and poems by Keble's early friend, G. Cornish, we read:—

'I do not think that I am in error when I say that they are so *tasteful!* and finished in composition . . . . that they would give pleasure to a larger circle if *they* were more generally known. I do not wholly despair that *this* may yet be done.'

And again, speaking critically of a tract which he attributes to Keble, Sir John writes:—

'Yet I will own *it* has interested me in reading *it* over again; and *it* can never be out of season, I suppose, to read *what* tends to elevate and sanctify *that* which the Church calls the state of holy matrimony.'

What would not the late Mr. Cobbett have given for such sentences when he was in one of his tearing moods for sacrificing men in high place, who were troubled with a loose slip-slop style of English composition?

To one other liberty which Sir John Coleridge has allowed himself there is even a deeper objection. It can scarcely by any latitude of allowance fall within the license of a biographer to make the narrative of a friend's life the occasion for endeavouring to controvert his strongest and most deliberate opinions. In one signal instance, at least, these pages exhibit such an attempt. On few subjects were Keble's opinions more deliberately formed or more constantly maintained than on the union which he believed should be maintained between the University of Oxford and the Church of England. This union he considered to be directly threatened by the Oxford University Reform Bill of 1854. What his opinions were on this subject Sir John well knew, from free intercourse with him on that subject both by letter and in person. To such argumentations Keble probably referred when he said, with one of his peculiar smiles, to Miss Wilbraham, 'Some of my friends don't agree with me, but I can't *always*, you know, look at things from the legal point of view.' * What Keble thought, Sir John, of course, tells us fairly and plainly. The language of the letters which he prints is, for Keble, unusually strong. He was, he writes (February 26, 1854, p. 370)—

* Recollections of Hursley, 'Monthly Packet,' part xlii. p. 576.

'Regularly scared at the draft of the bill. I much fear that it will make a sadder disruption of parties than ever. The constitution it enforces will leave us . . . . entirely at the mercy of the tutors and professors, the latter a completely new sort of folk to be as such an organic part of the body. . . . Then the plan is expressly anti-collegiate, it goes on the principle that it is actually good *cœteris paribus* to have a lot of students who are not alumni of some old founder, but disciples of Arnold, or Marriott, or Newman, or whoever he may be, as if this was not the immediate way to encourage party of all sorts, &c. With the colleges it deals *rather* less radically, but all through with a notion that *examination* and talent are everything; and with another notion, which I deprecate from my very heart, that natural preference, for home and kindred, &c., are not to be allowed in eleemosynary endowments. I think it is an indication of a certain hard priggishness which I fear is getting to be characteristic of this generation. But, *Ohè jam satis*, especially as I know that on this subject if I were to write for a year I should only make my heart and wrists ache for nothing.'

Again he writes, after the appointment of Sir John as one of the Commissioners under the Bill, 'I trust that, if it please God, you will be enabled to do a good deal towards drawing the sting of it; that a sting it has, and a snake's forked one, I wish I could doubt,' &c. There can be no doubt, after reading such sentences as these—and there are many more like them—that Sir John does not say at all too much when he concludes that 'the strong opinion of Keble's mind was obviously to preserve Oxford, so far at least as regarded resident students, to members of the Established Church.' Now, there is no reason why his biographer should agree with him in this judgment; though it is intimated that there was a time when they did agree, and that the biographer's reaching a different view was accomplished 'by slow steps, not very willingly taken.' But it is surely scarcely consistent with the just limits of biographical liberty that there should follow such statements as these a long essay to justify the biographer's own last conclusions, and suggest that Keble's 'opinions' may be regarded 'as out of date.' Such 'digressions,' as the author himself terms them, seem remarkably out of place, break the harmony of the narrative, and tend to obscure, if not to misrepresent, the character the volumes are intended to exhibit.

Yet, with all these deductions which we are forced by a sense of justice to make, we have to thank Sir John Coleridge for a most interesting and instructive contribution to our biographical literature. If it does not exhibit Keble's great intellectual power—and our main disappointment in the volume is its seeming to do the opposite of this—it shows us a singularly pure, bright, and holy character, as it is unfolded in letters to one he valued highly and dearly loved, whose own and whose family life gave many opportunities for calling out all the sympathy and tenderness, and beauty, of a most loving and unselfish nature.

John Keble was born on St. Mark's Day, April 25, 1792, at Fairford, in Gloucestershire. His father, of the same name, was Vicar of Coln St. Aldwin's; the vicarage of which being a mere cottage, he lived at Fairford, about three miles distant, in a house of his own, till his ninetieth year, and took a part in the service of his church till within a very few months of his death. Here he himself trained and taught his children. He was a scholar and a Tory, and he bred up his son under his own hand, and with his own traditions. Of the boyhood of the younger John Keble no anecdotes have been preserved, except his bearing, at the neighbouring house of his godfather, the soubriquet of John the Good. He won a Scholarship at Corpus Christi College, Oxford, in December, 1806, when he was only fourteen years and eight months old. The memory of this first launch into the world abode fresh with him till old age. Here is an instance of this, in one of those pictures which perhaps only a woman's hand can draw, and which greatly relieve the gravity of Judicial Biography:—

'In 1859, I had a passing glimpse of Hursley vicarage and its dear trio —Mr. Keble and his two wives (as in a note he playfully called them).

Miss Keble, whom I then saw for the last time, looked frailer, and slighter, and more transparent, but cheerful, and full of quiet observing interest in all home events, as well as in those Church questions which so affected her brother. My last and most vivid remembrance of her is as she stood by Mr. Keble's chair, with one pale little hand on his shoulder, and the "soft smiling eyes" beaming with amusement. He gave an animated account of that memorable first journey to Oxford, in 1806, with his father, when he was a "raw lad" of fourteen and a half, and tried for a scholarship, and won it. His descriptions of various dignitaries, to whom his father thought it well to introduce him, and of the awe they inspired him with (Dr. Routh of Magdalen amongst others . . . . an elderly man even then), were exceedingly entertaining. His gentle sister grew quite eager on the subject, and reminded him of trifling circumstances he had forgotten, and added pretty touches of her own to the narrative.' *

He went at once to reside, and joined at Corpus Christi a small, select, and remarkable society. Edward Copleston, afterwards Provost of Oriel and Bishop of Llandaff, had come to it, like himself, from the home tuition of a country parsonage; and whilst Keble remained at the college its numbers were augmented by Sir John Coleridge himself, by Thomas Arnold, George J. Cornish, Noel T. Ellison, Charles Dyson, and others. It was a remarkable sodality. No wonder that one of its surviving members, glancing after the lapse of years at their activity in the studies of the place, at the simplicity and ease of their social intercourse, at the delights of their walks, and the intellectual interest of their earnest talks together, should see everything 'distance-mellowed and softened, perhaps glorified.'

The impress of these days was deeply marked upon the young student. 'Keble's character through life,' we read, ' was but a strict development of his character in youth, and his early friendships were among the more powerful agents in its formation. His disposition was social, his affections very warm.'

In 1810, being then only in his nineteenth year, Keble

* 'Monthly Packet,' part xlii. p. 565.

was placed at the public examination in the first class of both the Classical and Mathematical Schools—a distinction never before gained except by the late Sir Robert Peel. On the 20th of April of the following year, being then not nineteen, he was elected to a fellowship at Oriel—the blue ribband of the University. The late Archbishop Whately was elected at the same time, and Copleston and Davison were leading members of the common room, in which, whilst yet a lad, Keble took his place. The society of that common room was marked by the highest intellectual power. Whately was fond of startling it with strange propositions, which he maintained with a somewhat biting sharpness of argument. Copleston's mind was more of the judicial cast, and at that time was by no means wanting in elasticity and play. But he was not rapid enough in his movements to escape his younger assailant. Davison stood plainly in intellectual power, and in vast and accurate erudition, at the head of the society. Years afterwards it was almost with a feeling of remaining awe that he was spoken of by his contemporaries.

Into this society the young fellow was launched, and with all his deep humility and reserve he well held his own in it. His succeeding University distinctions soon justified his election into that high company.

It is interesting, as fixing the point which his intellectual and poetic powers had reached, to see how he expressed at this age his feelings on the first sight of the sea. Here are some of the lines:—

> 'Visions of vastness and of beauty! long,
> Too long have I neglected ye: content
> Nor to have soothed my soul to rest among
> Your evening lullaby of breeze and wave,
> Whilst the low sun retiring glowed from far,
> Like pillared gold upon a marble plain;
> Nor yet, wild waked from that deceitful sleep,

> When the storm waved his giant scourge and rode
> Upon the rising billow, have I sate
> Listening with fearful joy and pulse that throbbed
> In unison with every bursting wave.
> Yet the strong passion slept within my soul
> Like an unwakened sense, e'en as the blind
> Mingles in one dear dream, all softest sounds,
> All smoothest surfaces, and calls it light.
> Such lovely formless visions late were mine,
> Dear to remembrance yet, but far more dear
> The present glories of this world of waves.'
> —*Keble's Poems*, p. 176.

The very next year he won—then an unprecedented feat—both the Bachelor prizes.

In 1813 he took a party of pupils to read with him in the long vacation to a picturesque cottage at Sidmouth, the property of the father of his old college friend G. Cornish. The Sidmouth of that day was widely different from the Sidmouth of the present. But it had its gaieties, and into these the young tutor entered, we are told, with 'a quick relish.' 'No one was better received, and no one seemed to enjoy more heartily the morning or evening parties, the concerts and dances which were frequent; the scenes and the society both found him impressionable.' This impressionableness seems to have given birth to some beautiful lines, which Sir John Coleridge says might have been a love song. Love verses from the author of the 'Christian Year' and the 'Lyra Innocentium,' of any quality, may be perhaps a surprise to some, even though his 'Love Song,' as Sir John reminds us, 'became, in his way of dealing with it, elevated' (perhaps, says Sir John, too elevated),—[We cannot help asking, Why too elevated?]—'and holy from the perpetual holiness and elevation of all his serious thoughts.' Our readers shall judge of this for themselves by its first stanza :—

> 'How can I leave thee all unsung
> While my heart owns thy sweet control,

> And heaven and love have o'er thee flung
> The softest moonlight of the soul?
> Oh, I have longed for thee to call
> Soft echo from the West Wind's Hall,
> Some notes as wildly blythe to seek
> As the wild music of thy voice,
> As the wild roses that rejoice
> In thine eye's sunshine on thy glowing cheek.'—p. 52.

On his return to Oxford he was appointed Public Examiner, and the year following was ordained on Trinity Sunday, 1815, a deacon; and on Trinity Sunday, 1816, a priest. How deeply he felt that solemn dedication, may be gathered from a letter dated eleven years later, in which he says, 'To-day I have been to an ordination for the first time since I was ordained myself, and I have almost made a vow to be present at one every year. I think it would do one a great deal of good, *like going back to one's native air after long intervals.*'

He began his pastoral career by taking charge, during six weeks of the long vacation, of two small contiguous parishes near to his father's residence.

His heart was at once in his parish work. How highly he rated the nobleness of his office his own words shall tell. 'Can there be, even among the angels, a higher privilege that we can form an idea of, than the power of contributing to the everlasting happiness of our neighbours to be specially delegated and assigned to us by Almighty God?' And whilst he thus estimated the office, his warm affections were drawn strongly forth by the needs and troubles and cares of every parishioner. He was not, however, at present able to continue this parochial charge. As a fellow of Oriel he felt bound, in 1817–18, to accept the College Tutorship which he was called upon to hold. He returned accordingly to residence at Oxford, and remained there until 1823.

Oriel was then beyond question the first college in the University; and no one did more than Keble to maintain its pre-eminence. He was not only great in the lecture-room, but—regarding 'tuition as a species of pastoral care, as otherwise' he would have deemed it 'questionable whether a clergyman ought to leave a cure of souls for it'—he may be said to have begun in that generation the system of dealing individually with his pupils. Amongst these we find many known afterwards to fame. Of some of them he speaks in his letters; as of 'Baring' [the second Lord Ashburton] 'and Fremantle' [since Sir Thomas] 'delightful fellows both, who come to me as peculiar grinder (I must have a little slang, though Davison's face should glare on me from the opposite panel).' Sir W. Heathcote, was another, and Isaac Williams, Archdeacon Robert Wilberforce and Hurrell Froude. In these years the foundations of much of his great after influence were laid, '*generavit patres*.' He formed the characters which were to form others, whilst his personal intercourse with them at the time their own characters were being moulded into their perfect shapes, gave him an influence over them which neither time nor altered circumstances could materially shake.

During this period his vacation rambles were his special delight, and there is strong internal evidence that we owe to them some of the most beautiful touches of the 'Christian Year,' which was now approaching to completion. Sir John Coleridge notices one of those instances, tracing up—

> 'The fitful sweep
> Of winds across the steep,
> Through withered bents—romantic note and clear,
> Meet for a hermit's ear'—

to an evening which Keble describes at Malvern, July 7, 1822, where he says, 'What a delightful feel it is to sit under one of the rocks here, and hear the winds sweeping with that peculiar kind of strong moaning sigh, which it practises on the bent grass. I never was so much struck with it as this evening.' All this time he was adding, as his soul welled forth in them, to the collection of poems which gradually formed the 'Christian Year.'

His natural tastes led him to store up abundantly such materials. 'What a quick eye,' says Miss Wilbraham, 'he had for anything great or small of natural beauty! A thorn-tree covered with green mistletoe, another tree leafless and blighted, but clothed with a lichen that looked like frosted silver. Nothing was lost upon him.'* From youth to age, without being in any sense a naturalist, he delighted in the life of Nature round him; watching it with a reverend spirit, and reading and storing up its manifold symbols of the higher life. Miss Wilbraham has fixed for us the sketchy outlines of one of his 'frequent talks about Natural History.' 'He spoke of the nightingale's fearlessness, singing by the highway side; of the same bird's harsh scolding note when disturbed or quarrelling; and then the mystery of its winter haunts unsolved at present, since we could hardly suppose the nightingales heard by Dr. Hooker in the Himalayas, in November, to be our summer visitors. He delighted, too, in an immense colony of sand martins that had established themselves not far from Hursley.'† These familiar thoughts again we may trace, repeating themselves in many instances, throughout the 'Christian Year.' Here is an example; for the verses for the first Sunday after Epiphany link themselves naturally with this conversation:—

> 'By the dusty wayside drear,
> Nightingales with joyous cheer
> Sing, my sadness to reprove,
> Gladlier than in cultur'd grove.
> *Christian Year*:—'*1st Sunday after Epiphany.*'

By 1823 he was evidently getting somewhat weary of Oxford, where he writes, 'We go on much as usual, criticis-

---

* 'Monthly Packet,' part xlii. p. 549. † Ibid., part xlii. p. 562.

ing sermons, eating dinners, and laughing at Buckland and Shuttleworth.' The death of his mother in the May of this year brought his college residence somewhat suddenly to a close. He returned to the service of his two old curacies and to residence at Fairford with his father, whom, with one scarcely-effected exception, he never left. again until the death of the aged man in 1835 broke up the family. The influence of his father's character and opinions may be traced everywhere in Keble. His political opinions, and in a great measure the character of his religious life, were impressed upon his early boyhood, and the lines were gradually deepened through these years of filial duty. He was full of natural affection; and during this reach of his life many family sorrows opened all the fountains of his heart. His mother's death in 1823 was followed in 1826 by that of a favourite sister. This at once brought him back to comfort his father and surviving sister, from the curacy of Hursley, upon which he had entered a few months before. They had been months of great happiness to him. The neighbourhood of Hursley Park and of Winchester gave him the society he needed. Parish work was always dear to him. He loved the country round him. His father and his sisters had been domesticated with him, and old friends had visited his first independent home. 'You may imagine,' he says, 'the pleasure it is to have my father and sisters here.' His brotherly love for each, with its distinctly individual tone, comes out in another letter, in which he distinguishes the elder, 'Not my wife Elizabeth,' from 'My sweetheart Mary Anne,' the younger.

Amongst other friends, 'Tom Arnold,' he says, then school-keeping at Laleham, 'ran down here like a good neighbour, and surveyed the premises and the neighbourhood presently after Christmas. How very unaltered he is, and how very comfortable and contented; he is one of the persons whom it does me good to think of when I am in a grumbling vein.'

How pleasant to read from Keble's pen such words as these before the bitterness of party conflict had clouded over with something of a morose severity the earlier geniality of Arnold's spirit. It seems as if there was some working already of what afterwards declared itself, since Keble adds of a review on schools and universities which Arnold brought with him, 'The covering of the jar is so very sweet and luscious, that I suspect there must be something terribly bitter below; but he only cackles and crows at anything anybody can say to him.'

This pleasant interlude was brought sadly to an end by the sudden death of his younger sister, Mary Anne, the very sunbeam of the family. At once he returned to Fairford to share and lighten his father's sorrows. It was a heavy blow, but borne with Christian submission. 'My brother and Bessie,' he writes from the house of mourning, 'are with us, and are the greatest support to one another, and to us; and the baby is like a little angel sent among us to shine in an overclouded place. Then we have our bibles and prayer-books at hand, and are sure of the affectionate sympathy of many dear friends.'

The poem in the 'Lyra Apostolica,' No. 50, on the burial-service, is the precious gum which this wound distilled from his soul. We read the very murmur of his own spirit in the lines—

> 'The deep knell dying down, the mourners pause,
> Waiting their Saviour's welcome at the gate,
>   Sure with the words of heaven
>   Thy Spirit met us there.'

The 'Christian Year' was published the year following. Its poems had been long preparing. His father, whose wishes in his present grief were now more than ever a law to his son, pressed their publication. Keble himself would have delayed it until his own death. He himself had formed a low estimate of the real worth of his poems. Thus, in 1825, he writes to Froude concerning them :—

'These are to thank you for the trouble you have taken about them—these things of mine—and still more for your telling me exactly what you think about them; for which I shall hold you in greater honour as long as I live. For, to say the truth, I look upon thorough honesty in this kind to be a rare thing in Critic-land. I am not so partial to my own crockery as not to be myself aware of the want of poetical depth and fervour which disqualifies many or most of them from being of use to imaginative people; but if they only serve as helps to the memory of plain, good sort of people, that is, in my mind, use enough, provided they do no harm by being untrue or obtrusive—of which last I am a little afraid.'

But besides his keen sense of their faults a far deeper feeling than an author's sensitive modesty lay at the root of this desire of postponement. He saw that the author and the poems must be identified in the reader's mind, and with the truest Christian humility he shrank from thus claiming inferentially the possession of a higher measure of the spiritual life than he believed himself to have attained. In this spirit he attempted to keep the authorship of the book a secret, and when, as soon happened, it transpired, he expressed deep pain at any commendations which the book brought him. This and the strong expressions of self-depreciation in which it found utterance, are a great trouble to his biographer, who seems almost unable to understand such feelings, and to fear lest Keble's character should suffer from their being known. But they were in exact keeping with the reality and entire humbleness of his spirit, to which they acted as a safeguard against the temptation of the sudden and unexpected popularity of his work. Not only was he himself quite unprepared for this, but it was almost as unlooked for by his friends. One of the ablest of them, announcing the publication to a relative then travelling on the Continent, added that a few persons would value the poems highly, but that they never could be generally popular; yet by January, 1854, 108,000 copies had been sold, and the same rate of sale has been amply maintained since both in England and America. They appealed to the religious heart of the nation, and at once won their way, not only with the different schools of thought within the English Church, but also with the leading sectarian bodies. The evening hymn, 'Sun of my soul,' is heard as often in the meeting-house as in the parish church, and is as dear to the worshipper in the one as in the other.

Whilst the 'Christian Year,' even as a literary work, stands plainly at the head of the religious poetry of the day, it is, in point of execution, of very unequal merit. The old jest, which designated it 'the Sunday puzzle,' pointed at a real fault. There is much obscurity which more labour might have removed. To the same cause is to be traced an occasional lack of melody, which is only the more striking from its contrast to the exquisite sweetness of so many of its notes. Yet what poems in the English language can compare with it for general popularity; what poems have ever influenced so widely and so deeply the religious mind of England? In forming an estimate of their merit, it is of the first importance to remember what these poems are. They are not hymns, and they do not owe their popularity to the same source to which hymns appeal. It is not as chants for united voices, or as common utterances of religious fervour, quickened in each by the sympathy of all, as it is with many of C. Wesley's, of Toplady's, and other hymns, that the poems in the 'Christian Year' have won the love of so many hearts. They are more nearly, perhaps, lyrical effusions than anything else. Occasionally, indeed, they rise into high flights of lyrical genius, as, for instance, in the description of Balaam :—

> 'O for a sculptor's hand,
> That thou might'st take thy stand,

Thy wild hair floating on the eastern breeze,
   Thy tranc'd yet open gaze
   Fixed on the desert haze,
As one who deep in heaven some airy pageant sees.

In outline dim and vast
Their peaceful shadows cast
The giant forms of empires, on their way
   To ruin: one by one
   They tower and they are gone,
Yet in the Prophet's soul the dreams of avarice stay.'
—*Second Sunday after Easter*.

The faults which may be found in them are, to a great degree, to be traced to the attempt to make them fit exactly into the course of the Christian year. The great bulk of the poems were the spontaneous outpouring of the writer's soul. They were composed through a long series of years, for some were shown to his most intimate friends as early as 1819. We can trace him in them as he rode along the hedge-side to his distant church, or, as in his long vacation rambles, he mused by the sea-shore or climbed the hill-side; or as he played in his friend's house with the children in whom he delighted; or as some passage in God's Word flashed out to his own spirit its more inward meaning; and in these poems there is often scarcely a word to wish altered. They flow on in one unbroken gush of melody, idea following idea like sunlit waves chasing each other under the breath of the breeze of heaven across the bosom of a lake. How clearly, to give but one instance, can we trace the record of an excursion amongst the mountains, in the beautiful verses for the 20th Sunday after Trinity:—

' Where is thy favoured haunt, Eternal Voice,
   The region of thy choice?
Where, undisturbed by sin and earth, the soul
   Owns thy entire control?
'Tis on the mountain's summit dark and high,
   When storms are hurrying by;

> 'Tis mid the strong foundations of the earth
> Where torrents have their birth.
> No sounds of worldly toil ascending there
> Mar the full burst of prayer;
> Lone Nature feels that she may freely breathe,
> And round us and beneath
> Are heard her sacred tones—the fitful sweep
> Of winds across the steep,
> Through withered bents—romantic note and clear,
> Meet for a hermit's ear—
> The wheeling kite's wild solitary cry,
> And, scarcely heard so high,
> The dashing waters, when the air is still
> From many a torrent rill
> That winds unseen beneath the shaggy fell
> Track'd by the blue mist well;
> Such sounds as make deep silence in the heart
> For thought to do her part.
> 'Tis then we hear the voice of God within,
> Pleading with care and sin.'
> —*Twentieth Sunday after Trinity.*

Here there is not a word to change. We can see him on the mountain-top awed into a silence, in which all these sounds sank into his soul to murmur forth at another time their most musical echoes. But when the whole set were to be gathered into a volume, which was to run parallel with every Sunday and Saints' day of the year, and to apply also to the occasional offices of the Prayer-book, it became necessary to add others: in these are the blemishes of which we have spoken, and which mark them as having been composed to meet a necessity, instead of having flowed, like the rest, limpid, clear, and complete, from the deep springs of their writer's being. It is to these last that we always revert with unflagging delight. In them may be traced the great charm of the volume. Their perfect naturalness, full as it is at every turn of a deep humanity, and so speaking home to every other human heart, combined, first, with a most unusual knowledge of Holy Scripture, and, next, with a marvellous appreciation of the beauties of the natural world, and a keen insight into its symbolical meaning, derived in a great measure from the writer's eyes being opened by his whole soul being full of true Christian doctrine—these seem to be, if we subject them to analysis, the main causes of the popularity of the volume. This is why men of different temperaments, of different schools, and already of at least two generations, class it apart from other books with the inner sacred few with which in their best hours of solitary musing they most love to commune. This it is which, so long as the English tongue continues what it now is, will maintain for it an undying value.

Sir John Coleridge enters with some warmth into the vexed question of the alteration made after Keble's death in the verses for 'Gunpowder Treason.' In the original edition the passage stood :—

> 'O come to our communion feast,
> There present in the heart;
> *Not* in the hands the Eternal Priest
> Will his true self impart.'

But in the first edition published after the death of Keble, the '*not*,' at the commencement of line 3, was, without note or comment to the text itself, changed into '*as*.' With a high chivalry Sir John Coleridge defends the 'widow and the nephew,' and, so far as we understand, justifies, though he 'cannot approve' of the change. We cannot assent to the justification he pleads. Even if Keble had been in the full vigour of his bodily health, and in the strength of his intellectual power, we think that no such alteration ought so to have been made. Sir John argues that no real variation in their real doctrinal value was imparted to the verses by the substitution of 'as' for 'not.' Again we dissent. It certainly seems to us that the doctrinal significance of the lines is largely varied. What change, indeed, could be more complete? The predicating of a local presence of 'the Eternal Priest' is surely in this matter a distinction between the Reformed Church and the Unreformed. The Church of England asserts as strongly, we believe with more consistent strength than the Church of Rome, the *reality* of the presence. Her words admit of no possible doubt when she defines the 'thing signified' to be 'the body and blood of Christ, which are verily and indeed taken and received by the faithful in the Lord's Supper.' But whilst with primitive antiquity she is perfectly clear upon this point, she is no less distinct in excluding all carnality of presence. In that sense she declares the body of the Lord to be in heaven. It is of a spiritual presence, a sacramental, a superlocal presence that she speaks; a presence '*not* in the hand,' because in the hand there *can* be only a local presence. The change, therefore, of 'not' into 'as' seems to us nothing less logically than a change of the whole doctrinal aspect of the passage. We do not believe that Mr. Keble held this other doctrine: and we do not believe that in the full vigour of his intellect he would have sanctioned the alteration. But we must say further, if no such change was intended, why were the verses altered at all? Sir John gives as the reason that 'a Right Reverend Bishop, citing the verse to grace the peroration of a speech, certainly was in fact the immediate occasion of the alteration.' We find, in 'The Chronicle of Convocation' for February 9, 1866, that the late Bishop of Peterborough is the prelate referred to, who, certainly, not as 'gracing a peroration,' but as pointing a main argument of his speech, referred to the authority of 'an honoured man, Mr. Keble,' as supporting in this passage his own views. We are not careful to settle what might be the amount of their difference on this point. No doubt it was not inconsiderable. Sir John says that the interpretation thus put on the words was at variance with what Keble originally meant to express and was known to hold, and he quotes the following words, from a letter writen by Keble in 1863, as 'setting the matter at rest.' 'In a note to the preface of the second edition of a book of mine, which nobody reads, on "Eucharistical Adoration," I have given my own commentary on it: that it is to be understood " not in the hands *only*," as against a carnal presence,—*vide* St. John vi. 63.' Now, without entering at greater length upon this difficult and mysterious subject, we must say that these words by no means 'set the question at rest.' On the contrary, they leave us quite at sea as to what Keble did mean to lay down on the subject. Indeed, the whole volume on ' Eucharistic Adoration ' (the least successful prose production, we think, of its author's pen) leaves the reader in very much the same perplexity as to what he is or is not to believe on the subject. All that seems clear is that the alteration was intended to teach some doctrine concerning the Real Presence different from that which all the world, in common with the Bishop of Peterborough, had gathered from the verses as they stood in all the multiplied editions of the 'Christian Year.' Now, our complaint is, that such a change should be made with nothing more than an appended note of explanation at the end of the volume, in a book of a large established circulation. Of course an author has a perfect right to change his opinion on any matter, and to express that altered opinion in a new edition of his works; still more, if his opinion has been mistaken, has he a right to remove any ambiguity of diction which has led to the misapprehension; but, in a matter of this moment, he has not a right to make the change almost *sub silentio*. He enters into a sort of alliance with the public; and if, when his work has obtained a vast stereotyped currency, and is admitted freely into a multitude of families, its teaching tone is without some very demonstrative notice of the change materially altered, a breach of the tacit compact on which it is received has surely been committed. But, if this be so as to the author himself, it seems to us still less admissible that others after his death should consider themselves at liberty to make such a change in order to carry out his supposed wishes.

It was in these years, from 1826 to 1835, at Fairford, that Keble's pen was the most active. In them the 'Christian Year' was finally completed and given to the world; in them his prelections as Professor of Poetry in the University of Oxford were composed and published. In them, too, he edited his edition of the works of Hooker. This edition of Hooker occupied him five years, from 1831 to 1836. Of all his prose works the introduction to this edition seems to us far the ablest. It shows great critical power both in the minuter questions which concern the authenticity of certain portions of the ecclesiastical policy, and in the broader subject of what Hooker's real opinions were upon the turning points of the long controversy he held with the puritan writers, and what the influences were by which they were shaped. This was a work to which his whole heart was given. For though he would call no man master, not even Richard Hooker, and where they differed stated with all boldness and sincerity the difference and its cause, yet he could not but perceive in Hooker's times of opposition and reproach that which shadowed forth to his inner consciousness the likeness of his own work in his own generation. This consciousness often re-appears in his pages, and adds a most life-like reality to them. Thus, when he is summing up the difficulties of Hooker and his associates in 'conducting the controversy with Puritanism on the side of the existing Church down to the middle of Elizabeth's reign,' he names with an evident pang of self appropriation 'the certainty. . . . that whatever they said and did would be tainted with the name and suspicion of Papistry; so easily affixed and so hard to shake off whenever men demur to the extreme of what are denominated Protestant opinions.' * He suggests, too, in several remarkable passages, the tendency of old error to reproduce itself under new circumstances, and the value, therefore, of a deep study of such times and such struggles as Hooker's for those whom the providence of God has set in our own day to guide the fortunes of His Church.

Another work of these years, his contributions to the 'Tracts for the Times,' leads us into one of the most interesting chapters of Keble's life—his connection with that deep internal movement in the Church of England which has so greatly shaped, and must continue to shape, the fortunes of that most important of all our great national institutions.

Dr. Newman has told us that he ever kept the day of the publication of a sermon on National Apostacy, preached by Keble at Oxford on occasion of the summer assize of 1833, as the commencement of this religious movement. Undoubtedly that sermon well represents the tone of its first originators. Nothing could be less intentionally connected with any Roman tendency than its earliest stages; it was half a political, half a religious movement. Keble himself, born and bred in a country parsonage, the tone of which in matters political was almost nonjuring, grew up with a feeling towards the whole Whig party, which was as near hatred as his tender spirit rendered possible. There was far more than a mere outbreak of fun in his writing to an intimate friend of the word 'delegates' as being 'a most disagreeable word, it puts one in mind of everything that is Whiggish and disagreeable.' This keen dislike for everything 'Whiggish' had been sharpened by the recent measures of the Whig Government affecting the Established Church. Lord Grey's advice to the English Bishops to put their house in order, coupled with what Keble termed 'the suppression' of ten Irish

* Editor's preface to 'Hooker's Work,' p. lviii.

Bishoprics, sounded to him like the voice of the trumpet summoning every churchman to do battle for what was the dearest to him. Hurrell Froude, who had been his pupil, and in some respects his favourite pupil, exerted a strong influence on him in the same direction. Froude was a man of rare ability. Although he had not the well-grown strength of Davison, or the logical sharpness of Whately, or the concentrated power of Newman, yet amongst all the great intellects then gathered at Oxford, his genius was—to use the word in the strictest sense—the most vivid. From a boy he had lived, as is the wont of such spirits, in a world of his own, nursing his high thoughts, speculating upon life, and correcting few of his ardent imaginings by converse with others. To Keble he submitted himself as to a saint, with a deep reverence for his moral intuition. Keble's inbred Toryism delighted the more impetuous nature of the younger man, who acted back again upon his old tutor, to a greater degree probably than either of them at the time knew. Keble was fired by Froude's enthusiasm, and Froude regarded the flights to which his temper and imagination exalted him as the sober certainty of truth when he saw them adopted by Keble. In Froude, hatred to the Whigs and to 'Whiggism' in every form was a passion. The heading, invented by him to describe the Whigs, for some of the poems which were afterwards gathered into the 'Lyra Apostolica,' as they appeared in the 'British Magazine,' speaks the whole man: Περὶ τῆς μισητοῦ στάσεως.

He did not confine his hatred under the veil of a Greek motto. The strongest words of the vernacular tongue gasped to express the strength of his political animosity. Thus he says:—'If it was not for a personal hatred of the Whigs, I should care comparatively little for the Reform Bill' ('Remains,' vol. i. p. 250). And again he thus expresses his sentiments:—'How Whiggery has by degrees taken up all the filth that has been secreted in the fermentation of human thought. Puritanism, Latitudinarianism, Popery, Infidelity, they have it all now, and good luck to them' ('Remains,' vol. i. 340).

From this mighty fervent of spirit sprang the Oxford Church movement of 1833. Looking forward then to the probable separation of Church and State, with which the language of the Whig Prime Minister intentionally threatened the body in which that movement took its rise, they saw the absolute necessity of turning the thoughts and trust of churchmen from that connection with the State, on which in the long spiritual deadness and apathy of a hundred and fifty years they had learned too exclusively to lean, to the internal and independent strength of the Catholic character and constitution of their Church. Of this attempt Keble was in a great degree the immediate author:—

'What think you,' he writes in August, 1833, ' of a kind of association (as quiet and unpretending as may be, if possible, without a name) for the promotion of these two objects: first, the circulation of primitive notions regarding the apostolical succession, &c.; and, secondly, the protection of the Prayer-book against profane innovation? We have, as yet, only written round to a few very intimate friends—Davison, Ogilvie, Tom (Keble)—and, as far as they have answered me yet, they seem to think it may do good. To give you a notion of the kind of thing, the first tract we propose to print will be a Penny Account of the Martyrdom of St. Ignatius, with extracts from his Epistles. *Pray* do not blow on it as being all *ultra*.'

From this small fountain-head sprang the 'Tracts for the Times,' and all their still advancing consequences. Keble himself contributed some of the earlier tracts, but his genius lay in a direction wholly different from such compositions, and they are by no means the happiest efforts of his pen. Those only who are old enough to remember the effect produced by the first numbers of the Tracts amongst the parochial clergy, can duly estimate the change which has since been wrought upon the clerical body. As a rule, with some exceptions great at once through their individual excellence and through their rarity, all earnestness in their spiritual work had been long well-nigh confined to that branch of the clergy which had acquiesced, not of late without some pharisaic self-complacency, in the title of evangelical. They, too, were beginning to pass from the pure zeal of their youth into a new phase of unreality and religious wordliness. To both parties the claims of their Church as a leading member of the great Catholic body were substantially unknown. Amongst the orthodox the existence of such claims was still held as a respectable tradition, dormant under the spell of worldly-mindedness, and without any living power; amongst the Evangelicals they were generally unknown and regarded as hindrances to that inner individual spiritual life which it had been the glory of their party to revive, and the great truths of which their younger generations were growing to treat rather as the flags of the battle-field than as the reproductive principles of an ever-germinating vitality. In many instances the earliest tracts met with a warmer reception from the latter class than from the former, because whilst the remaining receptiveness of life was most awake amongst the younger Evangelicals, the older and more lethargic party feared even a threatening external change less than an internal awakening. Accordingly, many of those who most eagerly received the new enthusiasm, had been bred up in the Evangelical camp. Foremost amongst these was John Henry Newman, the man to whom a later age will point as the chiefest agent in the whole developed movement. Newman and Keble had been brought together for the first time by Hurrell Froude. He was wont, according to his manner, to speak of the accomplishment of this reunion as the great action of his life.

At this stage of the movement it had developed no Romeward tenancy. Hurrell Froude, whose impetuous ardour might have driven him from the inevitable tameness of an

Established Church, was even vehemently anti-Roman. And when the search for health had driven him into countries under the Roman obedience, all that he saw and heard and observed, deepened and strengthened his hatred to the system, claims, and practice of the Papacy. Thus, in the course of an argument, when a friend remarked that the Romanists were schismatics in England, but Catholics abroad, he replied—'No, they are wretched Tridentines everywhere,' vol. i. 434. And he writes home from abroad:—

'These Catholic countries seem in an especial manner κατέχειν τὴν ἀλήθειαν ἐν ἀδικίᾳ, and the priesthood are themselves so sensible of the hollow basis upon which their power rests, that they dare not resist the most atrocious encroachments of the State upon their privileges. . . . I have seen priests laughing when at the confessional; and indeed it is plain that unless they habitually made light of very gross immorality, three-fourths of the population of Naples would be excommunicated. The Church of England has fallen low, and will probably be worse before it is better; but let the Whigs do their worst, they cannot sink us so deep as these people have allowed themselves to fall while retaining all the superficials of a religious country.'—*Froude's Remains*, vol. i. p. 293-4.

And, as the climax of his condemnation, he writes again, 'Since I have been out here (Naples) I have got a worse notion of the Roman Catholics than I had. I really do think them idolaters' (Pref. p. xiii.).

Keble judged Rome in a gentler spirit, and expressed himself about 'our sister's fall' more calmly, but with no less distinctness of condemnation. All his traditions and convictions were eminently anti-Roman, and such they continued to the end. Thus, in 1841, he writes to Coleridge—'I cannot go to Rome till Rome be much changed indeed.' And again, 'As to Rome, I thought I had said in my letters to you that come what will it would be impossible [twice underscored] for me to join it until it is other than it is at present.'

With Keble's own views so distinctly anti-Roman, it may

well be asked how could it happen that in a body in which his influence was so great there could be developed so strong a Romeward tendency amongst members of the tractarian party. To no small degree the evil inclinations to which these extracts point may account for many of the perversions. Some fell through unreality, more through impatience and temper. A very large proportion of the leading perverts had been bred up in the Evangelical school, and the vision of which Keble speaks of the one Catholic and Apostolic Church had dawned upon them with all the startling grandeur of a new discovery. Intoxicated with this glory, they were unable to bear any delay of their longings or any contradiction of their theories; and as the Sorceress of the Seven Hills promised them the instant fulfilment of their dreams, they drank of the cup of her enchantments, and some at least shared the fate of those who quaffed of old the draught of Circe. Amongst the higher spirits who passed from the Evangelical school to the Church of Rome may be mentioned such leading names as those of J. H. Newman, R. I. and H. W. Wilberforce, H. E. Manning, Mr. Dodsworth, Faber, and Anderdon.

But another powerful influence in the same direction was early at work, and it was one against which, from certain peculiarities in his own character, Keble was ill fitted to strive. The strong master mind of the whole movement was that of J. H. Newman. Upon that mind, in spite of passionate efforts of his own to counteract it, the bias early passed. This bias, which even his most devoted followers could then perceive to be really that of his own mind, he read as an impulse providentially imparted to the whole movement, and therefore to be yielded to without resistance as coming from God. In him too, alas! contradiction, misunderstanding, loneliness, did their work. With a mind naturally impatient of that external rule which belief implies, he reached a point when either the rule must be absolute or belief would become impossible; and then at last, with a reluctance hardly to be overborne, he took the fatal step. Those whose minds he had thoroughly mastered, one after another followed him. Early in the movement, if Keble had placed himself determinately on the opposite side, much of this might have been prevented. But he was of too loving a nature to do what such a course implied. When, with much real ground for censure, Tract XC. and its author were made the objects of misrepresentation and persecution, it was not possible for Keble to forsake his friend. Tenderness to the man modified his language towards the doctrine, and the opportunity was lost: and so the bias of that firm will and vast capacity crossed the movement and passed for a season upon its whole flow. From time to time, as we have shown, so long as he lived, Keble's influence was used to quiet uneasy minds and to prevent the spread of perversion. But it was now too late to prevent a certain Romeward inclination being imparted to the whole course of the current. Upon the present aspect of the movement it is not necessary to enter in dealing with the life of Keble. It has been enough here to trace the connexion of Keble with the publication of the 'Tracts for the Times' and with the religious movement of which Dr. Newman holds him to have been indeed the author.

This reach of his life was ended by the death in January, 1835, of his aged father. Until this happened, he declined everything which would have taken him from soothing, with all a son's piety, those declining years. His father's death broke up the scheme of his life. He and his surviving sister were left alone in the world and had to choose a new home. From his people at Coln St. Aldwin, and from the scenery which he had learned to love, he could not be torn without a pang. There was indeed nothing romantic about it, but the willowy stream of the Coln had charms for him. Sir John

Coleridge, in one of his least felicitous phrases says, 'he had a *sort of filial fondness* for this river,' and quotes to prove it words which would have been almost the last in the language in which such reverend love would have been expressed by Keble. 'I got to Bibury about half-past six and walked leisurely home, and really some of the spots which I passed on *our jolly river* Coln are quite beautiful enough to recompense one for a much longer walk.'

At the very time when he was thus cut loose from Fairford, the vicarage of Hursley was again offered to him. He was, too, engaged to be married; an engagement the fulfilment of which for sometime past had only waited the release of his life from the care of his father. He announced, says Sir John, this engagement to his nearest friends in letters which seemed to be but the prose version of those beautiful lines:—

> 'But there's a sweeter flower than e'er
>   Blushed on the rose's spray,
> A brighter star, a richer bloom
> Then e'er did western heaven illume
>   At close of summer day.
> 'Tis love, the last best gift of heaven,
>   Love, gentle, holy, pure;
> But, tenderer than a dove's soft eye,
> The searching sun, the open sky,
>   She never could endure.'
> —*Christian Year: 4th Sunday after Lent.*

He was married October, 1835, to Miss Charlotte Clarke, and took possession of Hursley Vicarage in January, 1836. It was in all respects the residence for him. The beauty of the country, the neighbourhood of Sir William Heathcote, than whom he had no dearer or more valued friend; the vicinity of Winchester; all made it in outward circumstance such a home as those who loved him best would have chosen for him. Sir John Coleridge well sums up some other of the smiling features of his life:—

'There were his brother's nursery, the children at the Park; the large fine family of his neighbour, Dr. Moberly; his own school, where he was a very frequent teacher; his cottage visits; the numberless opportunities which presented themselves to him in his rambles from hamlet to hamlet; and all these presented to that receptive spirit and faithful memory inseparable from the true poetic nature.'

Such Hursley was to him. There he lived for thirty years, and, in spite of many recurring anxieties, enjoyed a large share of calm happiness. His wife's very feeble health leading latterly to long enforced absences from home, and the troubles of the Church round him were his main trials. But these were borne with a gentle submission which turned them into blessings to his own spirit. His letters picture forth this life in touching sentences, like the following: 'My wife, I am thankful to say, continues on the whole a little stronger than she used to be at Cirencester; but the autumn makes itself felt a little both by her and the trees, gently as it is coming on.'

In his parish he was a most diligent, loving, and wise pastor; using every effort to win the young especially to him. He himself taught diligently in his Sunday school. He sought to use the help of the teaching of ladies, believing it to be 'often the most effective with boys, because it roused the dormant chivalry in them.'* Perhaps the most distinctive feature of his ministry was the degree in which he ever sought to deal with those committed to his care as individual souls who could be reached only by the direct influence of a personal ministry. It was perhaps, as Sir John suggests, owing to his longing more effectually to prosecute such a course with them, and to the difficulties which his exceeding modesty threw in his way, and which his self-depreciation magnified, that he somewhat overlooked the terrible evils of the confessional, and at times longed to be able to employ

---

* 'Monthly Packet,' part. xlii. p. 556.

more freely what he terms 'the arm of confession.' It does not indeed appear that he ever desired to restore compulsory or formal confession after the Roman model, but rather to encourage those who were conscious of sin to return to the more frequent voluntary use of such an aid. We may, it seems, conclude that he probably meant to express no more than his longing for the existence of a fuller spiritual confidence than his great reserve on the deepest matters rendered easy between himself and those committed to his oversight. Such seems to be the meaning of such words as these: 'In short our one great grievance is the neglect of confession. Until we can begin to revive that, we shall not have the due severity of our religion, and without a severe religion I fear our Church will practically fail.'

In his parochial charge, besides care for the living Church, Keble was a great benefactor to his parish in its material arrangements. He built, or procured the building, not only of schools but of churches and parsonages, at Otterburne, and Ampfield, the two larger dependent hamlets of Hursley, and of a school and chapel at a third and smaller hamlet; and he turned the parish church, from being a most debased specimen of George III. architecture, into as beautiful a building as any country parish can exhibit. Such a work, defrayed as it was out of the profits which came to him from the 'Christian Year,' was surely a most appropriate destination of funds so raised.

His pen was ever busy during these years. We have in the appendix to the second edition an interesting glimpse of him in the process of composition:—

'He liked Mrs. Keble to play to him while he was writing . . . . he said it helped him. He was very fond of bits from "Acis and Galatæa" and other works of Handel. . . . . He hardly ever used his study for writing of any sort, but carried his papers and books into the drawing-room, setting himself between the window and the door, which in summer were usually both open; there he seemed to hear everything that went on without being disturbed by it; even reading aloud he liked whilst he was writing, occasionally taking the book from the reader and going on himself for a little while, making quaint remarks as he read, and then returning to his work. ..... His book on Eucharistic Adoration was entirely written on scraps of paper and backs of envelopes, and was afterwards fairly copied out from these by Mrs. Keble. He seemed unable to write about what he felt most deeply, except in this way and at odd times.' *

In 1839 he published the least successful of his works—though one which had cost him great labour—a metrical 'Version of the Psalms.' Parental fondness did not blind him to the real quality of this one of his literary offspring. In the preface to it he says, 'The Version was undertaken, in the first instance, with a serious apprehension, which has since grown into a full conviction, that the thing attempted is strictly speaking *impossible*'—a conclusion adopted and happily expressed by Archbishop Howley in the words, 'Mr. Keble's work has demonstrated the truth of his position.' The shades of Tate and Brady may rest in peace. After John Keble's ill-success let us trust that no one else will attempt to invade their undisputed supremacy in having disfigured and debased the Royal Psalmist's inspired utterances. Further he took an active part in the library of the Fathers—published a volume of sermons; a volume on Eucharistic Adoration; a Life of Bishop Wilson, besides pamphlets, some of them of great merit, on the passing events of the ecclesiastical world.

In 1846 he published—a dangerous act for the author of the 'Christian Year'—another volume of poetry under the title of 'Lyra Innocentium.' Sir John Coleridge does not expect, he tells us, a general agreement in his own judgment of it, which is 'that if not equal to the "Christian Year" as a whole, it is at least more than equal in some parts.' We are amongst those who fulfil the expectation here expressed. Certainly the judgment of his countrymen is plain from the

* 'Monthly Packet,' xlii. p. 602.

difference in the circulation of the two volumes, as to their respective merits. Who does not turn again and again to the 'Christian Year'? How few comparatively know the exact place on their library shelves of the 'Lyra Innocentium'? There are many beautiful lines in the volume—many deeply touching, many ennobling thoughts beautifully expressed. How could there fail of being such in anything written by John Keble? But on the whole, in our judgment the excellencies do not equal those of the 'Christian Year,' whilst the blemishes of the former volume are more frequent and more marked in the latter. The verses seem less commonly than of old to be the unbidden outpourings of the poet's heart.

The great sadnesses of his later life were all more or less directly connected with the trials and prospects of the Church whom he served with such unswerving fidelity and unfaltering love. Sir John Coleridge has stated Keble's position as to this, in words which it does not seem possible to improve:—

'All his associations, early and late, were with the Church of his fathers—the loyal and affectionate language in respect of her to be found everywhere in "The Christian Year" was not merely poetical, it was sincere. But he had grown up in the High Church school, and as a High Churchman naturally will do, he looked upwards through the Reformation to the Primitive and the Undivided Church. He loved his own Church as on the whole a faithful representative on earth of that Church; the more truly and exactly she represented it, the more did he think her excellent and to be beloved; the more she admitted what he called puritanical doctrine or practice, the less loyal and dutiful could he be. Coln and his father on the one hand, Fairford and its incumbent on the other, were ever in his recollection.'

The principles in which he believed ever intertwined themselves in him, as they do more or less in all entirely real and affectionate men, with the persons whom he loved. For this reason, the secession of such a friend as John Henry Newman from his fathers' Church cut Keble to the heart.

The shadow of the coming evil had lain broad and heavy on the very spring of his life from the time when his first apprehension of it rose. He had done all in his power to prevent the step; he did not undervalue its too probable consequences upon others; but his first grief was for the dishonour to his Church, and for the evil to his friend. With his habitual self-restraint in the use of language, he speaks of it as 'the desolating anxiety of the last two years;' and long after the event, he pointed out to a friend a chalk-pit which they were passing as connected with perhaps the saddest event of his life, which he afterwards explained by saying that it was there, after carrying it with him all day, afraid to open it, that he had at last opened and read the letter which announced to him that his friend was lost to him. They met again but once. Within a few months of his death at his vicarage at Hursley, were gathered the three— himself, Dr. Pusey, and Dr. Newman—who had in earlier years lived in such unbroken communion and almost unequalled intimacy. It is hardly possible to contemplate that meeting, and read the then aged man's account of it unmoved:—

'E. B. P. and J. H. N. met *here* the very day after my wife's attack. Trying as it all was, I was very glad to have them here, and to sit by them and listen; but I cannot write more of it now.'

Hardly less moving is the account given by the other long separated friend. Newman writes:—

'I made my appearance at Hursley without being expected. Keble was at his door speaking to a friend. He did not know me, and asked my name. What was more wonderful, since I had come purposely to his house, I did not know him, and I feared to ask who it was. I gave him my card without speaking. When at length we found out each other, he said with that tender flurry of manner which I recollected so well, that his wife had been seized with an attack that morning, and that he could not receive me as he should have wished to do; nor indeed had he expected me; for "Pusey," he whispered, "is in the house as you are aware." Then he brought me into his study and embraced me affectionately, and said he would go and prepare Pusey, and send him to me. I think I got there in the forenoon, and remained with him four or five hours, dining at one or two. I recollect very little of the conversation that passed at dinner. . . . Mr. Gladstone's rejection at Oxford was talked of, and I said that I really thought that had I been still a member of the University, I must have voted against him, because he was giving up the Irish Establishment. On this Keble gave me one of his remarkable looks, so earnest and so sweet, came close to me and whispered in my ear (I cannot remember the exact words, but I took them to be), "And is not that just?" . . . . . Just before my time for going . . . I was left in the open air with Keble by himself. . . . . We walked a little way, and stood looking in silence at the church and churchyard so beautiful and calm. Then he began to converse with me in more than [query 'of'?] his old tone of intimacy, as if we had never been parted; and soon I was obliged to go.'

What a meeting, and what a parting! The three men; the dying wife; the calm churchyard; the deep life-long sorrow; the impassable separation; the parting, to meet again only before the great white throne when the shadows shall have fled away.

More than once after this first great loss, Keble had to suffer again, in its measure, the same smart. And even in instances which happily did not reach to final secession, much of the burden and sadness of the times fell on him. He was referred to, consulted, leant upon by all who were in doubt or trouble. A great portion of his time was spent in allaying such doubts. He could not enter coldly into such cases; they ate into his very heart, whilst the management of them consumed large portions of his time. The more he saw of such cases, the more he felt the danger of unsettling souls by changes in the order or constitution of the Church, so that he became painfully alive to the evil which was threatened by every one of these shocks. Every trouble, therefore, which passed over the Church through his remaining years, touched Keble to the quick. The alteration of the law of divorce was one of these which he felt most deeply: and he published on the occasion two pamphlets against repealing the laws, which treat the nuptial bond as indissoluble.

Any assault upon the purity and sharpness of the Church's doctrine moved him most, and after that any such alteration in her constitution as seemed to him to lessen her power of resisting future inroads on her dogmatic teaching. On this account, 'the decision,' says Sir John Coleridge, 'in what is known as the "Essays and Reviews" case, gave him in all its circumstances, as well as the decision itself, great pain.'

Yet with all this distinctiveness as to doctrine, and with his inherited Toryism, Keble thought and acted for himself. Two instances may suffice to show how resolutely he did so. The first is, his unvarying and zealous support of Mr. Gladstone as the Member for the University of Oxford, down to the very last time when he contested that seat in 1865; the second, the way in which he speaks of the temper and of some of the tenets of those who doubtless consider themselves to be the legitimate successors of the writers of the 'Tracts for the Times.'

Speaking of the attempts made to restore a higher form of service in our churches, he says :—

'The success will be more complete, and the satisfaction more perfect, when those who have the work at heart shall have ceased to indulge themselves in invidious comparisons and scornful criticisms on such amongst their brethren as do not yet see their way to it, and when on certain kindred subjects they have learned to make candid allowance for the difference between our circumstances and those with a view to which the primitive canons were framed. I allude particularly to the disparaging tone sometimes used in speaking of mid-day communions. . . . Again, I cannot but doubt the wisdom of urging all men indiscriminately to be present at the Holy Mysteries, a matter left open so far as I can see by the Prayerbook, and in the ordering of which it may seem most natural to abide by the spirit of the ancient Constitutions which did not willingly permit even the presence of any but communicants, . . . the rather that there appears some danger of the idea gaining ground which meets one so often in Roman Catholic books of devotion of some special semi-sacramental grace connected with simply assisting devoutly at mass over and above that promised to all earnest and faithful prayer.'

Would that such candid, charitable, moderate, and anti-Roman views were more widely spread amongst those who, setting themselves up as the great lights of the Church, now-a-days, consider themselves qualified to revile our reformers, contemn our offices, and lampoon our bishops. Such was not John Keble's temper; no trait of all his character was more remarkable than his humility, and it increased even to the end. This was evermore re-appearing. 'One of us,' Miss Wilbraham records, 'alluded to Easter Eve as "her favourite day in the whole year, though a Fast." "I love that day best too," Mr. Keble answered; then, after a pause, he added, with indescribable sweetness of look and tone, " perhaps because it is a Fast; the days of humiliation seem to suit one best as long as one is here."' * What again can be more instructive than to hear the writer of the 'Christian Year' speaking of himself as at the time of writing it not having 'understood the doctrine of Repentance, or that of the Holy Eucharist, or that of Justification?' It was in great measure this deep humility, and the tenderness which grew out of it, which gave so unspeakable a charm to his society. Yet he had enough of human applause to have endangered that great virtue. One of the troubles of his latter years was the perpetual influx of strangers, who came as on pilgrimage to Hursley; and this, not from England only, but also from America, where the 'Christian Year' has reached a circulation little less than it has attained in England.

Sir John Coleridge mentions one characteristic instance of such an American worshipper who, as they were leaving the ivy-clothed porch, drew him apart, and asked if Mr Keble would take it amiss if he begged of him a branch of the ivy cut with his own hand. He received the coveted gift, and

* Monthly Packet,' xlii. p. 557.

said as they walked away, 'You may smile at my request, but I could name persons at home who would give me (I am afraid to mention the sum) for every leaf I have in my hand. So it was alike from young and old, at home and abroad. The homage due to genius, love, and saintliness, was tendered to him abundantly. One of Mr. Forbes's children records in simple words what all who came near him felt: 'He is old and short, with white hair, and rather plain features; but he has such a sweet, heavenly expression. His voice is rather low, we cannot hear him unless he is close to us. He is so kind, and takes such interest in the little ones; aunt calls him her good angel.' Latterly Mrs. Keble's health required him to be much at Penzance; he occupied a house 'in the very best position for seeing the whole of Mounts Bay, and hearing all that the wild waves had to tell us.' Here he met his usual welcome, and to his joy found clergy with whom he could entirely sympathise, and for whom he was always ready to preach. He asked to have a district assigned for his visiting, only covenanting, that it might be entirely amongst the poor. Mr. Tyacke, one of these clergy, has well caught and happily expressed some features of his character, when he speaks of 'his humbling humility and kindliness, especially respecting the Dissenters.' A letter to the other clergyman, Mr. Hedgeland, is a beautiful instance of the way in which Mr. Keble received such acts of kindness: 'One word of thanks for you and your parishioners' very great kindness to us. Such it was as must make the very bends and turnings of the streets—let alone the mount and the bay, and the lanes, and flowers, and moors, and cairns, and crosses—most pleasant to think of.'

One effect of Mrs. Keble's increasing weakness was that his residence at Hursley became necessarily shorter, until he proposed resigning the vicarage, and being 'summer curate,' so as still to minister to the flock he loved. Meanwhile his care and tenderness towards the fragile invalid were unwearied. How deeply her illness told upon him all his letters testify, and yet he was ever cheerful, ever ready to rejoice with those that did rejoice. Mrs. Keble once gave the history of his cheerful placidity in these remarkable words: 'He lays aside his anxieties with his prayers. He does what he can; the issue is with God, with whom he is content to leave it; therefore he is still, and sleeps like a child.' Here is a glimpse at one of their evening readings at Penzance:—

'What a beautiful and comfortable circumstance it is of this great development of our missions, that quiet people are come naturally and without writing *in a tone* to pour out their hearts mutually to those whom they suppose to be like minded, from the other side of the world, just as the old folks did in the very old centuries—St. Cyprian *e.g.*, not to mention St. Paul. I say this apropos to the South Pacific and South African letters, which have been so much our reading of late. It really does seem to help one in a very special way, to realise the communion of saints, and to feel (D.V.) one, not only with the distant living, but with the holy dead.'

This was with him one of those favourite subjects of thought on which, with subdued voice and a fixed intensity of eye, he would from time to time open with those who loved him best. Miss Wilbraham, after the death of his second sister, thus beautifully records his state. After speaking of Mrs. Keble, she continues:—

'Mr. Keble was aged and shaken; yet there was a wonderful peace and elevation of feeling, mingled with their sense of loss, as though they had gone down to the very brink of the dark river with their sister, and been granted a glimpse of the pleasant land beyond. Mr. Keble more than once condescended to share these thoughts with me, and to speak of that intermediate state as one of loving, waiting, resting, and prayer—prayer for the speedy coming of His kingdom; prayer, too, for those on earth for whom when with us, they used to pray; we have no hint given us, he thought, that they discontinued that.'*

For the fulness of this communion he was manifestly ripening. To those who loved him best, and witnessed his

* 'Monthly Packet,' part xlii. p. 564.

evident drawing nearer to his rest, 'the thought brought no bitterness with it. Who would not wish the golden grain to be housed when it is ripe? Who that had witnessed Mr. Keble's deep delight in the promise, "And sorrow and sighing shall flee away," as sung by sweet treble voices in Winchester Cathedral, could wish to keep him back from the Presence in which alone that hope can be realised?'*

The end was not long delayed. In the midst of his ministering to Mrs. Keble, he was himself struck down by paralysis; and, though he recovered to a certain extent, yet his active powers were much diminished. He was unable to attend the last confirmation at Hursley; but wrote a touching letter to the newly-confirmed, closing with words almost prophetic of his own coming end. 'So doing you will abide in Christ, and be sure He will abide in you. There may be sorrow on the road, but all will go right in the end, for you will see His face with joy.'

So doubtless it was with him; on the 29th of March, 1866, he fell asleep; on the 11th of May his wife followed him. Their graves are in that quiet churchyard at Hursley, which looked 'so beautiful and calm' to Dr. Newman as he gazed on it with Keble but a few months before. In the Church of England, we cannot write it without shame, he was but the Vicar of Hursley. Once only by any patron was there offered to the author of the 'Christian Year' one distant dignity, the Archdeaconry of Barbadoes, which he could not forsake his father to accept. His only Church preferment was the gift of a lay friend, upon whose tomb—may it be years before it can be written—amongst many honourable memories not far from the highest might well be graven, 'The sole patron of John Keble.'

Such he was: so he lived amongst us : so he passed away from us. Never aiming at acquiring influence, he exerted it in

* 'Monthly Packet,' part xlii. p. 576.

its highest measures on every one who came within his reach, and widely beyond his immediate sphere upon the Church at large. He took a resolute part in all the most stirring controversies of his time; and yet no one could ever point to a word of his, written or spoken, which had inflicted one needless wound upon any one opposed to him. He gave England's sacred literature the high boon of 'The Christian Year.' He gave England's Church the learning of a deep divine, the love and trust of a loyal son, the labours of a devoted priest, and the pattern of a saint; and he died, as he had lived, the Vicar of Hursley.

EAST AFRICAN SLAVE TRADE.
(*October*, 1872.)

THERE is a peculiar propriety in the time at which the discovery of Dr. Livingstone has been accomplished. Lost as he has been to the civilized world for these past years, as completely as the arrow shot into the darkness, the weight of his authority against the maintenance of the East African slave-trade was beginning to diminish. There was a perceptible slackening of general interest even as to the great geographical problems, to settle which it seemed but too probable that he had sacrificed his life. Another buried in those sands! Another lost in those swamps! Another stricken down by the irresistible fever! Another victim to Arab treachery! till the heart of England somewhat sickened at the mention of the subject, and many were ready to acquiesce in the great traveller's own account of the African estimate of his researches, and to say with those whose answers to his eager questions concerning the fountains of the Nile he reports, as 'We drink our fill of the river, and let the rest run by;' delivered with a look which meant 'This poor White is afflicted with hydrocephalus.'

But the voice of the living man sounds again in our ears. Mr. Stanley's courage and perseverance have enabled him

* 1. 'Report from the Select Committee of the House of Commons on the Slave-trade on the East Coast of Africa, 1871.'

2. 'Despatches addressed by Dr. Livingstone to Her Majesty's Secretary of State for Foreign Affairs, 1870, 1871, and 1872.'

3. 'The East African Slave-trade, &c., as viewed by Residents in Zanzibar, &c.' London.

4. 'A Letter to the Select Committee of the House of Commons.' By H. A. Fraser.

5. 'The Slave-trade in Africa.' By Étienne-Félix Berlioux, Professor of History in the Lyceum of Lyons.

to renew the long-suspended communications, and David Livingstone speaks to us out of Central Africa from the seven hundred miles of the great river's watershed, a 'bird's-eye view of which resembles the frost vegetation on window panes,' and trusts, by the sacrifice of one year more, to verify the assertion of old Herodotus as to the fountain-heads of the mysterious stream. It was in the temple of Minerva, at Sais, the old historian says, that he was told by the Steward of the Sacred Things, that from between two mountains, rising each to a peak, bearing the names of Crophi and Mophi, rise from unfathomable depths the sources of the river. Herodotus throws in the doubt whether the Steward of the Sacred Things was not laughing at him in his narrative. If perseverance can accomplish the object, Livingstone will be the revealer of the long hidden mystery.

All this is of deep interest in the cause of scientific Geography; but for a yet higher cause we deem the sounding of this voice in our ears to be, at the present moment, singularly apposite. The mind of the nation is just beginning to awaken to a sense of its duty in relation to the East African slave-trade. In both Houses of Parliament attention has been called to it. In the Lower House a most valuable Report of a highly intelligent and diligent Committee was printed in August, 1871; and in the House of Lords, after waiting till July for the papers on the subject, which are annually laid before Parliament, an Address to the Queen upon the subject was moved by Lord Campbell, and seconded by the Bishop of Winchester. The debate upon this motion led to an emphatic declaration from Lord Granville of the interest felt in the subject at our Foreign Office, and a declaration that most of the measures suggested by the Bishop of Winchester were, or would be, adopted by the Foreign Office, so far as that office could secure the co-operation of the Administration—declarations which were well followed by the notice of the subject in the Speech put, at the close of the Session, into the mouth of the Queen, which committed the whole Government to exertion in this cause. 'My Government has taken steps intended to prepare the way for dealing more effectually with the slave-trade on the East Coast of Africa.'*

Happily these exertions are not confronted—as those were by which, after so fierce a conflict, the West African slave-trade was abolished through the labours of Wilberforce, Clarkson, and their allies—by any great domestic interest. Though, as we shall have to show, there is too much reason to fear that British capital does surreptitiously aid in maintaining this detestable traffic, yet it can no more openly parade the injury which it will suffer. Lord Brougham's Bill of 5 Geo. IV. c. 113, has made it felony for any subject of Great Britain openly or secretly to take part in the vile trade in the bodies of men. This difficulty, therefore, is gone. But still no Government, even if it were united and determined in the cause, could, without national support, incur the expenses of bringing to a successful issue a contention like this: waged at a distance from home, entangled with many conflicting interests, and liable to be represented as one not immediately concerning our own national obligations, and so to incur the easily-whispered reproach of being a busy and unnecessary interference with others, suggested to unpractical minds by a dreamy and sentimental humanity.

The necessity of counteracting this inevitable tendency by engaging in the great cause the hearty interest of all who will attend to the claims of justice and mercy, must be our excuse for stating plainly, in the first place, the actual evils of the existing trade; we shall then show our readers how we are nationally connected with it, and end by suggesting the best modes which present themselves to us for relieving

* Queen's Speech, August 10, 1872.

humanity from this scourge, and setting free legitimate commerce from all the evils which are inflicted on it by such a horrible rivalry.

The trade in negroes from the East Coast of Africa is, so far as export goes, now almost confined to the different ports within the dominions of the Sultan of Zanzibar. There is an internal traffic along the coast-line from Zanzibar, but by far the greater portion of the traffic is with the Coast of Arabia, a certain amount with Persia, and a yet smaller with Madagascar. The Zanzibar dominions extend along the East Coast of Africa, from the Equator to ten degrees South Latitude, about 350 miles, and include the islands of Momfia, Pemba, and Zanzibar; this last being the seat of Government, separated from the mainland by a channel about twenty-five miles wide—about five miles farther than the distance of Calais from Dover.

A port named Kilwa, almost at the southern border of the Zanzibar dominion, is the place at which nearly all the slave caravans arrive from the interior, and where the victims of the traffic are put on board the dhows which are to convey them to the slave-market at Zanzibar.

Leaving then, for the present, the slaves who reach the Zanzibar slave-market, let us travel back with them from their native territory, and glance at the horrors of their capture and their transit. The mode by which the slaves are obtained is described in an official communication from Brigadier Coghlan to the Chief Secretary of Government at Bombay; quoting the words of the eminent African missionary, Dr. Krapf, he says:—

'To the South of Pangani, is the territory of the heathen Wasegua tribe and the great centre (in 1860) of the slave-trade. The Arabs of Zanzibar come here, and promise the Wasegua Chiefs a number of muskets and shot for a certain number of slaves: so, when a chief has entered into the contract he suddenly falls on a hostile village, sets it on fire, and carries off the inhabitants; among these tribes the slave-trade has hitherto flourished to a frightful extent, chiefly owing to the encouragement of the Arabs of Zanzibar. From 10,000 to 12,000 slaves are said to pass yearly through Kilwa on their way to the various ports of the Sowahili coast and to Arabia, and we saw many gangs of from six to ten slaves chained to each other, and obliged to carry burdens on their heads.'—*Appendix to House of Commons Report*, p. 115.

Again, Colonel Rigby, her Majesty's Consul at Zanzibar, says,—

'The Arabs go into the interior with large numbers of armed followers on purpose to procure slaves, and whole districts are systematically hunted to procure them; the cupidity of the native chiefs being excited by the muskets, gunpowder, and cotton cloth they receive from the Arabs in payment.'—*App.*, p. 116.

The Rev. Horace Waller gives the same evidence:—

'I can speak distinctly to the fact of its being the chief aim of the slave-traders to set one tribe against another, in order that they may bring on war and the consequent destruction of the country, which produces just the state of things which makes slaves cheaper.'—*App.*, p. 87.

Mr. Allington, one of the witnesses, gave an instance which fell within his own experience, when he was residing with Bishop Tozer in the neighbourhood of Lake Nyassa, of one of these acts of violence:—

'I remember going into a native village near Mount Mollumbala. The slavers were there just before we got there, and on our approach they fired some shots and took to their heels, carrying away with them some men out of the village. When I got to the village there was an old chief hiding in the bush, afraid to come back to the village on account of these slavers. I have not the slightest doubt that whilst I was there parties of slavers attacked villages with the view of obtaining slaves.'—*Ans.* 1326, 1327.

Again, the Rev. Horace Waller gives the evidence of an eye-witness:—

'I have seen as many as three villages burning in one morning within two hours, and I have seen hundreds of captives carried away from those villages. The villages are set on fire, and in the confusion the men, women, and children are captured.'—*Ans.* 945, 946.

All this is abundantly confirmed by the fell seal of

depopulation and destruction which has been set by these deeds of iniquity upon populous and thriving districts. Here is an official report to Lord Clarendon:—

'On arriving at the scene of their operations, they incite and sometimes help the natives of one tribe to make war upon another. Their assistance almost invariably secures victory to the side which they support, and the captives become their property, either by right or purchase. In the course of these operations thousands are killed, or die subsequently of their wounds or of starvation ; villages are burnt, and the women and children are carried away as slaves. The complete depopulation of the country between the coast and the present field of the slave-traders' operations attests the fearful character of these raids.'—*Report of House of Commons*, 1871, p. iv.

This utter depopulation, as if fire had passed over the land, is made the more horrible by the contrast which it presents to all that was going on in the same district before the ravages of the slave-trader swept it with the besom of destruction. It is thus that Dr. Livingstone describes the aspect of the country before the advent of the man-stealer. 'We crossed Kirk's Range, and got amongst Manganja in the primitive state, working in irons and spinning buaze, and sowing grain extensively.' 'Buaze,' adds Mr. Waller, 'is a fibre used for nets. Dr. Livingstone is speaking here of a population which had not been visited by slave-traders.' *

There is the like testimony from every quarter. 'The land is as the garden of Eden before them, and behind them a desolate wilderness.' The evidence of Major-General Rigby (who was Consul at Zanzibar and Political Agent of the Indian Government from 1858 to the end of 1861) before the Committee of the House of Commons, may be considered as settling this question for ever :—

'The vast and rich country,' he says, ' from Lake Nyassa to the south is becoming depopulated. Banians who have been for years at Zanzibar have told me that they remember, when they first came to the coast, the whole country was densely populated down to the sea-coast, and now you have to

---

* 'House of Commons Report,' Ans. 1352.

go eighteen days' journey inland before you come upon a village almost. That is fully confirmed by Baron Von der Decken and Dr. Rosher, who travelled that route. Baron Von der Decken talks of miles and miles of ruined towns and villages; the whole way up to Lake Nyassa, where there is now no population at all. . . . Dr. Livingstone recently travelled through the Manganja country, where the whole population was engaged in the cultivation and working up of cotton, and he said that he had never seen such a wonderful cotton country in his life, or such a fertile country. A year or two afterwards, he went through the same country, and found it entirely depopulated, all the huts being full of dead bodies. The children had been carried away, and most of the adults slain. That is one of the worst features of the slave-trade in that country. . . . The slave-traders kill all the men and women, and burn the villages, and carry off the children, who are driven more easily . . . . the men they lose more by desertion on the way.'—*House of Commons Report*, p. 48, Ans. 611.

Here, then, is the curse with which Central Africa is cursed by the slave-trade. Intestine wars created, promoted, aggravated; scenes of peaceful, useful and active industry broken in on rudely by the cupidity of the man-stealers; whole villages burnt to the ground, whole districts depopulated; and, by this terrible whirlwind of physical suffering sweeping over the land, all possibility of the increase of civilization, and, even more, of the spread of a better religion, rendered absolutely impossible.

From year to year, moreover, these terrible evils are extending themselves further into the land. Through the depopulated country the slave-trader has to press on for his victims to a further tract of land, which is as yet prosperous and peopled, because the curse has not yet reached to them. 'Every year,' says General Rigby, 'this slave-trade is extending further and further inland. A great number of the slaves are now brought from the western side of the Lake Nyassa; the Arabs have got dhows in the lake on purpose to convey their slaves across.' * Here is the completion of

* 'Report,' p. 48.

this portion of the picture. This march of death is perpetually advancing onward. The ring of fire is widening its circumference, and gathering within its folds of destruction more and more of the doomed land. Districts rich in all manner of natural fertility, in iron, in cotton (so abundant that all the people of both sexes are busily employed in spinning and weaving), in all sorts of grains and vegetables, in sugar, in dyes, in the Sim-Sim tree—from which most of our finest olive-oil is made, which goes very largely to Marseilles—in gold and in copper,—this land is being reduced to barrenness and utter desolation. 'It was formerly so thickly populated that you might have travelled for seventy or eighty miles and have come to a village at every half-mile—thoroughly well-watered; a flourishing cotton-growing country. Two years pass over it, and you may cross a tract of 120 miles and not find a human being of any kind; and all this damage and misery caused by the slave-trade.'*

But there is another sad chapter of this misery into which we must pray our readers to have the courage to look a little with us. We ask them to follow with us the caravan of misery, the collecting of which brings this utter destruction upon so wide a district of God's earth. It is indeed a march of death, the horrors of which every successful raid increases by prolonging the distance over which the captives have to be conveyed before they reach the sea-shore, whence they are embarked for the slave-market at Zanzibar. When the emigration towards the coast begins, 'the slaves are marched in gangs, the males with their necks yoked in heavy forked sticks, which at night are fastened to the ground or lashed together so as to make escape impossible. The women and children are bound with thongs: any attempt at escape, or to untie the bonds, or any wavering or lagging on the journey, has but one punishment—immediate

* 'Report of House of Commons,' Ans. 947-950.

death. The sick are left behind and the route of a slave caravan can be tracked by the dying and the dead.'* Thus they have, now that the man-stealers' hunting-ground has been forced by depopulation further back from the coast, to traverse a distance estimated as 500 miles, occupying three months of almost unequalled misery. We will not shock our readers by the detail of horrors which they may find in the answers of the witness before the House of Commons Committee. The imagination can supply, it cannot exaggerate, the actual scene of cruelty and blood. The earth cries aloud to Heaven against it. 'The road between Nyassa and the coast is strewn with the bones of slaves that have been killed or abandoned on the road; and for every slave brought to Kilwa there is a loss of four or five additional lives;'† or, as it is estimated by Dr. Livingstone, not unfrequently of ten, for every victim who reaches the coast.

When the diminished remains of the caravan reach the sea-coast of Zanzibar, at the Port of Kilwa, they are embarked in Arab dhows, and the greater number are transported to Zanzibar, to be sold either in the open market or to private dealers. On this voyage, though the special character of their sufferings is changed, it would be difficult to say that they were diminished. In the words of the Report of the House of Commons, 'The sea passage exposes the slave to much suffering, and, in addition, to the danger from overcrowding and insufficient food. . . . Between Kilwa and Zanzibar a dhow lately lost a third of the slaves; there were ninety thrown overboard dead, or dying, many of them in a terribly emaciated state.'‡ Here is a picture of this voyage from the hand of an Officer in Her Majesty's Navy

* Report to Earl of Clarendon, quoted in 'House of Commons Report of 1871,' p. 5.
† 'House of Commons Report,' pp. 287, 288.   ‡ 'Report,' p. iv.

who has been himself engaged in the naval prevention of the trade:—

'The dhows or vessels generally used by the Arabs for the transport of slaves vary in size from 30 or 40 to 120 tons, and carry from 100 to 250 slaves. They are for the most part more or less unseaworthy, and badly fitted and equipped. The slaves are packed literally like herrings in a barrel. In one dhow of 37 tons captured by me, I found 160 slaves, of which number four were dead—the dead being packed in tightly with the living. Several more died within a few days from the effects of previous starvation and ill-usage, many of the poor creatures suffering from frightful sores and ulcers, caused by the abrasion occasioned by slave-irons.

'Whilst in these dhows they are given barely sufficient food to sustain life: a handful of—very often unboiled—rice or sesamum and a cocoa-nut shell of water form their daily meal, and in consequence many of them appear like living skeletons. Men, women, and little children (generally more of the latter) are huddled up together; women with infants at their breasts, who from utter weakness and exhaustion are hardly able to stand upright when brought on the decks of a man-of-war.

'The dhows for the most part generally skirt along the coast, and on being chased by a man-of-war, or her boats, invariably try to run on shore. In this they very often succeed. Regardless of all risk, they deliberately run into the boiling surf, which in a few minutes reduces their vessel to a total wreck, and as may be expected, numbers of lives are lost. I myself, on several occasions when landing to secure slaves, have seen the beach literally lined with the bodies of little children and women who perished miserably whilst trying to struggle with the terrible surf. The Arabs generally succeed in making their escape with the able-bodied men and women, but, as may be expected, the children and weaker women perish in great numbers. In many instances, from the nature of the country where they run on shore, great numbers must ultimately die before the Arabs can reach any town or place of safety with them. On one occasion, when I was fortunate to capture 69 slaves, chiefly women or children, out of some 150, after having pursued them five miles into the interior, I found that the unfortunate creatures had then been two days without water; and of course the ones who escaped, some 60 or 70 more, must have been in the same plight. They would have, at least, 80 miles to march before they could hope to reach either food or water, so most of them must have left their bones on the road.

'The Arabs, on being chased by a man-of-war, invariably tell their wretched cargo that the English will cut their throats and eat them, and by these means succeed in making them run away when the dhow is run on shore. The saddest of all sights is to see the bodies of the little children washing about in the surf. I have seen the rough Blue-jackets almost crying whilst picking up the bodies before burying them.

'I have watched the slave-ships come into Zanzibar harbour, under the very guns of the English men-of-war (which, in consequence of our treaty with the Sultan, were powerless to touch them), and discharge their wretched cargoes at the Custom-house. The vessels were brought as close to the shore as possible, generally grounding in four feet of water, and then the slaves shoved overboard and left to struggle on shore the best way they could. Many of the poor wretches were so utterly exhausted, that on reaching the shore they fell down on the sand, some of them never to rise again; their masters looking on, affording them no help, and merely waiting to see whether it was worth while to pay the custom dues for them or not. If it appeared to them that their case was hopeless, they were left to die where they fell, or to be drowned by the incoming tide. All this I have seen myself, and on remonstrating with their owners and some of the Custom-house people, have been only laughed at for my pains. As long as the Government allow the Sultan to carry on the slave-trade such scenes will always exist.'—*Private Letter.*

Those who survive this voyage are sold either to private dealers or in the open market of Zanzibar. To describe this last abomination, what can be added to the words of the Hon. C. Vivian before the Committee of the House of Commons? 'I visited the slave-market here yesterday, and a more painful and disgusting sight I never saw. Hundreds of poor negroes of both sexes ranged about in all sorts of conditions, some living skeletons, others fat and well dressed, pulled about with a crook stick, and examined just like sheep or other animals in a market.'* From this market are distributed first those who are needed to supply the internal wants of the dominions of the Sultan of Zanzibar. But these form a small proportion of the whole number. Mr. Vivian, Sir Leopold Heath, and others, estimate the whole number of slaves annually exported from Zanzibar as amounting to 20,000; whilst the number retained within the Zanzibar territory does not exceed 1700. Here, then, begins a new set of horrors for these miserable creatures. The export trade is

* 'House of Commons Report,' p. 13, Ans. 186.

a violation of the treaty obligations of Zanzibar with Great Britain; and the cruisers of Her Majesty watch for the slave-dhows, and, if possible, capture them. This of necessity entails on the wretched Africans all the horrors of being the living subjects of a contraband trade—greater crowding on shipboard, less provisions taken, with the probable chance, if the slave-dhow is sighted by a British cruiser, that the slaves will be thrown overboard to prevent the condemnation of the vessel. Here we may end our inquiries into this dark history. With the after-expatriation and foreign servitude of those who reach the Arabian, Persian, and Muscat slave-markets we have not directly to do. It suffices for our purpose to have shown this accursed traffic devastating and depopulating Africa, making impossible its civilization or conversion, destroying the possibility of lawful commerce, and inflicting upon its immediate victims, in their convoy to the coast, in their voyage from Kilwa, and in their ultimate transportation to the shores of Asia, an amount of helpless, hopeless suffering, from the thought of which humanity revolts.

But then arises the question, What have we to do with this system of iniquity? When the eloquence of William Wilberforce awoke against the slave-trade from the West Coast of Africa, it was against the crime of his own countrymen that he inveighed. It was to purge from this deep criminality the commerce of our own land that he devoted his life to the cause of abolition. This, it is urged, was our own concern. But what right have we to constitute ourselves the curators of the purity of Arabian commerce, or to trouble ourselves as to the slave-trading iniquities of the Imâm of Muscat or the Sultan of Zanzibar? There is something plausible in the argument; and addressing itself, as it does, to the practical mind of Englishmen, which, in spite of occasional paroxysms of enthusiasm, naturally revolts at all mere Quixotic undertakings, it is likely, if it is not answered, to hang as a drag upon any national efforts to put down this trade. Can it, then, be answered? We have no doubt that it can, and will proceed to allege what seem to us convincing answers to it.

In the first place, we are nationally concerned in this trade. Dr. Livingstone—no slight authority upon the matter—asserts positively that the trade is absolutely maintained by the capital of our East Indian subjects. In one of his letters, just published by the Foreign Office, Livingstone says:—

'The subject to which I beg to draw your attention, is the part which the Banians of Zanzibar, who are protected British subjects, play in carrying on the slave-trade in Central Africa. The Banian British subjects have long been, and are now, the chief propagators of the Zanzibar slave-trade; their money, and often their muskets, gunpowder, balls, flints, beads, brass-wire, and calico, are annually advanced to the Arabs, at enormous interest, for the murderous work of slavery, of the nature of which every Banian is fully aware. Having mixed much with the Arabs in the interior, I soon learned the whole system that is called "Cutchee," or Banian trading, is simply marauding and murdering by the Arabs, at the instigation and by the aid of our Indian fellow-subjects. The canny Indians secure nearly all the profits of the caravans they send inland, and very adroitly let the odium of slavery rest on their Arab agents. As a rule, very few Arabs could proceed on a trading expedition unless supplied by the Banians with arms, ammunition, and goods. . . . It strikes me that it is well I have been brought face to face with the Banian system, that inflicts enormous evils on Central Africa. Gentlemen in India who see only the wealth brought to Bombay and Cutch, and know that the religion of the Banians does not allow them to harm a fly, very naturally conclude that all Cutchees may safely be intrusted with the possession of slaves, but I have been forced to see that those who shrink from killing a flea or a mosquito are virtually the worst cannibals in all Africa. The Manyema cannibals, amongst whom I spent nearly two years, are innocents compared with our protected Banian fellow-subjects. By their Arab agents, they compass the destruction of more human lives in one year than the Manyema do for their fleshpots in ten; and could the Indian gentlemen who oppose the anti-slave trade policy of the Foreign Office but witness the horrid deeds done by the Banian agents they would be foremost in decreeing that every Cutchee found guilty of direct slavery should forthwith be shipped back to India, if not to the Andaman Islands.'—*Livingstone's Despatches.*

Now whilst it is not entirely correct to class, as this letter does, the inhabitants of Cutch, who are not British subjects, but the subjects of a protected State, with our actual fellow-subjects in Bombay, yet the force of the argument that the criminality of the trade is nationally ours remains altogether unshaken, whilst Bombay merchants and Bombay capital are really maintaining these horrors in Central Africa. And even as to the Cutchees themselves, the charge of moral complicity lies undoubtedly at our door; for there can be no doubt whatever that we could at once, if we so desired, conclude a treaty with the ruler of Cutch and the other protected States, which would bring their subjects under the operation of our own anti-slave-trade laws. Indeed the more accurately we estimate the full extent and character of this Banian trade, the more clear becomes the case by which our moral complicity with it is established. The Indian traders generally known as 'Banians' are of several castes and classes. Some are Hindoos, of various sections of the great trading castes, who may be termed 'Banians' proper; others are Mahomedans of various sects, generally reckoned heretical by the more orthodox, and retaining some rites and peculiarities which are accounted for by the tradition that their ancestors were Hindoo traders converted to Islam, many of whose old Hindoo customs they retain. But all these various sections of the 'Banian' community have many points in common.

The whole trade of the East African Coast passes through their hands. They are to be found, in greater or smaller numbers, at every port on the coast, as far south as Delagoa Bay; numerous and influential in the ports under the Sultan of Zanzibar, more sparingly in the Portuguese ports. They collect from the native traders all the country produce for export, and prepare it by packing, sorting, &c., for sale to the European merchants on the coast, or for direct export to

India, and other foreign parts. In like manner they are the immediate customers of the European or American importer of foreign produce, purchasing his goods wholesale, and preparing them for the native markets. There is very little trade between Europe, America, or Asia, with East Africa, which does not pass through the hands of some branch of the Banian community. From their knowledge of local customs and language they are on that coast necessary intermediaries in all commercial transactions between Africans and foreigners. They have long held this position. The oldest historical records relating to the East African Coast testify to their presence, and apparently to their monopoly of all foreign trade. When the Portuguese first doubled the Cape, they found Indian Banians established, and possessing all the trade—then very great—at every large port. It was they who taught Vasco de Gama and his successors the secret of the easy approach to India by the aid of the trade-winds.

But, in spite of this long possession of the coast-trade, the head-quarters of all these trading communities are in India: thence their capital comes; and thither the accounts of their trade are periodically transmitted. There reside all the heads of the firm; almost without exception at some Indian emporium; whilst the younger men, who are for the time resident on the African Coast, are either British subjects, or are under some sort of British consular protection. This last element must be thoroughly apprehended, in order to estimate aright our moral responsibility as to the slave-trade. What, then, we mean is this: the official aid of the British representative is continually needed by these traders. It can, too, be almost always secured. The different members of the 'Banian' community are so closely connected, that almost every one has some unquestionably British subject with whom he is so identified in partnership or interest that, through him, the influence of the British official can be secured. Now, as all the strings of commerce—that of France, Germany, America, as well as our own—pass through the hands of Banian traders, who lean continually not only along the African Coast, but through all parts of India nearer to their homes, on the goodwill and aid of British officials, we have, in fact, an overpowering hold upon the whole community, and cannot possibly escape the responsibility which the possession of this power involves as to all the trade which so greatly depends for its existence upon our protection. The argument, then, that this Eastern slave-trade is no concern of ours, and that the zeal of England against the Western cannot properly burn as hotly against the Eastern, is absolutely false in its very first proposition. We are nationally engaged in the perpetration of these wrongs; our own commerce is defiled, and the moral purpose which extinguished the Western should never rest until it has swept away utterly from us the contamination of the Eastern trade.

But further, we cannot, in other respects also, cast off the responsibility in this matter, which follows by necessary consequence from the maintenance of our Indian Empire. Paradoxical as it sounds, there is great truth in the assertion that the Queen of England rules over the greatest Mahomedan kingdom on the earth. Whilst we continue to govern India the moral consequences of the acts which flow from the necessary effects of our maintaining that empire come back with all their responsibility upon us. And as to the Eastern slave-trade, certain political conditions of our imperial rule bring this specially home to us. For this Indian dominion, as it has mixed us directly up with so many Oriental dynasties, so it has specially connected us with the rulers of those states which form the basis of the internal African slave-trave, and from whose ports the victims of the trade are shipped and re-shipped. We have long cultivated the friendship of the ruler of Muscat,—the superior State, of which Zanzibar was formerly a conquered dependency. The old Imâm, Syud Saeed, father of the present sovereigns of Muscat and Zanzibar, was a special friend of ours; faithful to us, and supported warmly by us. His death left an open question between his two sons Syud Thoweynee and Syud Majeed as to their succession to their father's sovereignty. War was imminent between the two chieftains. It has always been our policy to prevent such wars, which, besides their other necessary evils, have in those Eastern lands a constant tendency to degenerate into piracy,—the enemy of all commerce and civilization, which it has been a part of our special efforts to suppress. We accordingly intervened, suggesting that the two Princes, instead of settling their dispute by arms, should refer the question to the arbitration of the Governor-General of India. The arbitration was accepted, and war between the two Princes prevented. The history of the conduct of this arbitration, the questions which it raised, and the mode of their settlement, is not only most interesting in itself, but some knowledge of it is almost essential to understanding the intricacy of our connection with the Oriental dynastic question, and so to our comprehending our real responsibility as to all that flows from it. We will, then, give a slight sketch of the entanglement and its solution.

The islands of Zanzibar, Mombasa, and Pemba, with Kilwâ, and other places on the coast of Africa, were not originally part of the dominions of Omân, but were taken from the Portuguese, between 1680 and 1698, by Syud bin Sultan, the Imâm of Muscat. The Imâm was the chief of the Arab tribes of Omân in Arabia, and, beyond his character of temporal ruler, was invested in their eyes with a certain sanctity, not indeed as possessing any direct religious authority, but as having a religious fitness to rule over pious Moslems; so that Imâm may not improperly be translated, as it is by Burton, 'the Prince-Priest.' Successive Imâms, in virtue of their succession to the rule of Omân, were also the rulers of Zanzibar and the other African settlements. The Imâm Syud Saeed, or as other writers Anglicize the Arab name, Sayyed Said, who succeeded to the seat of empire early in this century, was a man of very superior abilities both in war and in civil administration. For his personal gallantry, in 1820–21, he received a sword of honour from the Governor-General of India; whilst he refused in successive years grants of money which we offered to him for the aid he gave us in the suppression of the slave-trade. By his force of character and by his success he both added to his African territories and consolidated greatly the dominion which he had inherited from his father, who, though he had nominally conquered the African provinces, had done little more for establishing his rule over them. He reigned for no less than fifty years. Though Muscat was the cradle and the head of his rule, yet, perceiving that Zanzibar was the living and flourishing part of his possessions, he, about 1840,* fixed his own residence there and made it the seat of government. By this step he greatly weakened his hold over the tribes of Omân; but, on the whole, his administration was eminently successful, especially as regarded the African provinces. He induced many Arabs from Omân to settle in them, and he promoted agriculture and commerce; he broke down the monopoly which had crippled trade; concluded, in 1835, a commercial treaty with the United States of America, which thus early discovered the riches of the country in ivory, copal, and hides; four years later he received a British consul, and in 1844 concluded a treaty of commerce with the French, and received a consul from that nation.

The fruit of these enlightened views was seen at once in

* Mr. Burton places this as early as 1832.

the growing prosperity of Zanzibar, which he found a mere line of huts and converted into a commercial town. So successful was he in this, that, whilst Zanzibar was described in 1834 as having little or no trade, it possessed in 1859 a trade which was estimated at 1,664,577*l.* sterling, with a revenue increasing at a proportionate rate. With a view, doubtless, to retaining the sovereignty in his own immediate family, he had in his lifetime appointed his second son Khaled—passing wholly over the eldest—to be Governor of the African provinces, and his third son, Thoweynee, to the government of Muscat. On the death of Khaled, in 1854, he placed a younger brother, Majeed, as his successor in the Government. In 1856 the wise old chief was gathered to his fathers in the odour of Mahomedan sanctity, bequeathing, in his last will and testament, ' 500 dollars to whoever washes his body with the washing of the departed. Also 1000 expiatory prayers, each expiatory prayer to be of the value of what will feed 60 poor people. Also remuneration to whosoever shall fast for him for the space of 50 months, in lieu of what was incumbent on himself for his transgression of the fast of the months of Ramadhân. Also remuneration to whoever shall perform in his stead the pilgrimage of the Mussulmans to the Holy House of God, which is in the renowned Mecca, and shall visit in his stead the tomb of our prophet Mahommed, upon whom be peace. Written by the hand of the vile Saeed.' *

When 'the hand of the vile Saeed,' as he describes it, rested in his honoured tomb, his two sons—Thoweynee, the elder, and Majeed, the younger—were in possession of the governments respectively of Omân and of Zanzibar; and, according to the old man's desire, each after his death retained the governorship of his own province. At that time Syud Majeed paid to his brother Thoweynee 40,000 dollars:

* 'House of Commons Report,' Appendix, 1871.

of brotherly affection and to equalize the inheritance, as he afterwards averred; as a tribute from Zanzibar as dependent upon Muscat, as was alleged by Thoweynee. It was but for a very short time that a good understanding existed between the two brothers, for, as early as 1859, the British Resident learnt that Syud Thoweynee was preparing by force of arms to dispossess Majeed, and unite the Asiatic and African provinces again into one dominion under his own rule. According to what we have already said has always been a wise part of our policy, namely, the prevention of such wars, which not only disturb the surrounding tribes, but have also an inevitable tendency to degenerate into piracy, and so, by a twofold operation, to interfere with that progress of commerce and civilization which it is our interest as well as our duty to promote,—we set ourselves to prevent this fraternal conflict. Propositions were accordingly made to both the brothers that the questions between them should be submitted to the arbitration of the Governor-General of India instead of to the issue of arms. Both consented, and the inquiry into their claims began. In order to adjust them, it became necessary to decide whether the old chief had in fact devolved either sovereignty on his successor; whether, if he had, he was by the laws and customs of Omân entitled to do so; whether the elder prince had rights of primogeniture which he could claim; whether Thoweynee ruled by election of the tribes of Omân; whether a like right of electing their sovereign ruler had devolved upon the Arab tribes in Africa, and had been in like manner exercised in favour of Majeed; and whether the 40,000 dollars were paid as tribute-money, or as an equalizing gift. On all these points papers, admirable for their learning and judgment, were supplied by Brigadier Coghlan and the Rev. P. Badger; and the questions having travelled up through the Bombay Government to the Viceroy of India, were solemnly settled by Lord Canning, in a judgment to which both parties submitted, and which ruled that each should retain his own dominion, and that the annual payment of the 40,000 dollars should be continued by Syud Majeed to his brother of Muscat, not as a tribute from a dependent state, but as an equitable adjustment of the unequal value of their several inheritances. So far our interference had adjusted these difficult relations. But one of those revolutions which belong to Oriental kingdoms threw all again into confusion. Syud Thoweynee was assassinated by his own son, who then usurped his father's dominion, but was soon driven out by a new pretender. Syud Majeed refused to pay the 40,000 dollars to the parricidal assassin of his brother, but paid it into the hands of the Bombay Government; who, now that the second usurper had been dispossessed, and another son of our old ally, Syud Saeed seated on the throne, will doubtless hand over to him the stipulated sum which the ruler of Zanzibar paid the Imâm of Muscat.

No intermixture with the affairs of another people and government can be more evident or closer than all this. And it is as a part of this system of direct interference with the internal affairs of these governments that treaties were concluded with us which professed to limit the slave-trade of Zanzibar and to prohibit that of Muscat. The Sultan of Zanzibar bound himself to enforce, and to allow us to enforce, within his own waters these limiting conditions of the trade. Here, then, we are met by facts which establish beyond all doubt our moral responsibility as to this detestable traffic. We have constituted ourselves in the eyes of Heaven, and of the world, the protector of the Negro, and we cannot shake off at will the responsibility which such a protectorship involves. We are bound, if the treaties we have made are shamelessly evaded, or are ridiculously inadequate for their declared purpose, to reconsider and revise them. Even further than this, if these treaties have been so evaded as to allow of the continuance and even increase of the trade which they were intended at first to limit, and ultimately to destroy, whilst we find by experience that they tend, through their recognition of the slave-trade within certain prescribed boundaries, to give to it even the semblance of a legal character which it would not otherwise possess, we are absolutely bound by every principle of national obligation to insist upon so altering the treaties we have made as to prevent their sheltering the abominations they were intended to root out. So that here again we are brought back to the same conclusion: we are nationally bound to take in hand the just demands of our acknowledged clients, and, before we can be ourselves blameless in the matter, to do for them all that the acceptance of such clientship involves. The judgment which is formed by those upon the spot, even though their interest is at stake in the preservation of the trade, as given to us in the vigorous words of Admiral Cockburn, can scarcely be read without a blush. 'I assure your Lordships it is a matter of sneer and jeer by the Arabs, our impotent attempts to stop that horrible abomination. Yes, my Lords, even the Sultan says the English will talk and bully, but can't, or won't, stop the trade.' *

But we venture to say that there is an obligation upon us to root out this crying evil from off the face of the earth, which rests upon foundations deeper, we had almost said more awful, than any of those on which we have yet touched. It is with nations as it is with individuals. Great talents call for great achievements. There is a reckoning for their use to which He who entrusts them summons every one who receives them at His hand. In one sense this is even more true and more apparent as to nations than as to individual men. For whilst there is a future retribution for the

* 'House of Commons Report,' Evidence, Answer 176.

individual, there can be no future life to nations, and so their retribution is here. Like almost all retribution, it is slow but it is sure. The pages of history, which record the downfall of once powerful peoples, is but the tracing out of the fulfilment of the doom—

> 'Raro antecedentem scelestum
> Deseruit pede pœna claudo.'

Self-destroyed, cut down by strokes of the axe of vengeance which their own hands have edged and wielded, have the mighty ones of the forest, whose shadow was cast over half a subject-world, one by one fallen and perished. Like the Jewish people, they 'knew not the day of their visitation.' They have ceased to fulfil the purpose for which they were raised up, and, even through their own instrumentality, the hand of Him that felleth has been lifted up against them. Pre-eminently has this been the case when nations have comprehended their mission, have undertaken to discharge it, have gone some way in fulfilling it, and then have fainted in their course. The Roman empire broke in pieces when the Roman people ceased to be the world's subduers for that world's natural regeneration; when they fought their battles with hired soldiers and conquered only to fill Rome fuller with the vices of the vanquished and the luxury of the subject-world.

And Great Britain has, before God and man, accepted the championship of the negro race, and taken up the man-stealer's gauntlet, and borne it high on her helmet, with the declaration that the slave-trade shall be abolished. In ten thousand British hearts the accomplishment of this deliverance of humanity has been accepted as a religious duty; it has mingled with their prayers, it has exalted their personal religion out of the selfishness with which, alas! it too can be infected, into a noble and beneficent enthusiasm; it has elevated low and commonplace minds—as the possession of one grand idea acted on only can—to a nobleness of passion; and it has diffused itself as an indwelling spirit through a generation. It raised Henry Brougham against precedent, and almost beyond belief, to the representation of Yorkshire; it lent a glory to the foreign administration of Lord Palmerston; it did exalt the generation who accepted the charge, and brought the charge they had accepted to a triumphant issue. The evil has broken out again; the same evil, cursed with the same destruction of life, the same infliction of utter misery on its innocent victims, the same stern and heartless prohibition of civilization and new life to the continent our fathers pledged themselves to deliver from its abomination. Woe unto us if we do not secure the fulfilment of their pledges and claim the inheritance of their deeds of light! The peculiar danger of a high and general civilization is, that selfishness should eat out the cement of society, whilst luxury, like some wasting rot, saps the strength of its foundation-stones. The presence of this insidious but mighty danger to the national life was no doubt what dictated to the prescient mind of Lord Bacon the statement that 'in the growth of a state, arms do flourish; in the middle of a state, learning; and then both of them together for a time; in the decline of a state, mechanical arts and merchandise.'*

Now, for a people who are, from the very fact of their great material prosperity, of necessity exposed to such a danger, there can be hardly any other safeguard equally sure and ready as the taking up, with a thorough purpose of heart, some cause which possesses strongly the character of unselfishness, which embodies in itself some high principle of humanity, and which presents itself for accomplishment, not of a mere Quixotic seeking, but as the natural accompaniment of its natural condition. Everything declares that

---

* Bacon's 'Essay on the Vicissitudes of Things.'

from exactly such outward circumstances, under such conditions, is this cause offered to us: let us fear to turn aside from it, lest another take it, and we, with our own fainthearted consent, be put into the lower room. Let us undertake it as our predecessors undertook the like charge when it was laid on them; let us heartily resolve to take no rest until it is accomplished; and most surely it may well be for the lengthening of our prosperity that we have undertaken its charge. This is the conclusion reached by no sanguine and enthusiastic advocates of universal intervention in the cause of philanthropy, but by the calm wisdom of the Governor of Bombay, Sir G. Clerk, and his Council, who solemnly 'resolved':—'The Honourable the Governor in Council is certain that the details furnished by Brigadier Coghlan as to the extent to which the slave-trade is carried on on the East Coast of Africa, will convince the British Government, which has ever been the chief instrument by which Providence has curbed this inhuman traffic, that its work is not completed.'*

It remains for us but to indicate briefly what appear to us to be the instruments which we should use in carrying out this great crusade.

Of these, the first appears to be that we should indeed make it a true crusade. The purchasers of these slaves are now all of them Moslem. Yet whilst this is so, we are reminded, in the Translator's Preface to M. Berlioux's work, that the Mahomedan Faith, whilst it does not forbid slavery, gives no countenance to man-stealing. In the firman on the Circassian slave-trade, in 1854, the Sultan, 'so far from offering any defence of slavery on the ground of the Ottoman Faith, uses these remarks on the religious bearing of the question: "Man is the most noble of all the creatures God has formed, in making him free: selling people is contrary

* 'House of Commons Report,' p. 122.

to the will of the Sovereign Creator."' The Pasha of Egypt spoke of slavery 'as a horrible institution, inconsistent with civilization and humanity, and that, therefore, it must be abolished.' Whilst the Shah of Persia, who raised some religious objections to the abolition of the slave-trade, was met by the opinions obtained from six of his chief Moollahs, who declared 'Selling male and female slaves is an abomination according to the most noble Faith, "the worst of men is the seller of men"—tradition of Mahomet—God it is who knows.'* What then we have to do in this matter is to bring our Moslem brethren up to the more humane standard even of their own Faith and to the tradition of their founder. What cause can be more worthy of the united action of Christendom, than the extirpation of this abominable wickedness? To accomplish this end, we need not arms and violence, like the Crusaders of old, but the noble warfare of bringing moral force to bear upon nations who are below us in religion, morality, and civilization. 'Turkey,' says the Hon. C. Vivian, in his evidence before the House of Commons, 'is always ready to do what we ask her, when we show her the particular point.' † What more encouraging state of relations than this? Persia has shown herself even more ready to second our views in this matter. The Shah has issued two firmans, one to the Governor of Fars and another to the Governor of Ispahan and Persian Arabia, peremptorily forbidding the introduction of negroes by sea into Persia. The firman recites, that at the request of Great Britain, 'with a view to preserve the existing friendship between the two exalted States, a decree should be issued from the Source of Magnificence, the Shah, that hereafter the importation of the negro tribes by sea should be forbidden, and this traffic be abolished.' Nor would the Government of the Shah allow

* Ans. 167.
† Preface to 'Slave-trade in Africa,' by M. Berlioux, p. vi.

any trifling with this abolition of the trade, for the firman continues:—

'In consequence of this it is ordered and ordained that, High-in-rank, after perusing this firman, which is equal to a decree of fate, will feel it incumbent on him to issue positive and strict injunctions to the whole of the dealers in slaves who trade by sea, that henceforth by sea alone the importation and exportation of negroes into the Persian dominions is entirely forbidden, but not by land. Not a single individual will be permitted to bring negroes by sea without being subjected to severe punishment.

'That High-in-rank must in this matter give peremptory orders throughout his Government, and not be remiss.'—*Appendix to House of Commons Report*, pp. 98, 99.

Beyond this the Persian Government has testified in the highest degree its sincerity in the matter, by permitting British ships of war, in order to prevent the chance of negro slaves being imported, to search all Persian vessels which are not Government vessels, the Persian Government pledging itself that—

'In no manner whatever shall any negro slave be imported in the vessels of the Persian Government. Treaties to the same effect have been concluded by our Government with many of the independent Arab chiefs, who have declared that the carrying off of slaves from the coast of Africa and elsewhere, and the transporting them in vessels is plunder and piracy, and the friendly Arabs shall do nothing of this nature.'

Further, they have also conceded to us the right of search in the amplest manner, agreeing that if these vessels ' come under the suspicion of being employed in the stealing and embarkation of slaves,' they may be detained and searched whenever and wherever they may be fallen in with by the cruisers of the British Government, and upon its being ascertained ' that the crews have stolen and embarked slaves, these vessels shall be liable to seizure and confiscation by the said cruisers.' *

In like manner the Queen of Madagascar binds herself in

* 'House of Commons Report,' App. p. 100.

the strongest manner to do all in her power to prevent all traffic in slaves, 'being greatly desirous of effecting the total abolition of the trade.' *

With the Imâm of Muscat and the Sultan of Zanzibar treaties or agreements have been made, with a view to restricting the internal slave-trade and extinguishing the foreign; of the observance of these we must speak presently, but, so far as a professed acquiescence in our views goes, they leave little to be desired as regards the export of slaves to Asia:—

'In deference to the wishes of her Majesty and the British nation . . . His Highness the Sultan of Muscat engages to prohibit, under the severest penalties, the export of slaves from his African dominions, and their importation from any part of Africa into his provinces in Asia, and to use his influence with all the chiefs of Arabia, the Red Sea, and the Persian Gulf, in like manner to prevent the introduction of slaves from Africain to their respective territories.'—*Appendix to House of Commons Report*, p. 163.

Finally, he permits the seizure and confiscation by our cruisers of all vessels bearing slaves, except between the allowed limits of the internal trade in the port of Lamoo to the north of Keeluha or Kilwa to the south.

The first instrument, then, we would see used is an agreement amongst all the maritime Christian powers to enforce, and where necessary to amend, these treaties. It is eminently the interest, as it is the duty, of the mercantile powers both of Europe and America to unite in this true crusade. The natural products of Africa would enrich greatly the European and American markets. There is no limit to the increase of this trade, if only the slave-trade were abolished. Livingstone's last discoveries show us that there exist, outside that fire-line of death with which the man-stealer marks his progress, tribes of a far higher physical and moral class than the more degraded specimens along

---

* 'House of Commons Report,' App. p. 105.

the coast-line whom we are accustomed to regard as the true specimens of the African race. All of these are devoted to commerce, and would welcome its legitimate development:—

'Markets,' says Livingstone, 'are held at stated times, and the women attend them in large numbers, dressed in their best. They are keen traders, and look on the market as a great institution; to haggle, and joke, and laugh, and cheat, seem the enjoyments of life. The population, especially west of the river, is prodigiously large.'—*Despatches*, p. 9.

And again, speaking of the cannibal tribe of Manyema:—

'The women never partake at a cannibal feast, and I am glad of it, for many of them far down Lualaba are very pretty; they bathe three or four times a day, and are expert divers for oysters.'

'The men smelt iron from the black oxide ore, and are very good smiths; they also smelt copper from the ore, and make large ornaments very cheaply. They are generally fine, tall, strapping fellows, far superior to the Zanzibar slaves; and nothing of the West Coast negro, from whom our ideas of Africans are chiefly derived, appears amongst them; no prognathous jaws, barn-door mouth, nor lank heels are to be seen. . . . They use long spears in the thick vegetation of their country with great dexterity, and they have told me frankly, what was self-evident, that but for the fire-arms, not one of the Zanzibar slaves or half-casts would ever leave their country. . . . The people are industrious, and most of them cultivate the soil largely. We found them everywhere honest.'—*Ibid.*

Even with its present hindrances, the trade of England with Zanzibar is increasing every day. The Hamburg and French houses send their vessels direct to England, and import into Zanzibar British merchandise. In 1867-8 the returns from the Zanzibar customs amounted to 433,693*l*. A large trade exists between India and Zanzibar, where 3710 British Indians, and subjects of protected States now reside. These, however, represent only a very small part of the commercial houses which are engaged in the Zanzibar trade. Sir Bartle Frere, a witness of the highest order, well explained this to the Committee of the House of Commons :—

'Almost all the banking business at the ports at Zanzibar and Muscat is done by natives of India, who have their homes in Scinde, Kurrachee,

Kutch, Kattewas and Bombay, and some as far south as Cananore and Cochin. They never take their families to Africa. The head of the house of business always remains in India, and their books are balanced periodically in India. . . . When you have that kind of network of indigenous activity existing as a mercantile agency, it is impossible but that the traders will be as ready to push legitimate trade as they have proved themselves to be in India.'—*Evidence*, p. 453.

From the same witness we learn that the German trade with that coast has become a matter of very great interest to all German mercantile men and political economists; whilst, until it was interrupted by the war, a large and increasing trade was maintained between this coast and America.

Thus the interests of France, Germany and America coincide with our own in substituting for the robbery of man that legitimate traffic which, by God's appointment, not only enriches nations with material prosperity, but bears inevitably with it the seeds of civilization, and with them the yet higher blessing of the introduction of the Christian Faith. A union of these Christian nations for the purpose of putting down the slave-trade would be irresistible. We rejoice, therefore, to gather from Lord Granville's reply to the Bishop of Winchester, in the recent debate in the House of Lords, that he is bringing all his practised skill in diplomacy energetically to bear upon the accomplishment of this great result of gathering up the moral energies of Western Christendom and of America, to deliver Africa from its scourge. This clearly should be the first step in this great work. The jealousy of other European nations, especially of the French, has been a serious impediment to our progress. A hearty unanimity amongst us would make a common failure impossible. We witness, therefore, with joy the stirring of the mind of educated France upon this matter. M. Berlioux, one of her distinguished professors, has written not only the smaller work translated by Mr. Cooper, but a larger volume,* in which he thoroughly discusses the whole subject. Nothing can be more distinct than his conclusions :—

'The Eastern slave-trade can no longer be tolerated. . . . If Europe is earnest, . . . she will prevent the transport of all slaves, and will, as a consequence, destroy man-hunting. . . . The embarkations which take place at Zanzibar under pretext of furnishing the Sultan's ships, will quickly be suppressed when the British Government shall have renounced those unfortunate treaties.' 'It is for Christian powers, forgetting their differences, putting aside their jealousies, . . . and engaging with firmness of purpose in the great work, to bring the force of a united public opinion to bear upon the gigantic evil, when, with the blessing of God, it will disappear from the earth.'†

Amongst the Powers whose joint action should be secured, we have not named Portugal; and yet surely we may hope that the time is come when Portugal also might be included in so beneficent a Confederation. No country has so direct and vast an interest in stopping the East African slave-trade as Portugal. The enormous natural resources of her South African territories would be at once developed if the slave-trade were suppressed, and the restrictions on commerce, which are the evil legacy of her old slave-markets, were swept away. Her coal-mines alone would be an inexhaustible supply of national wealth. If the life of the late King had been prolonged, there can be no doubt that this would have been his action. And it is not too much to hope that with the general enlightenment of the nation, her Government may co-operate with Europe and America in substituting a wholesome commerce for this trade in degradation and death.

Second only in importance to this, we hold the next step to be to enforce upon our own Indian subjects, and, by means of agreement, upon the subjects of the protected Indian States, an absolute separation of every kind and degree from

* 'The Slave-trade,' &c.   † M. Berlioux, pp. 62-64.

participation in the trade. The Act 5 Geo. IV. c. 113, gives to our Bombay Government all the power which it can need to enforce such an abstinence; and perfect, unmistakeable separation of our own subjects from the trade must be the first step to convince the Arabs, under whose jeers we now rest, that we are in thorough earnest in the matter. Every British subject taking any part, direct or indirect, in the trade, is guilty of felony; and if this is distinctly known, and it is known also that every effort will be made by our Bombay Government to trace home to the offender any such act, and if need be, to punish it with the utmost rigour of the law, we shall at once have done much to destroy the infamous traffic. For Dr. Livingstone is no doubt perfectly right in saying that, whilst the Arabs are ready enough to find the men who will conduct the actual risks of the trade, they have not the wealth necessary to advance the capital required.

'It is well known,' he declares in a despatch to Lord Granville, received, on the 18th of August of this year, 'that the slave-trade in this country is carried on almost entirely with the money of Ludha Damji, the richest Banian in Zanzibar, and that of other Banian British subjects. The Banians advance the goods required, and the Arabs proceed inland as their agents, perform the trading or rather murder; and when slaves and ivory are brought to the coast, the Arabs sell the slaves; the Banians pocket the price, and adroitly let the odium rest on their agents.'—*Despatches*, p. 10.

Moreover, as the Customs are farmed at Zanzibar by Banians, many of whom are British subjects, or living under British protection; and as a very large proportion of these Customs is levied openly and avowedly from the duty on slaves here in another way, the subjects of the British Crown are mixed directly up with the forbidden trade in its most open manifestations.

Diligence then, fearlessness and, if need be, severity, is what this country has an absolute right to demand in this matter from the Indian Government.

A third means to which we should have immediate recourse is a revision of our treaty obligations, or agreements, or whatever we may term them, with the rulers of Muscat and Zanzibar. The shameless violation of existing obligations by their subjects, even if not connived at by themselves, gives us most clearly this right. To us it matters not whether the Sultans and their governments actually connive at the entire neglect by their subjects of the engagements which they have contracted with us, or whether it be that they are altogether powerless to repress what they have agreed with us to prevent. Probably both causes are at work. But the result is the same: that is not done which we have abundant treaty right to require shall be done. Lieutenant-Colonel Rigby doubtless does not overstate the case when he says, 'Daily experience more and more convinces me of the utter impotence of the Sultan of Zanzibar to stop the trade, and that the treaties for its suppression entered into by the late Imâm and the British Government are now and always have been practically null and void.'*

The way being thus cleared for new treaty engagements, the question is what should be the conditions they enforce. We have no hesitation in saying that their one leading feature should be the absolute prohibition of the slave-trade. This should include the abolition of all local slave-markets; the absolute prohibition of the transport of any save domestic slaves, duly registered and certified as household servants of African or Arabian subjects; and the sweeping away of all customs and duties for the public revenue levied upon any sale of slaves whatever. We have a perfect right to insist upon this: not to dwell on treaty obligations, the shameless breach of which entitles us to demand compensation, the Western nations have abstractedly the right to insist on sweeping the abomination utterly away. This is no question

* 'House of Commons Report,' Appendix, p. 121.

of the mere internal usages of another people; if it were, however bad we thought them, we should transgress the law of national right if we compulsorily changed them. But the Arab tribes of Muscat and Zanzibar can have no national right to enter countries outside their own dominions to kidnap men, women, and children, to burn and destroy peaceful villages. We have by solemn legal enactment, as well as in a multitude of treaties, declared the slave-trade to be piracy, and Christendom has added its seal to our award. We have ever held that every nation has a right to put down piracy in all waters, because piracy is the right of no nation, and is a deadly crime against all nationality. Why, as a matter of right, should the piracy of these Arab tribes be an exception to the universal treatment of the same offence elsewhere? Instead of being marked by any mitigating circumstances, this piracy is perhaps the rankest specimen of the foul brood to which it belongs. Its area is the widest; its destruction of all lawful commerce is the most complete; the cruelty which is inseparable from it proves it to be the most horrible. We have seen what is its track of horror, from the capture to the sale in the slave-market of its miserable tortured victims. What is its climax in that market may be read in the words of a letter handed in to the Chairman of the House of Commons from Bishop Ryan (late of Mauritius):—

'They were as naked as on the day of their birth; some of them with a long fork attached to their neck, so arranged that it was impossible for them to step forward. . . . Others were chained together in parcels of twenty. . . . The keeper of this den utters a hoarse cry: it is the order for the merchandise to stand up; but many do not obey. The chains are too short; the dead and the dying prevent the living from rising. The dead can say nothing, but what do the dying say? They say that they are dying of hunger. Let us look at some of the details: who is the creature that holds tightly in her arms a shapeless object, covered with filthy leaves? On looking close, you see it is a woman, holding to her dried-up breast the child of which she has just been delivered. . . . And the man who is working with his hands a piece of mud, which he is continually putting to his eye, what is the matter with him? Our guide tells us "he is a troublesome fellow, who sets a bad example, by throwing himself at my feet this morning, and saying with a loud voice, 'I am dying of hunger.' I gave him a blow which burst his eye; he is henceforth good for nothing; and," he added with a sinister look, "he won't be hungry long." '—*Appendix to House of Commons Report*, p. 110.

In the name of our common humanity we declare that this foulest form of piracy is an insult and injury to God and man; and we claim for civilized Christendom the sacred right of taking its victims into her protection, and declaring the curse abolished.

But not only have we the right, we have the power also so to do, and are therefore responsible for a gross neglect if we refuse to use it. The fiat of England, France, Germany, and America has but to be uttered to be obeyed. In fact, the Arab mind has for some time been apprehending such a result. Lord Palmerston's noble despatch has long since been translated into Arabic, and read repeatedly in the Durbar to the Sultan. In it the Arab chiefs were warned 'that the traffic in slaves was doomed to destruction; that Great Britain was the main instrument in the hand of Providence for the accomplishment of this object; that it is useless to oppose what is written in the Book of Fate; that the slave-trade shall stop, and that we will be the instruments in stopping it.'*

Some have proposed that, either by purchase or by other means, we should annex Zanzibar to our dominion. Others less violently have proposed that we should free the Sultan of Zanzibar from his stipulated payment to the Imâm of Muscat by taking it upon ourselves. To the first suggestion we altogether object. In our judgment the injustice of such an act would be as great as its impolicy. Nothing could be devised which would throw such a suspicious character over

* 'House of Commons Report,' Evidence, pp. 574-583.

all our attempts to extirpate the trade or alienate more hopelessly from us those through whose instrumentality and aid we must act against it. But though great names can be quoted in support of it, none greater for all reasons than that of Sir Bartle Frere, yet neither do we assent to the second proposal; for though the suppression of the man-stealing iniquity would, even for the increase of our lawful commerce, be cheaply purchased at the 8000*l.* a year which this would cost the nation, and though our undertaking such a payment might at the first moment remove some difficulties, yet we hold that neither right nor necessity requires the sacrifice. That we are entitled to demand and not to purchase the abolition we have already shown. And our demand would suffice to accomplish it without the addition of a bribe. General Rigby is strongly of opinion that the acceptance of such a payment might greatly endanger the Sultan's life. In truth, we have nothing to compound for. We should be conferring, in the very destruction of the traffic, an inestimable boon on Zanzibar. It is true that the head-money paid as tribute on each slave must be abandoned. But, instead of this, Zanzibar would receive the lawful profits of honourable commerce (already the customs yield to the Sultan 24,000*l.* a year more than they did twelve years ago), whilst she would be delivered from that influx of the lawless northern Arabs whom the slave-trade draws into the country; whose presence makes life uncertain, trade feeble, and the paralysing grasp of universal peculation irresistible. Relieved from this, 'Zanzibar would become a second Singapore or Kurrachee for that part of the world.'*

But, further, not only is the entire abolition of the trade the right, but it is the only course. The principles of righteousness on which we protest against this trade, make any connivance as to it, or any regulation of it, morally

* 'House of Commons Report,' Evidence, p. 970.

impossible. And even if this were not so, experience has convinced every one who has been engaged in the attempt to check it, that it is impossible to introduce any effective restraint upon it whilst its continuance in any shape is permitted. For, as the House of Commons Committee report,* 'Any attempt to supply slaves for domestic use in Zanzibar will always be a pretext and cloak for a foreign trade.' It must never be forgotten that the whole population, from the Sultan's highest officer down to the lowest Arab, are personally interested in defeating all attempts at enforcing any restrictive regulations; whilst the restless intriguing and treacherous nature of the Arab eminently fit him to succeed in such a course.

Geographical peculiarities, moreover, enforce the conclusion, that whilst the trade may undoubtedly be stopped, it cannot be regulated. By our present treaty, slaves may be carried, without interference from our cruisers, between Kilwa, on the south (S. lat. 9° 2'), and Lamoo, on the north (S. lat. 1° 57'), or along the whole extent of the African territory of Zanzibar. The vessels, therefore, which conduct the contraband trade can only be stopped after they have cleared out from Lamoo. But in these seas, with the help of the unvarying monsoon winds, it is, practically speaking, impossible that our cruisers should prevent the escape of dhows enough to pay, by the high price of the slaves landed on the other shore, for the loss of those whom we had captured, or whom, in even greater numbers than these, the fear of capture has caused to be thrown into the sea. The only way to make the sealing up of the coast possible is to allow the seizure of slave-dhows everywhere; and for this the trade must not be licensed within certain degrees of latitude, but absolutely forbidden everywhere. If only this absolute prohibition were required, and our cruisers were made somewhat more numerous, and

* Page viii.

were fitted with the steam launches which are essential for following the dhows into the creeks and bays in which they conceal themselves, the profits of the trade could be at once reduced to a point at which it would no longer pay to retain it.

We are brought to the same conclusion by the absolute necessity, of which we have spoken already, of wholly divorcing British capital and subjects from partaking in the trade. For when we attempt to do this, we are met at once by the extreme difficulty, from the indirectness of their connexion with the trade, of bringing home the offence to those who are subject to our laws. Against all avowed participation the enactments are stringent and comprehensive enough —more stringent than is always convenient to those who, with the best intentions, meddle at all with the traffic. Captain Fraser furnishes us, in the Letter the title of which is prefixed to this article, with a good instance of this. He was one of a firm who, in 1864, set on foot the cultivation of the sugar-cane and the manufacture of sugar by steam-machinery at Zanzibar. For this purpose the firm entered into partnership with the late Sultan Syud Majeed. The Sultan was to supply 500 unskilled labourers, allowing, if he fell short in his supply, the firm to engage elsewhere the number of labourers necessary to complete the stipulated complement. These labourers were of course, slaves, sent by their owner the Sultan, according to the use of Zanzibar, to labour for the firm in which he was a partner. This contract was certified by the British Consul and Resident, and was declared afterwards by the Law Officers of the Crown at home to have infringed none of our enactments against the slave-trade. The co-partnership, however, was by joint consent terminated after a few months; and the firm, having obtained the requisite machinery at a large expense, looked about for another mode of employing it. They first endeavoured to obtain free labourers from the Comoro Islands; but these would steal, and would not work. Then the firm fell back again upon the employment of slave labour. But this time they entered into a contract with the Arab owners of the gangs of porters who were to supply them with slaves bound to work for five years, after which they were to obtain their freedom. The firm had not perceived the difference between entering into partnership with a native who employed his own slaves, and undertaking to receive the 'transfer' for five years of a gang of slaves to themselves: an operation decided by the Law Officers of the Crown to be a violation of the Act 5 of George IV. c. 113. Thus the firm had involved themselves unawares, and, as Captain Fraser argues, with most humane intentions, in a most serious violation of the law; from the penalties of which they escaped only by the Sultan manumitting the slaves in question, in consequence of which no penalties were sued for against the firm. Captain Fraser casts his uttermost scorn on this act of manumission—most unfairly, as it seems to us; and for himself and his firm most ungratefully, as that act of prerogative alone delivered them from the very serious complications in which they had become involved.

But dangerous as it is for a British subject to connect himself in any way directly with the traffic in slaves, yet, to bring home the indirect traffic criminally to them is, whilst the trade is legal at all, well nigh impossible. The Consul at Zanzibar may easily prove that a Banian house there, itself a branch of another great house at Bombay, and both of them of the very highest commercial character, fitted out a caravan for a most respectable Arab merchant, with the cloths of Hamburg, or the beads and wire of England and America, to go into the interior and trade for ivory. Evil rumours may soon abound as to the conduct of the caravan; that its conductors are stirring up wars amongst the inland tribes and practising the slave-trade with its most aggravated enormities; but the Consul is utterly powerless as to interfering with it. After two years, perhaps, the Arab reappears; slaves in numbers, as well as ivory, arrive; who are sold for the mainland, whilst some to go to Zanzibar, some to Arabia. It is clear as the sun at noonday that all this is the direct fruit of the employment of British capital in the felonious trade; but how can he bring home the guilty complicity? How can he obtain evidence where the whole feeling of the place is against any inquiry?

Captain Fraser's own letter to the Select Committee of the House of Commons is a curious instance of the universality of this feeling amongst residents at Zanzibar. In the evidence given before the Committee, the Rev. Horace Waller had deposed that 'the fact of Captain Fraser employing slaves led to everlasting murmuring on the part of the natives.' 'One morning they would see us burning the dhows which were engaged in the slave-trade, and the next morning they would see an Englishman working factories and plantations with the slaves safely landed. . . . . The poor slaves were hired in gangs from their Arab masters. . . . . It was encouraging the slave-trade.' Our readers will remember Captain Fraser's defence of the transaction. But Mr. Waller's evidence stings him to the quick, and he 'protests against the injustice done him by receiving and placing on Parliamentary record such statements,' and claims earnestly 'the rehabilitation of his character for the great injury done to him.' Captain Fraser, therefore, considers, as most Englishmen would, that to be charged with having in any way promoted the slave-trade is a brand upon his character. And yet even upon such a mind the effect of a residence in the midst of slavery can too plainly be traced in the picture which he draws of the slave's life on the plantations at Zanzibar. It is the old story with which all who remember the struggle with West Indian slavery were so familiar. The comfort of the slaves, their ease, and the like: with, however, incidentally, the terrible admission as to the most prolific race in the world, that 'some children, not many, are to be seen amongst them.'* This is 'the East African slave-trade and its results as viewed by residents in Zanzibar.' The vital difference between slavery and freedom, —the degradation of humanity which is involved in men and women being happy because, though the property of a master as much as any other of his chattels, they have a 'good supply of poultry and perhaps a goat or two,'—seems almost to have faded away from the writer's view. If this is the effect of living in such a moral atmosphere upon a high-minded British merchant, we may conceive what it must be upon the natives of India and Arabia, who live by the abominations of the trade, and how impossible it would be for the most zealous consul to obtain, in such a state of society, evidence which could lead to the conviction of the covert slave-trader.

Only in the fewest instances would it be possible to prove the guilt which he knows to exist. Legal slave-trading must, whilst it exists, effectually shelter the felonious act, and only by the trade being declared universally unlawful, can any general attempts to punish British subjects be successful. We are brought to the inevitable conclusion: the Sultan must be induced to give up a partial protection of the trade.

But if, without exception of any kind, the transport of slaves was absolutely forbidden, all these difficulties would cease. Nor would any evil accrue to Zanzibar. The British cruisers, acting in concert with the native Government, could, without any difficulty, prevent the acts of violence which are sometimes apprehended as a consequence of abolition from the Northern Arabs. Nor need any difficulty

---

* 'The East African Slave Trade.' &c., p. 17.

arise as to the supply of labour. The engagement for their manumission after a brief time of service, made by Captain Fraser as to the negroes his firm proposed to hire, might be universal, and a term of apprenticeship might terminate in freedom. The abolition of slavery would of itself substitute the far more useful exertions of free for the proverbial idleness of slave-labour; whilst, if in the Seychelles, at the Mauritius, and other places more remote from a labour-market, sugar and other exports can be grown without slave-labour, far more certainly could they be at Zanzibar.

When once this new condition of treaty obligation had been established, the Governor-General of India could act upon the whole Banian community in a way which is now entirely impossible. If the Viceroy could notify, first, to the vast Banian confederacy, some members of which are to be found at every emporium of trade in India, and then through their respective chieftains (such as the Rao of Cutch, the Nawab of Jafferabad, and others) that the British Government was in earnest in its intention of suppressing the slave-trade, and that it would exert its power of punishing any Indian subject who might be convicted of participating in the traffic, the effect would be seen in every branch of the great mercantile community. The effect of such notifications in India cannot be overlooked. As in the case of suttee, infanticide, and many other abominations, the clearly expressed will of the Imperial power carries immense weight even into the family and counting-house of a Banian subject of an independent chief.

One other suggestion, earnestly pressed by Dr. Livingstone, might, moreover, be most usefully adopted. He considers that the most beneficial measure which could be introduced into Eastern Africa would be the moral element which has done so much for suppressing the Western slave-trade. He quotes the report made by Colonel Ord, and laid before

Parliament in 1865, as establishing the fact that, whilst the presence of a naval squadron has had its share in the work, after all, the suppression of the trade around the English settlements on the West Coast is mainly due to the existence there of settlements of free Christian Negroes. If, he urges,

'the native Christians of one or more of the English settlements on the West Coast, which have fully accomplished their object in suppressing the slave-trade, could be induced by voluntary emigration to move to some healthy spot on the East Coast, they would in time frown down the duplicity which prevails so much in all classes that no slave-trade treaty can bind them. Slaves purchase their liberty in Cuba, and return to unhealthy Lagos to settle as petty traders; men of the same enterprising class who have been imbued with the moral atmosphere of our settlements would be of invaluable benefit in developing lawful commerce.'—*Despatches*, p. 22.

He suggests that the Sultan can, without interference with any native rights, give ground for such a settlement, and is quite ready to do so, on the mainland opposite to the island, which in many places is perfectly healthy, and that all which our Government need do would be to provide an able man to begin and lead the movement; or at most to transport existing officials in a man-of-war, and to advance on loan part of the passage-money, and give rations and house-rent for the earliest infancy of the settlement. In this view Mr. Churchill, who has resided between two and three years as Political Agent and Consul at Zanzibar, entirely agreed in his evidence before the House of Commons,* and recommended, as Livingstone does also, the island of Momfia to be acquired from the Sultan as the best place for such a settlement.

The Rev. H. Badger, whose acquaintance with the whole subject makes his opinion worthy of the utmost weight, suggests Iniack island, in Delagoa Bay, with the surrounding

---

* Pages 416-420.

country of Tembé, undoubtedly British property, as the fittest for such a purpose. Iniack island, he urges,*

'is admirably adapted for trade, whilst the two navigable rivers in its immediate neighbourhood, the Mapoota and Manice, are said to give access to the Zulu country, and to the territories of the Transvaal Republic. Should the result be favourable, Iniack island would bid fair to become an important commercial emporium, whilst the adjoining country of Tembé, also British territory, might afford an eligible settlement whereon to locate the slaves captured by our cruisers on the coast. In short, the healthiness of the climate once proved, a British station in Delagoa Bay might occupy, on this side of Africa, a position analogous to Sierra Leone on the Western Coast; and should the scheme proposed be found feasible, benevolent societies at home would not be backward to crown the humane efforts of the Government in behalf of the liberated Africans, by corresponding endeavours to impart to them the blessings of a Christian civilization.'

Yet still, even when the assent of the Sultan of Zanzibar and of the Imâm of Muscat has been given to treaties which absolutely abolish the slave-trade, our work will not all be done. No great and long existing moral evil can ever be extirpated without testing, by the need of prolonged exertion, the real steadfastness of purpose with which it was assailed. How long and how exhausting was the struggle with the West India slave-trade! It is of the nature of such evil that it lowers the general standard of opinion to its own level. So many are interested in maintaining the abuse, so few are willing or able to assist in its destruction, that even when suppressed it must for a time be liable, like a half-extinguished fire, suddenly to blaze forth again with all its former intensity. For all this we must be prepared. We must maintain for a season our cruisers on the watch, and if only the Treasury will give them the support they must have, the authorities at the Admiralty know well how, and are thoroughly ready to do what is required of them. But, beyond the simply repressive powers of our naval force, we must be prepared for other exertions. Accurate information

* 'Pall Mall Gazette,' Aug. 13.

and concentrated command are two of the most essential elements of success in our undertaking. For the first it is essential that our Consul at Zanzibar should have an able and thoroughly trusty agent, whose field of action should be between the sea-coast and the Lake of Nyassa. His actual location might be left to his own determination. But he should be where he could for himself observe, and so prevent, every attempt to renew the trade. The command of such means of information by our Consul is absolutely essential to any successful attempt to prevent the revival of the trade, even were it once destroyed. Until lawful commerce has established itself, and proved to the petty native chieftains how far better for them is honourable trade than felonious man-stealing, this watch must be kept; and, to make it effectual, there must be concentration of command. In every cause which demands for success rapid and determined action, divided command is the sure secret for securing weakness in execution; and these evils are increased when a wide distance is interposed between the different centres in which command is lodged. For this reason we hold it essential to our success in our great endeavour that the proposition of Sir George Clerk should be adopted, and all political and consular officers from Zanzibar to the Persian Gulf be placed under the orders of the Governor of Aden, who should be invested with the authority now exercised through the Governor of Bombay by the Government of India, and be allowed to communicate directly with the Viceroy and with the Foreign and Indian Offices. This would at once put an end to the division of authority and responsibility between India and England which now paralyses exertion, and causes interminable delays which make it impossible for the political agent at Zanzibar to know what instructions he may receive from Simla, Calcutta, or Bombay, till months after the duplicates of the despatches on which instructions are needed have reached London. All these delays might be at once terminated by the political agents at Zanzibar, and along the coast to Muscat, being instructed to correspond, through the political agent at Aden, with the Foreign and Indian offices; whilst the Indian Government, and the Government of Bombay, were instructed to abstain from giving orders to those authorities on matters relating to East Africa without previous reference to Her Majesty's Government in London. With this concentration of command, and the now meditated line of postal steam-communication between Aden and Zanzibar, and Zanzibar and Natal, the increased powers of our officers to check the slave-trade would be immeasurably increased. Of all the suggested means for putting an end to it, this would probably be ultimately the most effectual, whilst it would be the most easily carried to completion. All that would be necessary would be the early protection which the presence of a judicious British consular agent would afford to the rising settlement. A firman from the Sultan or native Prince on whose territories the settlement was effected would give it the necessary status. Materials of increase would naturally gather round such a centre of protection, and, after its taking root, there need be no more outlay of British money or exertion of British power than in a Turkish port in the Mediterranean.

Another great and difficult question might thus at the same time find its solution. Perhaps the most anxious duty which our watching the Coast of Africa now imposes on us is the treatment of the slaves whom our cruisers capture. The whole process of the capture is one of sorrow and perplexity. The slave-dhows when pursued and threatened with capture by our cruisers, begin, as we have seen, by throwing into the sea the least vigorous of the slaves, and often never cease their work of death till all are thrown over, or the dhow itself stranded upon the rocks. But, as to the comparatively few whom we do rescue, surely it is difficult to conceive more direct self-constituted responsibility than is ours towards these wretched creatures.

It is impossible to deny that at present we have, with all our good intentions, but ill-discharged these duties. On this point the 'Resident at Zanzibar' speaks in terms of most unmeasured and not we fear wholly undeserved, severity:—'Up to this point I have confined my remarks to the Report of the Commission, but I would fain go beyond it, to record my feeble protest against the inhuman and selfish policy that has throughout characterized the national effort to suppress the East African slave-trade.' Strong words, but not more so than justice demands. It is not the mere expenditure of a certain yearly sum, to support a squadron for the repression of the traffic, that will relieve the country from the reproach of acting selfishly, nor will the release of any number of slaves per annum save it from the stigma of inhumanity. Contrast the slave located in Zanzibar with the slaves liberated by Great Britain! We have already quoted the description of the slaves located in Zanzibar: here is the contrast. 'Where shall we find the freed slave under the protection of Great Britain living in equal comfort? Where shall we look for any such evidence that he is well cared for and contented? Alas! we may search in vain: the prison islets of Aden, the stews of Bombay, the plantations of Mauritius and Seychelles, tell alike the same disgraceful tale.

'There is no future provided for the "protected" freed slave, unless one infinitely more hopeless and brutalized than the lot from which he was forcibly torn. Is it for this so much treasure is lavished—so much innocent blood shed?'*

A free settlement of men of their own race and blood

* 'East African Slave Trade,' &c., p. 18.

would, under proper safeguards, form the fittest home for at least a large proportion of the captives. The Church Missionary Society, which has long, so greatly to its honour, provided schools for training the children whom our energies have rescued, will, we may be sure, be represented at such a new home of freedom; and the more recent efforts which at Zanzibar itself have been made under the superintendence of Bishop Tozer and the Central African Mission, might co-operate with it. Dr. Christie bears some remarkable testimony as to the rapidity with which even adult slaves, into whose nature the curse of slavery had eaten deeply, might, by judicious kindness and regular employment, be transformed into useful citizens of such a settlement :—

'On my arrival,' he says, 'I resided on the estate nearly two months. The negroes were exceedingly filthy in their habits. . . . . Many of them came from the same place and belonged to the same tribe, but they seemed utterly indifferent regarding each other. I was not prepared to see this, as I thought that a common affliction, viz., Slavery, would have produced a common sympathy. . . . Since I first came to the place, there has been a great change for the better in the condition of the people in every respect. At the time of their manumission by the late Sultan, not one elected to leave the estate. . . . The progress made by these people in the short space of six years is wonderful, and Messrs. H. O. Fraser and Co. have solved the problem completely as to what can be done with negroes in such a short space of time who have lived till the time of maturity in a savage state.'— *Appendix to a Letter, &c.*, p. 18.

Here is well-grounded hope that, in a friendly free settlement, even the poor degraded beings who have been rescued from the slave-dhow may become happy and useful members of a society of industrious freemen. Such a settlement of free negroes would not only be the greatest direct barrier yet interposed in the path of the slave-trade, but it might also be a principal means of opening these paths of honourable commerce into the centre of Africa, to which we must mainly trust at last for destroying in its interior districts the tendency to steal and sell men. When the native chieftains find by experience that men are more lucratively valuable to them as the producers and exporters of articles of commerce than they are by being sold into a foreign slavery, the temptation to internal warfare, to slave-hunting, and to welcome the slave-dealer will have passed away. Africa may be at peace within herself, her vast resources may enrich the markets of the world, and her now miserable children may know the blessings of freedom, security, and abundance; whilst along the highway which Commerce shall have opened, Christianity may speed upon its higher errand yet, of gathering in the nations to the knowledge of their God.

We trust that both the Indian and the Home Government will well weigh these suggestions, and will act with vigour in the matter. It is one which, from its own character and on account of the interest which will be raised concerning it in the country when the facts of the case are well known, will not brook listlessness and half-measures.

There are, in the evidence taken before the House of Commons and in the Report of their Committee, allusions of a painful kind to differences between different departments of the Government as embarrassing our action, and so preventing our success, and making our present expenditure on the cause useless and ridiculous. This must not continue. It is a case in which half-economy is entire loss. There must be no squabbling between the Government of India and the Administration at home as to the payment of officers needful to promote the objects of both; no frustrating by the Treasury, in one of its parsimonious fits, the more statesman-like proposals of the Foreign Office; no starving down of the squadron employed, so as to disgust its gallant commanders and give the nation the cost of maintaining it, and yet, through a paltry economy, maintaining it in vain.

On this question any Government which would act with a

generous vigour would have the whole country with it. It is one as to which internal wrangling and the great waste of petty savings may heap up against the sure day of reckoning, to the injury of any Administration, a large accumulation of reproaches. It is one from which rightly-handled resolution, skill, and diplomatic success may reap no little harvest of honourable estimation. Great as would be the merit of having solved by geographical discovery all the problems which yet perplex us as to the mysterious deserts and mighty rivers of Central Africa, how far grander would it be to have delivered these even unknown tribes from this deadly and greatly aggravated curse of the slave-trade! This is the great discoverer's own estimate of all his own labours. The noblest passage, as it seems to us, in his last despatches expresses, in his strong straightforward words, this as the utterance of his soul,—' Baker came further up the Nile than any other in modern times, but turned when between 600 and 700 miles short of the *Caput Nili*. He is now employed in a more noble work than the discovery of Nile sources; and if he succeeds in suppressing the Nile slave-trade, the boon he will bestow on humanity will be of far higher value than all my sources together.' *

* Livingstone's Despatches, p. 8.

THE END.

www.ingramcontent.com/pod-product-compliance
Lightning Source LLC
Chambersburg PA
CBHW050838230426
43667CB00012B/2044